Therapeutic Ways
with Words

OXFORD STUDIES IN SOCIOLINGUISTICS
Edward Finegan, *General Editor*

LOCATING DIALECT IN DISCOURSE
The Language of Honest Men and Bonnie Lassies in Ayr
Ronald K. S. Macaulay

ENGLISH IN ITS SOCIAL CONTEXTS
Essays in Historical Sociolinguistics
Edited by Tim W. Machan and Charles T. Scott

COHERENCE IN PSYCHOTIC DISCOURSE
Branca Telles Ribeiro

GENDER AND CONVERSATIONAL INTERACTION
Edited by Deborah Tannen

SOCIOLINGUISTIC PERSPECTIVES ON REGISTER
Edited by Douglas Biber and Edward Finegan

THERAPEUTIC WAYS WITH WORDS
Kathleen Warden Ferrara

Therapeutic Ways with Words

KATHLEEN WARDEN FERRARA

New York   *Oxford*
OXFORD UNIVERSITY PRESS
1994

Oxford University Press

Oxford   New York   Toronto
Delhi   Bombay   Calcutta   Madras   Karachi
Kuala Lumpur   Singapore   Hong Kong   Tokyo
Nairobi   Dar es Salaam   Cape Town
Melbourne   Auckland   Madrid

and associated companies in
Berlin   Ibadan

Copyright © 1994 by Kathleen Warden Ferrara

Published by Oxford University Press, Inc.
200 Madison Avenue, New York, New York 10016

Oxford is a registered trademark of Oxford University Press, Inc.

Library of Congress Cataloging-in-Publication Data
Ferrara, Kathleen Warden
Therapeutic ways with words / Kathleen Warden Ferrara.
p.   cm.—(Oxford studies in sociolinguistics)
Includes bibliographical references and index.
ISBN 0-19-508337-7—ISBN 0-19-508338-5 (pbk.)
1. Psychotherapy patients—Language.   2. Psychotherapists—
Language.   3. Discourse analysis.   4. Psycholinguistics.
I. Title.   II. Series.
RC489.P73F47   1994
616.89'14—dc20   93-2170

1 3 5 7 9 8 6 4 2

Printed in the United States of America
on acid-free paper

To Beth, my daughter

Series Foreword

Sociolinguistics is the study of language in use. Its special focus, to be sure, is on the relationships between language and society, and its principal concerns address the functions of linguistic variation across social groups and the communicative situations in which women and men deploy their verbal repertoires. In short, sociolinguistics examines discourse as it is constructed and co-constructed, shaped and reshaped, in social interaction, and as it creates and reflects the social realities of daily life.

Some linguists examine the structure of sentences independent of who is speaking (or writing) and to whom, independent of what precedes and follows in the discourse, and independent of the setting, topic, and purposes of the discourse. By contrast, sociolinguists investigate language as it is embedded in its interactional and institutional contexts. Not surprisingly, almost all interest in language matters among observers outside the field of linguistics is likewise focused on language in use, for it is only in natural discourse that language mirrors the intricacies of social structure and illuminates the strategic influences that make it so extraordinary and subtle an instrument of achievement and change.

In offering a platform for studies of language use in communities around the globe, Oxford Studies in Sociolinguistics invites significant treatments of discourse—whether spoken, written, or signed. The series hosts studies that are theoretical or descriptive, analytical or interpretive, synchronic or diachronic. While most volumes will report original research, a few may synthesize or interpret existing knowledge. All will aim for a style accessible beyond linguists to other social scientists and to humanists.

In the present volume, Kathleen W. Ferrara analyzes therapeutic discourse, a topic of great interest for many readers. Relying on her transcriptions of talk between psychotherapists and clients, she explores connections between the linguistic character of therapeutic discourse and its likely therapeutic value. Among the linguistic phenomena whose role in the therapeutic process she examines are "mirroring" by therapists and "echoing" by clients, along with "aligned speech" and metaphor. Dr. Ferrara recognizes the fascination that the content of therapeutic discourse holds for readers, and she offers an analysis of its linguistic expression that earns for psychotherapy a place alongside medicine and law as a rich site for the study of discourse in the workplace.

Therapeutic Ways with Words is empirically well grounded, methodologically innovative, and humanly compelling. It holds interest not only for sociolinguists and applied linguists, but for practicing psychotherapists as well. It helps bridge the gap between the professionalized study of language in the academy and the ordinary use of language in the workaday world. We are pleased to offer *Therapeutic Ways with Words* to readers of Oxford Studies in Sociolinguistics.

Edward Finegan

Acknowledgments

I am immensely indebted to Joel Sherzer and Barbara Johnstone for the time they took to read and comment on entire drafts of this work as it progressed. I appreciate the time and talents of John Baugh, Tony Woodbury, Madelaine Maxwell, and Steve Finn, who offered valuable criticisms of various portions. Neal Norrick, Deborah Tannen, and Keith Walters also gave me the gift of their critical insights on drafts of parts of the book. This book is the better for their time and attention, despite the remaining shortcomings of my own.

I am greatly appreciative of the rigorous training I received at the University of Texas at Austin Department of Linguistics and the many excellent teachers there. My insights into discourse could not have developed without their scholarship. I thank especially Joel Sherzer for opening my eyes to the language, culture, society nexus, John Baugh for introducing me to the work of William Labov and David Fanshel, Tony Woodbury for the depth and breadth of his linguistic knowledge, Carlota Smith, and Robert Bley-Vroman for stringent critical analyses and encouragement. I am grateful to Greg Urban and Steve Feld for use of the equipment in the Anthropology Lab.

My thanks go to the many courageous people, friends and strangers, who offered me their ideas and feelings about therapeutic discourse. I am especially grateful to the clients who were willing to let their lives come to light. I could not have written this book without the help of the many psychotherapists who contributed their time and talents. I greatly appreciate their allowing me access to their work and wisdom. Some people whose help has been invaluable in other ways throughout the course of writing are Becky Brown, Birna Arnbjörnsdottir, Jane Lowenstein-Mairs, Felice Coles, Valerie Balester, Matt Ferrara, Larry Mitchell, Bill Haddock, Guy Bailey, and Dana Kovarsky.

A sufficient amount of writing was done while on teaching leave in Koriyama, Japan, and I thank the directors there, John Norris and Bill Stout, for their help, as well as my colleagues, Elizabeth Mathews, Chuck Taylor, Harriet Merriman, Ron and Nancy Midkiff, Tom Patterson, and Yi-Noo Tang. I thank Larry Mitchell for facilitating that leave and the College of Liberal Arts at Texas A&M University for a Summer Research Award and uninterrupted time for writing in Summer 1991.

My thanks are also extended to the superb staff at Oxford University Press, especially Cynthia Read, Susan Hannan, Beth Hanlon, and Peter Ohlin, who were so pleasant and professional.

Contents

Therapeutic Ways
with Words

1

Introduction

Although thousands of people daily seek the benefits of talking with a psychotherapist throughout Austria, Germany, Canada, Great Britain, the United States, Australia, and New Zealand, relatively few people know what types of discourse actually occur in a therapy setting or how language is used by clients and therapists to create a therapeutic climate for change. Despite a general awareness on the part of the public about the availability of mental health resources, the practice of psychotherapy is still opaque because almost no reports are available to the general public that contain samples of the actual words used. Most people know that therapists listen to people discuss their problems, that they are trained to do so, and are paid for their services. Yet few people know what really goes on in therapy sessions or have any idea about how talking to a stranger can be beneficial to mental health. What is it about therapeutic discourse that is so therapeutic? Why is the therapy hour so powerful in the lives of troubled people if all they do is talk? What do clients receive for their money besides a few "Mmhmms"? Who gets to talk, and what do they talk about? These and other questions intrigue many people.

Given the evanescent nature of language, its tendency to fade in seconds, unless psychotherapy sessions are tape-recorded, even the participants involved may not be aware of skillful and creative uses of language to accomplish their aims for therapeutic effect.

However, language is, paradoxically, both the method of diagnosis and the medium of treatment in this cultural practice. Psychotherapy depends on language, but despite this central fact of its essence, almost no research includes actual samples of dialogue. Thus, this book, which takes actual discourse as a focal point, contributes to an understanding of how the reality of everyday lives is presented and represented to us and by us through the filter of discourse.

This book is a discourse analysis of the situated uses of language between clients and therapists in individual psychotherapy sessions in the American Southwest. The therapeutic uses of language between ten different clients engaging in therapy with four experienced psychotherapists and two clinical psychologists in training are analyzed.

I have two principal goals for this book. First, I want to elucidate the speech event of psychotherapy from an ethnographic standpoint, that is, a standpoint in which an outsider seeks to come to know about a speech event and a culture that supports it through the eyes of the participants in the speech event and through participant observation. There is a need for an understanding of the health care practices of not only exotic cultures, but of the tacit assumptions underlying Western culture and its health practices as well. I want here to explicate the nature of psychotherapy, an emerging speech event of the twentieth century, to discover what speech acts, interactions, and genres are appropriate to the event and to understand how the norms of interaction come to be established through the discourse that constitutes the speech event. The focus is on characteristic uses of these discourse strategies in psychotherapy, but I claim that their use is not confined to therapeutic discourse. The study is complementary to the pioneering work of Labov and Fanshel (1977), *Therapeutic Discourse: Psychotherapy as Conversation*, because it incorporates new insights and techniques of discourse analysis that have arisen in the decade and a half since its publication. Because psychotherapy is a highly complicated activity, to penetrate its complexity, studies from many differing perspectives are called for.

Second, I want to use some of the insights here to contribute to the field of discourse analysis, a linguistic subfield that has taken as its focus stretches of speech or writing, that is, language in context rather than language in isolated words or sentences. The discourse data here are very rich and provide an opportunity to address several issues in an emerging area. The field of linguistics and the professions, or "language at work," is a growing one (Shuy 1984), but investigation of language use in law and medicine has proceeded more rapidly than has investigation of the important area I deal with here. Thus, this book contributes to an emerging subfield of discourse and the professions by shedding light on therapeutic uses of language. An ancillary goal is to provide a new perspective, that of sociolinguistics, to clinical practitioners to heighten awareness of how they are accomplishing their aims through language.

To accomplish these goals, I analyze 48 hours of tape-recorded, naturally occurring, individual psychotherapy sessions between ten different clients and four experienced therapists and two clinical psychologists in training from a discourse-centered ethnographic perspective. The data were collected in Texas and Oklahoma. All of the clients who volunteered to participate in the study are ordinary people, all are employed, and all are paying for mental health services. They are neither schizophrenic nor hospitalized, but people whose personal problems compel them, willingly, like thousands of others, to seek the help of a trained therapist in individual therapy sessions. All of the participants gave signed permission in advance. The therapists are representative of the type of people who conduct therapeutic discourse. Additional information about the background of the participants is given in Appendix A. (Readers may find it helpful to familiarize themselves with the brief biographical sketches.)

The thesis of the book, borne out in the central chapters, is that speakers can employ two cohesive aspects of discourse, repetition and contiguity, for strategic social purposes. Repetition and contiguity are manipulatable resources of language that speakers can recombine in various ways to create meaning within a given social context. I develop this thesis by focusing on the many ways in which these cohesive devices are utilized in therapeutic ways of speaking. Because cohesion, like other aspects of discourse, exists on both local and global levels, it can be thematic, structural, or lexico-semantic. The central chapters examine various ways of speaking that are characteristic of therapeutic discourse, which employ repetition on different levels of language, or which exploit contiguity or a combination of repetition and contiguity to achieve meaning.

The central theme of the book is that language and discourse are jointly constructed by interlocutors as they each take up portions of the other's speech to interweave with their own. If therapists are like most people, they probably think of discourse as a series of ordered steps: (1) one person saying something, (2) the other person computing the meaning of that, (3) the second person saying something, and (4) the first person computing the meaning of that, and so on. I try to show here, and to remind discourse analysts, that language is interactive; discourse is really mutually constructed. Discourse is more complex than the simple concatenation of monologues into conversation. People create meaning for each other. Reality is jointly constructed as bits and pieces of one's own and other's talk are interwoven in dream interpretation, jointly created extended metaphors, and even jointly produced sentences.

Specifically, the thesis is developed and the theme carried out in the following way. The book begins with an introduction to the goals and purpose, gives a brief sketch of the various participants in the study, and outlines the framework and data collection procedures. Chapter 2 presents a discussion of how psychotherapy is different from conversation and other speech events on seven dimensions and gives an overview of the history and development in the twentieth century of psychotherapy as a widely available, brief, focused mental health practice. Chapters 3 to 7 take as their starting point the real words of real people in therapy and provide a discourse analysis of two somewhat familiar and three somewhat less well known discourse strategies. Discussed in Chapters 3 and 4 are the two aspects that may be familiar, retellings of personal experience narrative, and dream telling and interpretation. This portion expands the path-breaking work on narrative by Labov and Fanshel (1977) who did not discuss these important variations on narration. In Chapters 5 to 7 I examine the less well known characteristic speech practices of using repetition, extended metaphor, and spliced sentences.

Chapter 3 discusses the nature of repeated tellings by the same person of a personal experience narrative and posits three types of retelling, each with different linguistic dimensions. In this chapter I explore global repetition by looking at how discourse participants can use and reuse the same events to make different points in their presentation of self and how they can use different events to underscore the same theme. This chapter addresses the questions of whether it is possible to tell the same story twice, whether retellings are expansions or condensations, and what counts as reportable in a specific setting. An extract illustrating one type of repetition present in two stories from different therapy sessions follows. Transcription conventions are explained in Appendix B. Analysis of this and other types of repetition is given in Chapter 3.

Short Sample of Narrative Retelling

Extract from First Story

KURT: (2) But that was the hardest thing. It was very
emotional

RALPH: Yeah

KURT: to try to get rid of it. Cause I
felt like it was just hanging around my neck like an
albatross.

Extract from Second Story

KURT: A:nd I felt so good after I finally got rid of it. You
know, it had been a dead weight to me

RALPH: Hm

KURT: for
about the last year or so. I never shoot it, you know.

Chapter 4 observes that although dreaming itself is a universal
occurrence, the telling of dreams, relating a quasi-visual experience
through the prism of language, is a culturally bound phenomenon.
Who receives dream tellings, who is authorized to interpret them,
and what their social import is all vary from culture to culture. From
analysis of dream narratives and discussions of their importance in
the therapy session I comment on their similarities to and differences from personal experience narratives and show how interpretations are jointly rather than unilaterally arrived at. An extract of
an example to be analyzed follows:

Example of Dream Telling and Initiation of Interpretation

SHARON: And last night I had the strangest dream. I was i:n:
Russia (1) ((tsk)) about to be married (.) and my
mother was there and some of my other relatives
were there too I think. My aunt was there and I think
one of my cousins, although my cousin was much
younger. And (.) I was very upset in the dream that
I was having a white wedding dress with (.)
black (.) pumps. I wanted different color shoes. I
was mad at my mother for not having gotten the right
colored shoes.

MARIAN: What do you make of that?

Chapter 5 takes up the situated and strategic use of local repetition and shows that two types, termed here *echoing* and *mirroring*, differ on three levels: (1) syntactic complexity—whether phrasal

or clausal, partial or whole, (2) discourse originator—either therapist or client, and (3) function—indirect request for elaboration or emphatic agreement. One strategic use of repetition of another's utterance displays solidarity and emphatic agreement (echoing). Another is the case of partial utterance repetition to encourage elaboration by the other (mirroring) (both to be defined). Two short examples, which are to be analyzed later, follow.

Example of Echoing

SHARON: He was in a bad mood, he was mad a lot of days and I didn't want to do anything to provoke him.

MARIAN: So you have to suffer when the big boys are angry.

SHARON: Yeah! Like he suffers when the big boys downtown are angry. It just you know—

MARIAN: **It's all a chain of command** with.

SHARON: **It's a chain of command** (.) literally. Kick the one next (.) down. (1) ((hmmph))

Example of Mirroring

JAKE: Buh uh, you know, it just seemed like (.) if you were gonna try to sit down and plan to do something, like planning on moving the trailer, uh she would jump into the middle of it.

BONNIE: Are you unsure that she would do that? Did it just seem like she did that? or [was that every time?]

JAKE: [She did that about] *everything*.

BONNIE: *Everything*.

JAKE: Very—she was very disorganized, you know. Uh ((throat clear)) you'd come home and try to find the mail, try to find the bills. Uh you may find them in the yard

BONNIE: ((laugh))

JAKE: You may find them anywhere in the trailer

BONNIE: Mmhmm

JAKE: You may find them in the trash.

BONNIE: How did you feel about that?

In Chapter 6 I further develop the claim that repetition and contiguity are manipulatable elements of discourse and that their strategic use has social implications. I show the various ways in which metaphors can be received in psychotherapy with examples from actual dyads. The chapter details metaphor misunderstanding and ratification, and features one type of jointly constructed, spun-out, metaphorical extension in which client and therapist mutually create figurative meaning by means of collocational cohesion of words, a playing out of word associations, with resulting therapeutic effect of insight. A portion of an extended metaphor showing mutual attempts to co-construct meaning follows.

Extract of an Extended Metaphor

JUDY: What's it like to be *floating down the river?* Tell me
           more.
HOWARD: (2) It's (1) comfortable. It's safe. Everything just
           keeps on an even keel, you know.
JUDY: Mmhmm.
HOWARD: You're just kinda *floating.*
JUDY: Kind of *in a canoe?* (.) *going down the river,* or-
HOWARD: No, more like *a great ole big barge* (.) *on a great old
           big* [*river*]
JUDY: [*barge*] very stable, kinda.

Chapter 7 further explores the mutual creation of meaning by looking at how two people, client and therapist, can jointly create a sentence, each contributing a portion to the other's discourse with split-second timing, as objectively measured by computer. The aligning of the speech and thought of two persons in a single sentence and its discourse effect of exhibiting empathy in the therapy setting are shown. This concatenation of the stream of talk in spliced sentences is called *Joint Productions* (where one speaker initiates an utterance and a second speaker completes or extends it). Also discussed are how such *Joint Productions* differ from interruptions and how their syntactic properties are exploited for social uses. Because each of the cases explored involves culturally recognized yet creatively achieved and innovatively situated uses of strategic speech options, the study advances discourse understanding of linguistic resources.

Example of a Joint Production

SHARON: The woman I worked with this afternoon will be my
           boss there. She's-
MARIAN: You like her?
SHARON: Yeah. I think we'll do okay. I don't like her calling
           me honey, though, and **I'm gonna have to FIND
           some way=**
MARIAN: **=to tell her.**

SHARON: to tell her. And this is not a person that (2)
           Somebody that's 40 years older than me maybe can
           call me honey, but this is a woman that's not even my
           <u>age</u>. She's mid twenties and she's calling <u>me</u> honey.

Chapter 8 is an afterword, which reports on the life of one of the participants in the study several years later. The afterword reiterates what linguists as early as Sapir (1927) claimed, that linguistics can make a contribution to psychiatry. By opening up what is clouded in secrecy to the view of outsiders, the book reveals not only important discourse practices but also enhances understanding of a complicated social institution by examining the speech event, psychotherapy.

The book will appeal not only to specialists in discourse analysis but also to ordinary people, to family and friends of participants in psychotherapy, as well as to participants themselves who are interested in how words are used in skilled and beneficial ways. The book will interest those with acknowledged curiosity about the "talking cure," because it reveals actual assumptions and practices and the very words they are based on. It will also be of interest to experienced practitioners of psychotherapy from fields such as clinical psychology, educational psychology, pastoral counseling, and psychiatric social work, because it focuses on skilled and often artful ways in which psychotherapists use language differently from ordinary conversationalists, to therapeutic effect. In this respect the book will be of use to therapists in training who want published and accessible examples of actual therapeutic ways with words. Therapists in training may find particular relevance in the interactive rather than one-sided approach to language use. Both clinical psychologists and psycholinguists will gain a new perspective on the power of language.

In addition to general interest, it will be of particular interest to linguists, anthropologists, sociologists of language, and communication specialists who concern themselves with situated uses of language.

Finally, the book will interest discourse and conversation analysts not only because of its methodological innovations of incorporating ethnographic perspective into discourse analysis and showing use of computerized timing but also for its treatment of various discourse issues from a data-based perspective. Some of the issues discussed are how the sentence can be jointly constructed, how narratives of dreams differ from personal experience narratives, how phrasal and clausal repetition of others is different from self-repetition, how reportability and expandability differ in the therapy setting, and how word associations are subtly played out. The book convincingly demonstrates that language use is interactive.

Specifically, a number of issues in discourse analysis can be considered more fully by looking at these discourse practices. Chapter 3 sheds light on the relationship of retellings to the original narrrative, illuminating whether retellings are expansions or condensations, shows the linguistic signals for chaining narratives together, and offers some insight on the nature of reportability. Chapter 4 offers an opportunity to see how language is used to convert a cinematographic experience into narrative syntax. I explore how dream telling is an oneiric recreation of a quasi-visual experience through the filter of language. Chapter 5 is informative on the issues of what forms repetition may take and why repetition has not been exhaustively studied. The chapter explores Johnstone's (1987b) observation that repetition is never exact and shows subtle differences in the various social uses to which repetition, a universally available language resource, can be put in specialized contexts. In Chapter 6 I investigate the symbolic uses of figurative language and explore the issue of whether meaning is individually constructed by following interactive uses of metaphor and their reception. Finally, Chapter 7 probes the nature of discourse by again questioning whether discourse is ever singly constructed by individuals by looking at co-authorship of such a basic unit as the sentence itself in Joint Productions.

My own interest in the unique discourse type has compelled me not only to collect tape-recorded samples of psychotherapeutic discourse but to find an adequate analytical framework to study the situated use of language. Early on I viewed the therapy setting as a site for investigation of narrative, since narrative episodes occur frequently and form a basis for the interaction. The narratives, likewise, seemed to be free of artifice, to be less self-consciously offered, and this seemed an advantage for a linguist to seize upon. But as I came to realize the complexity of the situation, my interest expanded to other types of language use such as repetition, metaphor, and dream telling as a type of narration.

The theoretical framework I use is the Ethnography of Communication [originated by Hymes (1962)], refined by Hymes (1964, 1967, 1972), and developed extensively by Bauman and Sherzer (1974, 1975, 1990) and others. I take the notion of speech event [developed by Hymes (1972)] as a starting point for investigation of some of the types of language involved in psychotherapy. A speech event is a culturally recognized occurrence that centers around language; the therapy hour is a naturally bounded speech event containing many varieties of language use. My investigation uses a discourse-centered perspective (Sherzer 1987) in approaching an understanding of what it is that people think they are doing, and acknowledges that words are both a reflection of and a means of creating social life. Discourse *is* the center of my analysis because discourse is the center of the psychotherapy exchange between client and therapist.

The approach I take to discourse analysis is a vigorously synthetic one. In addition to being conceived within the framework of the ethnography of communication, the study actively draws upon and integrates several useful models that have been proposed for dealing with discourse level phenomena, including Goffman's (1974) frame analysis, Sacks, Schegloff, and Jefferson's (1974) conversation analysis, Gumperz's (1982a,b) interactional sociolinguistics, and especially the ground-breaking discourse analysis approach of Labov, as exemplified in his collaboration with Fanshel in *Therapeutic Discourse* (1977), and the methodological extensions to that approach advanced by Ochs, Schiffrin , Tannen, Sherzer, and others. The research recognizes the mutual influence of each of these significant approaches and demonstrates that they can be fruitfully combined.

The advantages of the current study and resulting theoretical significance are that the research provides a model of how insights from major frameworks, the ethnography of communication, discourse analysis and conversation analysis, interactional sociolinguistics, and frame analysis, can be successfully synthesized. The study is a contribution to the ethnography of communication because it elucidates aspects of contemporary American society, in particular, the important yet little understood institution of psychotherapy. The study lays the groundwork for future cross-cultural comparative work on health care practices, which, no less than the well-studied political and educational realms, are universal human domains worthy of consideration.

I intend for the research to be a contribution to discourse analysis in several ways. In addition to shedding light on specific issues, the research expands the field in several directions. For example, the research extends the study of cohesion from written and monologic text to spoken and dialogic discourse and shows how speakers can manipulate inherent aspects of language for social purposes. The study expands discourse analysis, which, for English, has largely centered on investigations of everyday conversation, to encompass another important form of talk in the real world, therapeutic discourse. Although it uses the same language components as conversation, therapeutic discourse differs markedly in interesting ways from conversation and is thus an excellent relief against which to view other forms of talk. The work can be seen as contributing to sociolinguistics, linguistic anthropology, and the growing subfield of discourse and the professions. This subfield has drawn most of its work from language use in professions such as law and medicine, and there is a need for focus on other professional contexts.

The study infuses discourse analysis with a deeper, richer sense of context with the addition of the perspective of the ethnography of communication, providing a model for other enriched discourse analyses. Other methodological contributions of the study are that it uses an innovative polyphase procedure of data collection, which combines nonobtrusive tape-recording by the participants themselves with ethnographic observation and interviews. A further methodological innovation is the illustration of the usefulness of computer-aided measurements of timing and volume to determine critical junctures of speech.

As a preliminary to the central chapters, I next offer a brief orientation to the major frameworks employed: the ethnography of communication and discourse analysis. Chapter 2 also provides an overview of psychotherapy, how it differs from conversation and other professional dyads on seven proposed dimensions, and how it has emerged and evolved in the last century. In this next background chapter, some of the issues discussed are the norms of interaction, the rights and obligations of the participants, the types of speech acts, interactions, or genres that occur within it; and the history of the speech event.

Cultural events constrain the uses of language. Some researchers, like Labov, see the social situation as the most powerful determinant of verbal behavior (Labov 1972b:11). The function of utterances depends in large part on the culturally defined expectations about the nature of the speech activity in which they occur. The theoretical framework for dealing with a culturally recognized social activity in which language plays a specific and specialized role exists in Hymes's notion of a speech event. For Hymes (1972:56) the term *speech event* describes activities or aspects of activities that are directly governed by rules or norms for the use of speech and may contain one or more *speech acts*. For example, a university lecture, which is a speech event, may consist of jokes, apologies, compliments, warnings, threats, announcements, all of which are speech acts. Hymes's model is based on insights of Jakobson (1960). Some of the factors that play a part are the setting or scene, participants, ends (both goals/purposes and outcomes), act characteristics (both the form and content of what is said), key (tone, manner, or spirit of what is said), instrumentalities (channel and code), norms of interaction and interpretation, and genres (categories or types of speech act and speech event).

These individual elements and their fluctuating importance in defining the salient characteristics of individual speech events can be viewed as resources for a community to manipulate in unique ways. A speech event is at once a unique occasioning, an unrepeatable instance of social interaction created by interlocutors through language, and an example of a generalized cultural system in a community that draws on these eight resources. The dynamic tension between the ready-made and the emergent aspects of discourse is at the heart of the discourse-centered approach to language and culture.

When the possibilities inherent in a culture are actualized as discourse, language "creates, recreates, focuses, modifies and transmits both culture and language and their intersection" (Sherzer 1987:295). These emergent qualities are equally as important as the eight components in the notion of speech event. A speech act is an utterance that is intended to perform a particular function, such as greeting, apology, request, warning. The notion is central to the work of Austin (1962) and Searle (1969, 1975, 1976) and has been the focus of speech act theory. The notion of speech act bears resemblance to the traditionally recognized term *genre*. The notion of speech event is a useful departure point for this study of language use in the setting of psychotherapy.

A related notion to that of speech act has arisen out of Labov and Fanshel's (1977) research. Their concentration on speech interaction highlights the dynamic aspects of speech as social action, rather than viewing acts as an inventory of resources. I make use of all three of these notions: genre, act, and interaction. For example, dream telling may be viewed as a genre, whereas the emphatic agreement evidenced by echoing (a strategic form of contiguous repetition to be discussed) may be seen as a speech interaction.

Hymes's notion of speech community has been used extensively in sociolinguistics, and the delimitation of a speech community raises important theoretical questions (see Baugh 1983; Irvine 1987 for discussion). Basically, a group or community that shares resources, norms of conduct and interpretation of speech and rules for at least one linguistic variety is seen as a speech community. We can regard therapy-users as constituting an "invisible speech community," because, although they are not overtly identified outside the community, they have become socialized to its norms of speech interaction. I will offer a glimpse of some of the resources shared by this community.

The last of the notions related to the notion of speech event is Hymes's (1972) influential concept of communicative competence. The question of how speakers in a speech community arrive at the ability to use language in both grammatically and socially appropriate ways is a fascinating one. What members of a society need to know to participate in a speech act and how they acquire this information are relevant aspects of communicative competence. In the case at hand, for instance, it can be observed that not everyone is familiar with the norms of interaction in psychotherapy: whether the participants sit or recline, who is allowed to speak the most, who initiates, what topics are appropriate, whether both participants can ask questions, what speech acts are characteristic, who controls the flow of topics, and other norms. Thus, socialization into the invisible speech community of psychotherapists and psycho-therapy-users does not happen overnight. According to a clinical trainer I questioned, a generally accepted tenet among therapists about clients is that it sometimes takes up to a year to learn how to do therapy. For clinicians, too, the training period is lengthy. Members of the speech community share norms and these norms are revealed through discourse.

Speech events, in addition to being culturally constrained and socially arrived at, can wax and wane in a given society over time. New speech events, previously unimagined, can arise; likewise, older speech events may decline in frequency of use or die out. For this reason, therapeutic discourse is of interest because psychotherapy represents an innovation—a new speech event—which for Westerners did not exist prior to 1900. As a major innovation it stands in contrast to obsolete speech events such as gathering around the console radio to listen to and comment on a radio program, or the declining speech event in which a young suitor formally asks a girl's father for her hand in marriage.

Each of the ensuing chapters investigates an aspect of cohesive language in therapeutic discourse in its own terms. Each chapter can be viewed individually. The various aspects of discourse that are studied are not exhaustive; rather, their variety is indicative of the ways in which language can be utilized to create meaning.

Data Collection and Methods of Analysis

I adopt the procedure of dual accountability for discourse segments through the explicit recognition of *distributional accountability* as well as *sequential accountability*, that is, I look at large segments or chunks of discourse as well as at the frequency of occurrence of selected phenomena. Schiffrin (1987b:19) explains the two complementary types of accountability:

> When an analysis provides a comprehensive understanding of the coherence in a text, we may say that it has sequential accountability. When an analysis provides an explanation of why an element occurs in one discourse environment but not another, we may say that it has distributional accountability.

Schiffrin argues that to be considered empirical an analysis must be accountable to a body of data and that two standards of accountability (distributional and sequential) are available. This approach has had an enormous influence on the types of discourse analyses that are currently being conducted. Whereas sequentially accountable analyses such as Labov and Fanshel's (1977) are essentially qualitative, the extension of discourse analysis to the examination of a particular discourse phenomenon [e.g., "well," Schiffrin (1985)] wherever it occurs, in a variety of discourse contexts, increases the potential for empirical quantitative assessments of numerous tokens of discourse phenomena. In this book I use both qualitative and quantitative approaches to discourse analysis.

Within a sociolinguistic tradition of progressively improving data-gathering techniques, the current research acknowledges the major contributions made by leading discourse analysts and attempts to expand on these approaches by contributing alternative ways of establishing a corpus of language use in context. The research offered here differs from the work of other discourse analysts in several important ways. Because methodological advances lead directly from comparison of various data-collection techniques, the assumptions that underlie them, and the consequences that follow, it is useful to examine how the data-collection procedures and methods of analysis used in this study are similar to and different from those of other analysts.

In this section I give descriptions of the selection of participants, their characteristics, the time and setting involved, the recording equipment used, and the analytical techniques employed. I also briefly comment on the observer's paradox and ethical considerations. The transcription conventions adopted are noted in Appendix B. Readers may find it useful to be familiar with these notations used in data extracts.

Principally, the corpus I collected consists of 48 hours of audio tape recordings of naturally occurring individual psychotherapy sessions between ten clients and six therapists (four experienced therapists and two in training). The book is representative of actual practice by both male and female therapists and clients; therapists and clients of both genders are included in my corpus. For the majority of the clients I tape-recorded six consecutive hour-long sessions. My intention was to have consecutive sessions so as to benefit from continuity of referents and associations. This procedure was not always possible but is true for the majority of cases. Most clients were recorded for six sessions, others for fewer. In two cases eight hours were recorded. The audio recordings were made with the full advance knowledge and signed permission of all participants. I offered transcripts and duplicate tapes in exchange for participation. I use pseudonyms throughout to protect the participants' anonymity.

The current research grows out of and is similar to the work described by Labov and Fanshel (1977) in *Therapeutic Discourse* in several important respects. I believe there are also some important differences. Both studies are empirical analyses of actual language use between dyads engaged in psychotherapy. One goal of both Labov and Fanshel and the present study is to arrive at general principles of discourse by looking at a specific type of situated speech interaction, psychotherapy, which relies principally on extended discourse. The present discourse analysis, like that of Labov and Fanshel, is basically qualitative rather than quantitative. While no one book could provide a complete account of the complex language behavior in the psychotherapy setting, this book offers a glimpse at the therapeutic ways of speaking while emphasizing that language and discourse are jointly constructed.

However, consistent with the focus on the speech event as the basic unit of analysis, the book is motivated by the basic questions: What goes on in psychotherapy? and What kinds of language use are characteristic of psychotherapy?

Unlike Labov and Fanshel, the present work does not concentrate on the extended discourse between one therapist (a psychiatric social worker) and one female patient (Rhoda P.), but attempts in three ways to provide a representative sample. I examine language use in a variety of dyads, including those in which both the therapist and client are male, those in which both therapist and client are female, and those which are of mixed gender. Likewise, the psychological problems presented by the clients in this study are diverse. Whereas the patient Labov and Fanshel studied suffered from the psychosomatic problem anorexia nervosa, which usually affects young females, the clients in the current study have a broad spectrum of problems, ranging from troubles with alcoholism, low self-esteem, childhood sexual abuse, pedophilia or marital problems. The research utilizes several segments from the different dyads to illustrate the various discourse phenomena discussed.

This report offers a representative reflection of psychotherapeutic discourse as it is currently practiced in the United States: three of the six therapists involved in the present study are clinical psychologists who hold Ph.D. degrees in psychology and professional licensing as clinical psychologists. A fourth therapist in the study is a master's level social worker with extensive experience in therapy, and two of the therapists are clinical psychologists in training to be therapists. As Garfield and Bergin (1986:5) observe, psychiatrists and clinical psychologists "have been the most influential people in psychotherapy," although a number of other professional groups (e.g., counseling psychologists, social workers, school psychologists, psychiatric nurses, and pastoral counselors) "participate in some type of psychotherapy or counseling." While Beutler, Crago, and Arizmendi (1986:286–287) state that no differences in outcome rates have been found among therapists of different disciplines, in many states insurance companies will not pay benefits if therapy has not been conducted by approved practitioners.

In addition, the clients in the corpus are voluntarily seeking the services of a psychotherapist, and as evidence of this personal motivation are themselves willing to pay for their psychotherapy. The profile of the nonhospitalized, usually employed client who seeks individual therapy and is willing to pay fits that of a large number of typical therapy-users, estimated to be hundreds of thousands in the United States.

The two different terms designating therapy-users, *client* and *patient*, are "emic" distinctions (that is, labeled distinctions used by the participants themselves), which help differentiate this work. My focus on therapy clients is different from Labov and Fanshel's study of a patient. From ethnographic interviews I learned that practitioners differentiate the two classes, client and patient, on the basis of (1) the setting in which services are delivered, and (2) the discipline of the therapy-provider. People seen in hospitals are termed *patients* regardless of the discipline of the therapy-provider. People seen in private offices by clinical psychologists are called *clients*. However, social workers with psychoanalytic (rather than psychotherapeutic) training often follow the medical model of psychiatrists and call the people they see professionally *patients*. Thus both terms have meaning in mental health contexts. All of the paying people engaged in individual therapy in private offices who participated in this study are therefore called *clients*. Because the subject in Labov and Fanshel's study was seeing a social worker who had undergone psychoanalysis, the subject was called a *patient*. This study is concerned with patterns of language use in individual psychotherapy sessions between client and therapist. By means of first understanding how language is used in this specialized variant of conversation, the study ultimately intends to contribute to a fuller awareness of principles of language use in general. Tape recordings are the primary data. An explicitly stated goal is to supplement this primary data with other observational materials. Tape recordings alone can provide data for an analysis, but I have made attempts in this book to enrich the discourse-centered analysis with ethnographic observations, for example, discussions of transcripts with therapists, observations of clinical training classes, and other techniques to be described.

Another crucial difference between this study and the work of other discourse analysts arises from the deliberate decision *not* to be present when the therapeutic interaction was taking place. This decision stemmed from the desire to reduce the effects of the observer's paradox, the concept that holds that the act of observation can alter the naturalness of a situation. Unlike important work on conversation by Tannen (1984, 1989) and Schiffrin (1987a,b,c), I was not a participant in the interaction I later planned to analyze. Thus, I have not generated nor instigated my own data. The central point I wish to make is that the interactions I analyze would have taken place anyway, whether or not I was present. In this regard, the speech analyzed here can be regarded as naturally occurring speech.

To collect data on psychotherapeutic discourse I could have chosen to enter therapy and to have recorded sessions in which I took part, but by not playing a dual role—that of participant turned analyst—the research gains three important advantages: (1) the potential for replicability, (2) the potential for increased objectivity, and (3) the potential to widen the scope of the speech community observed.

First, analyzing the speech interaction of others to whom the researcher is not intimately known or related, or with whom the researcher has extended social contacts, in conversations in which one is not a participant, forces the researcher to rely on the internal evidence of the data themselves to gain access to the hearer's interpretations and the speaker's interpretations, that is, to be discourse-driven. Analysts with nonparticipant status cannot appeal to privileged knowledge of the situation or intentions and are less likely to have discourse analysis colored by ongoing social relationships with the people involved or by possible subjective reactions to memories or feelings evoked by their participation in the speech interactions. It is important to point out that measurement of phonological, morphological, or syntactical variation *can* be objective despite the analyst's level of involvement in the data generation, and that sociolinguistic interviews are effective means of gathering data for this type of analysis, but sociolinguistic interviews are less suitable for discourse analyses that involve statements about speakers' intentions. There is also less likelihood that a researcher will influence or skew the natural speech interaction if she or he is not a participant.

Second, because two or more analysts can look at the same data (to which they were not parties) and potentially arrive at the same conclusions without appeal to privileged knowledge, there is increased possibility for replicability of studies, an important attribute of current reliable scientific discovery. In other words, any skilled observer of language use in context might arrive at similar findings if he or she recorded and analyzed similar spoken interactions.

A third advantage to not analyzing language use situations in which the researcher was present is that having others tape-record speech interactions (as the therapists did with their clients here) allows discourse analysts to probe deeper into the general speech community than their own social networks would allow. The real strength of this method is that researchers thereby do not confine analyses to the speech patterns of those who share the same sociocultural assumptions as they do. I have initiated and would advocate the methodological practice of having discourse participants self-record in natural speech interaction situations and then supplementing these data with ethnographic studies. The widening scope thus afforded is illustrated by the inclusion in the present study of several lower-class speakers, who because of their rural backgrounds, lack of education, or unusual problems (e.g., pedophilia) might not usually be members of researchers' social networks. Likewise, the practices followed here permit data collection in a situation where, although discourse is the principal focus of interaction, outside observers have traditionally had extremely limited access.

Thus, the practice followed here of having discourse participants self-record and then gathering additional information ethnographically may not only help reduce the effects of the observer's paradox but may also expand the types of language situations that are available for discourse analysis to those that are highly confidential (e.g., psychotherapy), highly dangerous (e.g., neurosurgery), or illegal speech events (e.g., betting with a bookie in some areas).

Heretofore inaccessible or hard-to-get data can be gathered in the manner just described, having informants self-record. The inherent limitation of such a procedure is that otherwise valuable information about the participants, the setting, or the norms of interaction must be collected in other, nonobtrusive ways at other times. To maximize the naturalness of the speaker interaction being tape-recorded, minimal disruption or distortion of the flow of talk is the goal. I have used a polyphase procedure of data gathering in which interactants are interviewed before or after the discourse situation, and many additional means of observation are used to supplement.

I engaged in various supplemental observations of psychotherapeutic discourse in order to (1) reduce the effects of the observer's paradox, and (2) add ethnographic insight about, among other things, the underlying assumptions of, the attitudes toward, appropriate settings for, and interactants' interpretations of therapeutic discourse.

The study was enhanced by a variety of ethnographic observational techniques. During the course of data collection I met many times with four of the therapists who agreed to participate in the study. In discussion with them I learned how members of the mental health community conceive of psychotherapy as a process that facilitates change. The therapists freely discussed their own backgrounds, the backgrounds of the clients, their goals for the

ongoing sessions they were conducting with the clients, problems
they encountered in doing therapy, and insights both they and the
clients had gained. The therapists were also helpful in interpreting
segments of discourse from their own and others' sessions and
answering questions. These discussions with the therapists lasted
from 15 minutes to one hour each visit, depending on the therapist's
schedule. They took place in their offices. I wrote up notes immediately after each discussion with a therapist. After the first visit I
made sketches of the office, the seating arrangements, and other
furnishings.

On some occasions I brought in transcripts I had made of previous sessions to discuss puzzling discourse phenomena. I was
attempting to tape-record six consecutive sessions for each client
and to provide therapists and clients with tapes and transcripts. As
an example, I asked therapists such things as what they thought
was happening when echoing behavior occurred, how they regarded
"sentence" (utterance) completions or extensions by themselves or
their clients, why clients would retell narratives, what they thought
about thematic repetition of core metaphors, and how they approached
dream tellings. I also asked about norms of interaction such as who
asks questions, how often, and whether jargon is acceptable.

For these discussion sessions with the therapists I always prepared written questions. However, the therapists were usually eager
to talk about their cases, their progress and setbacks, and each case's
similarities to other cases, and I was ready to listen to anything
I could learn, so the list of questions I had prepared was never
exhausted. In this regard, I term these information exchanges discussion sessions because they did not resemble the usual interview
situation.

I interviewed one of the female clients in the study prior to
recording her session and received a request from a male client in
the study to meet. Soon after the second session recorded with the
female client whom I had interviewed, however, she asked to withdraw from the study, so I discontinued the practice of speaking to
the clients. This client, nonetheless, granted permission to use the
tape recordings of the two sessions she completed and was given
transcripts. In light of this, and in an attempt to overcome the
observer's paradox while gaining ethnographic data, I interviewed
five other therapy-users who were not being tape-recorded, and
either took notes or tape-recorded our talks. I held further discussions with an additional ten therapy-users. I thus gained insights

on therapy-users' attitudes toward the language used in therapy. In addition, I conducted informal interviews with ten undergraduate non-therapy-users about their knowledge about and assessment of psychotherapy. Over the course of several years I have benefited from discussions about psychotherapy with a dozen other therapists who are not a part of this study but maintain an interest in language and psychotherapy. Their insights have been very useful.

Another unobtrusive observational technique I employed was to watch an initial psychotherapy session between a clinical psychology trainer and an undergraduate female through a one-way mirror. The demonstration was given to a class of clinical psychology trainees who also watched behind the one-way mirror. I attended the class discussion that followed in which the clinical psychology trainees shared their differing interpretations of the session they had witnessed, and I later discussed my interests in language usage with them.

To learn more about the setting in which voluntary, individual psychotherapy is conducted, I made a practice of arriving early for discussions with therapists in order to sit for an extended time in their waiting room (which all but one therapist had) to observe the types of people who came in along with their behavior. On one such occasion, I inadvertently met a coworker who pretended not to notice me in the therapist's office but later at work voluntarily acknowledged having seen me and asked me not to reveal his whereabouts during work hours.

Because I have ongoing social ties with several clinical psychologists, I have observed them in a number of informal and recreational occasions. In discussions with psychologists and after presentations to psychologists I have received many helpful comments and a great deal of encouragement to explore an area that holds interest but has received little attention from psychologists previously. I further gathered information on issues of concern to therapists by reading, over a two-year period, professional newsletters, research journals, and books of this profession. The professional newsletters in particular are a rich source of insight on just what kinds of concerns therapists have, and I learned that psychotherapists can make light of their profession from the following piece of humor in print.

A: How many clinical psychologists does it take to change a lightbulb?
B: I don't know. How many?
A: One, but the lightbulb has to really *want* to change.

In addition, I have watched video tapes of group therapy, read how-to manuals for beginning psychotherapists (e.g., Lewis 1978; Zaro, Barach, Nedelman, and Dreiblatt 1977), listened to a therapist's telephone conversations with suicidal clients, and briefly tried participant observation by engaging in psychotherapy for a short time. In summary, while the tape recordings constitute the primary data and the transcripts are the auxiliary data for the current discourse analysis, a variety of supplemental observational techniques has been developed to enhance the quality of this inquiry into situated language use.

The research reported here was not conceived as a case study nor as an experimental situation. From the outset I determined that the principal criterion for selection of the therapists involved would be that they were experienced therapists who enjoyed good reputations in Austin, Texas, the community I was researching. I planned to have two female and two male therapists participate. I collected data from these four therapists from January 1986 to June 1986. In addition, the therapist Marian provided me with two tape recordings she herself made for an advanced licensing exam and two tape recordings of herself with another client. I transcribed these, talked with her about the cases, and have drawn examples from them. I later added eight sessions I transcribed from two female therapists in training from data collected in Oklahoma in 1980, and make use of examples contained in them. I wanted a corpus representative of what psychotherapists themselves would recognize as good psychotherapy.

Because others may be interested in how they might obtain confidential data, I will discuss my initial steps in data gathering. I asked therapists I knew to name members of the therapeutic community whom they respected. I planned to ask them to tape two clients each over six consecutive sessions. I was not prepared for the number of therapists who declined to participate. The first two therapists I approached to request their participation I had previously met briefly. One was a graduate of the small liberal arts college I attended and the other was the father of a child I had tested in a child language acquisition study. I counted on their previous knowledge of me to smooth the way. However, these early requests were met with refusals. One psychotherapist commented, "How can I ask people I charge $80 a session to make tape recordings?" This woman, after admitting her discomfort with being tape-recorded herself, told me of a friend of hers on an examining board for professional certification who might know area therapists who had some familiarity with tape-recording their sessions as part of the advanced professional certification process. This referral proved useful and the board member I contacted gave me the name of a highly respected, local, female therapist in her early fifties whom I did not know. I contacted her and explained my research objectives. This therapist, Marian, expressed a positive attitude toward research of the kind I described and was familiar with the work of Fanshel. She agreed to meet me to discuss the possibility of participating. Meeting her for the first time in a university office, I learned that she was a research-oriented person. She read over my research proposal and the release forms and gave me two tapes that she herself had recorded of psychotherapy sessions as a basis for her professional licensing. (I later supplemented the tape recordings that were made expressly for the current study with transcripts I made of these volunteered tapes and two others Marian provided.)

In convincing the therapist to participate, I explained that my interest was not clinical, but involved language use. There can be no doubt that my social ties helped me gain access. Finding therapists was only part of the battle. Thus, I spoke with three therapists before finding the first therapist who agreed to participate.

As is often the case, obtaining the participation of the second therapist was somewhat easier after I mentioned that another (unnamed) therapist in the community was willing to participate in the research. Ralph, a therapist in his late thirties, works in a psychotherapy center that serves holders of company-paid health insurance policies. Like Marian, he is widely known in the community of clinical psychologists and has held local offices. Like Marian, he holds a Ph.D. in psychology and is from the Northeast. Unlike Marian, Ralph had not tape-recorded his sessions before but agreed to try to find clients who would cooperate. I was not surprised, given the positive attitude toward research by Ralph, to receive a phone call two days later from a social worker, Gerald, who did therapy in the same mental health center as Ralph. Gerald asked to be part of the study. In a meeting shortly after with Gerald, I learned that he frequently tape-recorded his sessions and had volunteered to participate because he had heard that I had promised to provide transcripts of the sessions recorded. He was interested in using transcripts in a professional workshop. Gerald is a social worker with a masters degree who frequently makes use of Gestalt techniques and employs hypnotic suggestion.

The fourth Austin therapist included in this study is Charlene, a very active clinical psychologist in her midthirties. Charlene received her training in the southeastern United States and has been an officer in the local psychologists' organization. I had met her before and knew that she was widely respected. She was not familiar with tape recorders and admitted to machine phobia in operating them. Each of these four therapists describes his or her style as eclectic, although Marian prefers to apply the term *amalgam*.

The two psychologists in training, Bonnie and Judy, also provided six hours each of psychotherapy tapes with signed advance permission from their clients. I transcribed eight hours of these and have drawn examples from them. Both trainees are in their late twenties and are pursuing a doctorate in clinical psychology.

Thus, despite initial refusals by two therapists, I was able to secure the participation of six therapists (two male, four female) interested in research on language use in psychotherapy. Undoubtedly, the general high regard for the field of linguistics and the offer of transcripts and duplicate tapes in return (Cf. Shuy 1983 on compensating participants) helped gain the cooperation of therapists. However, securing the permission of clients, who, after all, were the ones whose problematic lives were to come under scrutiny, was much more difficult and occurred over a matter of months. Each of the four therapists broached the subject of participation with new and ongoing clients. I originally intended for all clients to be at the initial stage of therapy, but because the therapists experienced problems in enlisting the participation of some clients who were new to them I later decided to also tape-record clients who had been in therapy longer. One therapist reported being turned down five times before securing the cooperation of the first client. Thus, five of the clients I recorded are in the beginning weeks of therapy and the rest have been seeing their therapist for varying lengths of time, up to two years. The clients were asked to allow tape-recording of six consecutive sessions. They were assured that their participation was entirely voluntary and that they could withdraw at any time. I did not offer any monetary incentive but offered to provide transcripts. Even the client who later withdrew asked for and was given transcripts. The therapists voiced eagerness to receive the tapes and transcripts, some using them for professional workshops or for the basis for their own publications.

At times I could not produce transcripts fast enough for the clients. Evidence of client interest in the transcripts is contained in recordings of their sessions where questions about the promised documents are made to the therapist early in each session. The three extracts below are from the client Kurt's fourth, seventh, and eighth therapy sessions with Ralph.

RK4

KURT: Did you ever get those tapes transcribed (.) yet?
RALPH: She's she's transcribing but I haven't gotten any back yet.
KURT: Mmhm.

RK7

KURT: Did you get those transcripts yet?
RALPH: Rest assured we'll get you those.

The overall positive attitude toward obtaining the transcripts is visible in the following segment.

RK8

RALPH: Here's the surprise I have for you:. [This is very exciting.]
KURT: Oh [This is goo:d.]
RALPH: Uh (2) There are two transcripts. These are the copies for you. And: uh I don't understand what the designation RK(4) is. It would seem that this one would be the later one, but in effect I think this is the earlier one and this is the later one.
KURT: Yeah.
RALPH: But these are. these are your copies. And I think that you'll find them interesting. As you read them bear in mind that everything you say, including uh the "uhs" and uh pauses and everything is documented in there.
KURT: What are these ( ) parentheses for?
RALPH: Oh, let me show you. I forgot to. (8) "Uninterpretable." I'll make a copy of that (.) legend for you. (2) It's like the gap in the (.) Watergate tapes ((laugh))
KURT: Yeah. I had noted that I punctuate my speech with a lot of "uh."
RALPH: So do I: So do I. (2) But by and large I think that when you read that you'll really get the flavor of our sessions. I think it really comes through.
KURT: Uh-huh.
RALPH: I think some good material in there. I think (.) will (.) go nicely in your journal.
KURT: All this is just the one hour?
RALPH: Yeah. You got two hours there. And I don't have the other transcripts back. and that's just two of them. (1) One of

those there is the session where you talked about the child pornography. So that's particularly uh (.) sensitive session. And I think that the transcription is very good.

Brief Description of Clients
Who Participated in the Study

The clients who agreed to participate in this study shared at least one characteristic in common: courage to allow a researcher access to their innermost feelings. They differ in the perceived problems that served as an impetus to seeking help through psychotherapy. These pseudonymed clients were recruited by their therapists to participate: Sharon, Kurt, Wilma, Norma, Lana, Katie, Shannon, Shelly, Jake, Howard. Their "presenting problems" (the problems for which they seek immediate help, which are not necessarily identical to what the therapist sees as their underlying problem(s), range from fear of suicide (Shelly) to low self-esteem resulting from sexual or physical abuse (Sharon, Lana), to alcoholism (Kurt, Lana), to pedophilic fantasies (Kurt), to marital disruption (Jake, Katie) to remorse over an abortion (Shannon) or leaving young children (Wilma), to grief over a parent's death (Shannon, Norma). The ages of the clients in this study range from 19 to 43. Unlike the majority of the therapists in the study, who are from the American Northeast, each of the clients is from the central portion of the United States. They come from Texas, Arkansas, Missouri, and Oklahoma. A brief sketch of the personal history of these clients is given in Appendix A. Readers will find these short histories a useful background, and I recommend reading these first. Many more details of the clients' lives are included in the chapters to follow as further background to the extracts discussed. More important, their backgrounds will unfold as the clients themselves describe the contexts of their lives to their therapists, continue to create their lives during the therapy hour, and relive portions of their lives, sometimes those previously hidden from their own understanding.

Time and Setting for Data Collection

I collected the core of 36 hours of tape-recorded data from January to June in 1986. The additional 12 hours were tape-recorded from 1980 to 1985. In general, the clients were seeing their therapists once each week, and I recorded consecutive weekly sessions. Biographical sketches of each of the ten clients are given in Appendix A. Two clients (Lana and Katie), due to financial pressures, asked to have sessions once every two weeks. All but one of the clients remained in therapy *beyond* the sessions I recorded. The one exception, Wilma, stopped seeing her therapist after the sixth session, stating financial pressures as her reason. In two cases therapists volunteered to tape weeks seven and eight.

As Labov (1972) observes, setting may be the most influential factor affecting speech. Certainly the setting for psychotherapy is an important determinant of the type of language use seen here. It is, in fact, unlikely that identical interactions would occur in any other type of locale. The homogeneity of the settings in which I recorded is therefore important to consider. I visited all of the offices where recordings were made many times. All of the tape recordings in Texas were made in individual therapist's offices. These four offices were located on the same street in two different professional buildings about two blocks apart in an area of Austin known as the "medical district." The offices were all carpeted and draped, furnished with comfortable chairs (ranging from traditional to modern in style). The therapists and clients sat facing each other, usually with a small table placed between the chairs. Each of the offices had a window, framed pictures and diplomas on the walls, and bookshelves filled with books. In addition, each room contained the therapist's desk. The two offices in Oklahoma were less plush, more austerely furnished, and were individual rooms with one-way mirrors on a university campus in training facilities.

Two of the therapists had clocks in prominent positions and all had boxes of Kleenex tissues on hand. By coincidence, the offices of two of the female therapists were next door to one another on the same floor of a professional building where 30 other psychiatrists or psychologists had their offices. At the time of recording, neither knew of the other's participation. (Clustering of offices is one way to insure privacy, e.g., that clients leaving the elevator will not unexpectedly encounter a friend going to the dentist.)

During the course of taping, the two male therapists moved to a different floor of the professional building they were in. Their building was in the same area of town, within view of the professional building that two of the female therapists occupied. Both male therapists had individual offices in the mental health division of a large employer-sponsored health maintenance organization, and they shared the same waiting room. Their offices were located down a hallway from the waiting room. Both male therapists knew of the other's participation. The interior decoration of the offices resembled that of the female therapists. I was given tours of the office layout, which included a conference room for the six therapists in the mental health division.

Recording Equipment and Setup

The therapy sessions in Texas were recorded with a Marantz Superscope CD-330 stereo professional tape recorder, using a Superscope EC-335 bidirectional electret condenser microphone. I brought the tape recorders to the therapists' offices and showed them how to use them. During the actual sessions only the therapist and client were present. Adjustments had to be made in several cases. I preferred to use 120-minute tapes, in spite of the problems ascribed to longer tapes, so that therapists, who were in charge of recording, would not have to turn the tape over in the middle of the session. With this consideration I hoped to minimize the observer's paradox, and to interfere as little as possible in the natural occurrence. As planned, most 50-minute sessions were comfortably accommodated without interruption, but one therapist consistently had sessions longer than 50 minutes and flipped the tape over during the session.

The clients always knew *in advance* that they were being recorded, and gave written permission. The large, circular receptivity of the bidirectional electret condenser mike allowed its placement anywhere in the small rooms. I suggested that the recorder be placed in full view, either on the small table or on the therapist's desk, and therapists typically did so. The microphone was a slim one that did not call attention to itself. The tape recorder was usually placed on the desk, but one therapist put it under the desk. I asked the therapists to turn the tape recorder on before the client appeared and to leave it on until well after he or she had left because, among other things, I wanted to record linguistic patterns for initiating and terminating sessions.

These arrangements were undertaken to minimize the effects of the observer's paradox. The anonymity of the clients was protected by not using video recordings. However, potentially valuable data on kinesics and proxemics had to be sacrificed.

Analytical Techniques

Discourse analysis is an open-ended process of discovery, and analysts typically return to the primary language data (usually video or audio tape recordings) again and again, often making corrections or new discoveries with each successive stage. Audio tape recordings are a mechanical means of freezing a slice of actual speech interaction for the purpose of later analysis. However, the tape recordings are but one aspect of the actual speech event.

I made a conscious effort to treat the tape recordings as the principal source of information and to regard the transcripts made from them as adjuncts, to be read in tandem with the aural experience of listening over and over again to the tapes. I have followed this discovery procedure throughout the course of analysis. I employ an adaptation of transcription conventions originally developed by Jefferson (Sacks, Schegloff, Jefferson 1974), which is shown in Appendix B.

I was fortunate to be able to listen to pilot tapes and to realize that narratives abound in therapeutic discourse and that therapists ask questions in a variety of forms. At the earliest stage I had no idea of what aspect of narrative would command attention or what other genres or speech acts would figure prominently in the data I was to collect. Allowing the data to largely determine what will be analyzed involves not deciding a priori what is unique, characteristic, frequent, problematic, or otherwise of interest. Thus, after collecting the tape recordings I listened to them over and over, jotting notes, forming impressions of recurrent patterns. Deciding on analytical categories was a long way off. Next, I made the first of many versions of a transcript. This process of becoming familiar with what occurs in psychotherapy, across therapists and across clients, by means of making a rough but complete transcript of each session was both a lengthy and valuable one. With rough transcripts in hand, I then listened to each tape with the written approximation in front of me.

Then I made systematic marginal notes on the transcripts and next compiled these notes into categories with a numbered referencing system where certain recurring features could be found. In this early stage I noted openings and closing, uses of jargon, metaphor, sarcasm, slips of the tongue, multiple types of question formation (e.g., disjunctive, chained, subsequently answered by question poser, etc.), retellings, narratives, dream tellings, utterance completions by another, parallel constructions, and exact repetitions. I also noted syntactic and phonological accommodation by therapist and client. Gradually I began to select which of these patterns to investigate and which aspects of these items were of interest. I was influenced at this point by conversations with the therapists and by the work of Gumperz (1982b) on discourse strategies. I saw speakers as often making choices among linguistic resources in order to convey meaning. The types of choices that appeared salient in therapeutic discourse were strategic uses of repetition and contiguity, but I was puzzled in many instances by what I found. Throughout the transcription and analysis I consulted with the therapists involved and discussed segments of their own and segments of others' transcriptions that resembled theirs or followed the same pattern to discover what they considered to be the underlying rationale for a phenomenon.

Thus I have three or four sources of explanation for a given phenomenon: (1) what the therapist involved said about a speech segment, (2) what other therapists said about that or similar speech segments, (3) what the reply to an utterance or subsequent discourse seemed to convey about the hearer's interpretation of what an utterance meant, and (4) what I as an analyst with linguistic training formulated about an utterance as one instance of many similar such cases.

I argue that the meaning of an utterance is sometimes displayed in interaction, in the participants' reactions to the utterance, sometimes available in how members of a community explain the utterance, and sometimes only apparent to an analyst in cases where participants themselves may not have grasped the meaning. The problem of conflicting interpretations, succinctly stated by Schiffrin (1987b:17): "What is one person's definition of 'what is going on' may differ markedly from another's," is less of a problem for the current discourse analysis than for earlier ones, because the main goal of this research is not to discover what is going on in a given segment but to learn what language patterns are typical of therapeutic discourse in general.

I discussed the effects of taping many times with the therapists. The therapist Ralph, who had not tape-recorded before, reported that he was surprised that both his beginning clients who participated in the study gave very revealing information about themselves in the first two sessions that were being recorded. For example, Kurt reported his involvement with child pornography and Lana recounted three instances with rapists. Ralph believes that these important revelations at a comparatively early stage in the therapeutic process might be attributed to the heightening effect of being recorded. He suggested to me that he finds this effect valuable and would like to continue to make tape recordings of his sessions.

Ethical Considerations

In accordance with Linguistic Society of America and American Psychological Association guidelines, no covert recordings were made and no deception was involved. Every effort to insure protection of the anonymity of the participants has been made. All potentially identifying references including names of hometowns and people have been changed. The participants gave signed consent and were informed that they could withdraw at any time.

In discussing the obligations researchers have toward the participants of a study, Shuy (1983:352) poses the question, "How can we, in good conscience, take away a piece of our informant's life without offering something in return?" With this in mind, in appreciation for the courage the participants showed in sharing details of their lives, I offered tapes and transcripts to the participants. There were numerous indications that this was a valuable exchange, and several of the therapists said that they would like to continue to record on their own. I have also received numerous invitations to speak to groups of psychologists about research on language use in psychotherapy. There is a great deal of interest in this area.

In summary, the discourse segments examined in the forthcoming chapters are extracts of data collected from naturally occurring individual psychotherapy sessions between four therapists and eight clients in a metropolitan area of Texas and two client-therapist dyads in Oklahoma. One contribution of the study is that it illustrates alternative ways of establishing a corpus of situated language use by employing a polyphase procedure for gathering ethnographic information to supplement the self-recorded discourse between clients and therapists and to help minimize the effects of the observer's paradox.

With focus on discovering the genres, speech acts, and other linguistic phenomena characteristic of the speech event therapeutic discourse, the units of analysis have been allowed to emerge from the data rather than being predetermined to be of interest. Many examples from a variety of speakers have been used to illustrate a given aspect of therapeutic discourse. Thus the study extends work on discourse analysis by following Schiffrin's (1982a,b, 1987b,c) suggestion of using distributional as well as sequential accountability. Likewise, following the tradition of Gumperz (1982b), the study broadens the spectrum of speech events that are subjected to discourse analysis beyond the analysis of conversation.

The present study differs in a number of important ways from previous discourse analyses of conversation. Principally, it differs in (1) its focus on dyadic rather than multiparty discourse, (2) its insistence on observing actual naturally occurring discourse that would happen regardless of the researcher's presence or absence rather than creating interaction to observe, and (3) its attempt to penetrate a speech community that has been relatively inaccessible to discourse analysts.

Therapeutic discourse is seen as an optimal place to reduce the effects of the observer's paradox because hour-long sessions are examples of extended discourse in often emotionally charged situations that might reduce audio-monitoring. To overcome the paradox of transcription as text, the audio tape recordings themselves were treated as primary data and the transcripts as auxiliary. Increased precision in timing was achieved by using a computer application. A climate of reciprocal benefit was fostered because the by-products of observation, both tapes and transcripts, were regarded by participants as of value.

2

From Out the Shadows: Background on Psychotherapy

It may be helpful to explain further the benefits of looking at psychotherapy as a speech event by providing background on how the speech event differs from other more familiar activities such as conversation, confession, or doctor-patient discourse. I likewise want to add some information about the history and development of psychotherapy and discuss its practitioners' status in the community.

A speech event is a recognized activity centered in discourse, which is known to and often labeled by members of a speech community. I insist on the distinction between "known *about*" by a community and "known *to*" a community, because recognizing a labeled speech event as one that helps comprise the total linguistic resources of one's own community does not entail complete familiarity with that speech event. For example, Protestants may have little knowledge of a Catholic mass, although they are aware of its existence. Likewise, Catholics may have heard of a Bar Mitzvah but might not be able to describe one, and Jews may be only slightly familiar with a Protestant baptism. When I began this research, for instance, I was unaware of the distinction therapists regularly make between *client* and *patient*. On questioning practitioners I discovered that *client* is the term used to describe someone who visits a psychotherapist in the therapist's private office and that *patient* usually refers to someone who receives treatment while hospitalized or who is seen by a psychiatrist or psychiatric social worker. The term used by psychoanalysts for people who undergo longer-term psychoanalysis is *analysand.*

In informal interviews with college undergraduates I discovered that the public still confuses psychoanalysis and psychotherapy and the variety of mental health practitioners: psychiatrists, psychotherapists, psychologists, and others. This confusion exists despite the fact that the institutions have so pervaded American culture as to be routinely featured in cartoons, jokes, television situation comedies, to have recognized epithets: "the talking cure," "the impossible profession," and to be known by the euphemism "professional help." Psychotherapists are frequently featured commentators on television and radio, as are psychiatrists, but few lay people know the differences in their training or credentials.

Both psychotherapy and psychoanalysis are paradoxical in that, for some people, or "users" or "consumers" as they are often labeled by the professionals, there is social stigma attached; for others, such as movie or rock stars, they become a status symbol, a sign of affluence. For some I questioned, seeking this type of help was not a last resort, it was unthinkable. The reaction of one person I questioned was similar to that of the author Richard Rodriguez's mother. With her strong familial and religious ties, she could not comprehend why anyone who was troubled would approach a stranger. The following short selection from Rodriguez's compelling autobiography, *Hunger of Memory*, illustrates both an attitude and a folk attempt to contrast two speech events: psychoanalysis and confession.

> "What is psychiatry?" my mother asks. She is standing in her kitchen at the ironing board....
>
> Psychiatry? I shrug my shoulders to start with, to tell my mother that it is very hard to explain. I go on to say something about Freud. And analysis. Something about the function of a clinically trained listener. (I study my mother's face as I speak to see if she follows.) I compare a psychiatrist to a Catholic priest hearing Confession. But the analogy is inexact. My mother can easily speak to a priest in a darkened confessional; can easily make an act of self-revelation using the impersonal formula of ritual contrition: "Bless me, father, for I have sinned...." It would be altogether different for her to address a psychiatrist in unstructured conversation, revealing those events and feelings that burn close to the heart.
>
> "You mean that people tell a psychiatrist about their personal lives?"
>
> Even as I begin to respond, I realize that she cannot imagine ever doing such a thing. She shakes her head sadly, bending over the iron-

ing board to inspect a shirt with the tip of the iron she holds in her hand. . . .

For my mother that which is personal can only be said to a relative—her only intimates. She makes the single exception of confessing her sins to a Catholic priest. Otherwise, she speaks of her personal life only at home. (Rodriguez 1981: 182–185)

For many people, not just Rodriguez's mother, incredulity is coupled with curiosity about the speech event and its potency. This curiosity is fueled because few treatments include actual samples of language use, and thus the need for this book.

Because of the implicit comparison of psychoanalysis with psychotherapy, it is instructive to note two features about the speech event of psychotherapy. It has undergone both diffusion and evolution. From its origin in Austria, it has spread to Switzerland, Germany, England, and from there to Australia, New Zealand, the United States, Canada, and other Western industrialized countries. Psychotherapy in its modern form has its roots in Sigmund Freud's late nineteenth–early twentieth century creation, psychoanalysis. Psychoanalysis is "the first distinctively recognized form of psychotherapy," according to Garfield and Bergin (1986). Labov and Fanshel (1977: 30) develop the notion that the largest class of speech events that psychotherapy falls under is the interview. They define an interview as a speech event in which one person, A, extracts information from another person, B, which was contained in B's biography. However, the extracting of information is not the primary interaction in the speech event psychotherapy, and a characterization as "interview" places emphasis on the therapist, not the client. I propose that psychotherapy is better viewed as subsumable under the larger class of speech events called *consultation*. Consultations occur when one person, A, approaches a specialist, B, to receive assistance in planning future behavior or action, action that can be medical, legal, financial, or other. Interactions with guidance counselors, travel agents, as well as professionals such as attorneys and physicians, can be consultations. Placing the speech event in a wider context of professional service encounters or consultations also helps elucidate the interconnection or web of speech events that constitute a complex industrialized "service society."

Members of the speech community *know* the rules of speaking for interviews. They expect to be asked a series of questions and to answer them, but new participants in therapeutic discourse do not know the norms. It is through discourse itself that they become socialized to doing psychotherapy. Therapeutic discourse is decidedly more than answering a series of questions. I see two major differences between therapeutic discourse and the interview. These differences involve the rules of interaction and interpretation. First, "the subject does not have the right to introduce topics in an interview" (Wolfson 1976: 192). However, in psychotherapy, clients are free to introduce any topic of interest to them that pertains to their situation. I find that the majority of topics are introduced by the client. Second, in an interview one of the participants has "the unilateral right to ask questions" (Wolfson 1976: 190), and the other(s) the obligation to answer them. My research shows that questioning is not unilateral in therapeutic discourse and that the clients do ask a variety of questions during psychotherapy: rhetorical, clarification, and substantive. For example, one of the clients in the study, Wilma, asked 20 questions in her first sesssion (in 43 minutes), comprising 4% of her utterances, whereas the therapist asked 117 questions, about 52% of his utterances. By the sixth session the therapist was making more declaratives, and the extent of questions decreased to 35% of the time (N = 72), while the client's questions remained about the same (3%).

In discussion with and observation of a clinical trainer modeling techniques to a class, I learned that therapists designate the first session with a new client, in which they gather background information and assess the nature and extent of the problem, as the "intake interview." In these initial sessions, certainly, questions do play a primary part, but, as therapy progresses, the second and subsequent sessions differ from the first. Although questioning is the primary modality of the therapist in the get-acquainted first sessions, it decreases in importance as actual therapy begins. As shown in Table 1, in the sixth session the therapist asks fewer questions and makes more declarative utterances than in the first session. Table 2 illustrates that clients are free to ask questions. For these reasons, psychotherapy as a speech event will be viewed as distinct from the interview.

Table 1 Therapist Speech Modalities

Session	Question	Imperative	Declarative	Other	Total
1	52% (N = 117)	1% (N = 2)	32% (N = 72)	15% (N = 34)	N = 225
6	35% (N = 72)	2% (N = 4)	44% (N = 91)	19% (N = 40)	N = 207

Table 2 Client Speech Modalities

Session	Question	Imperative	Declarative	Other	Total
1	4% (N = 20)	0% (N = 0)	77% (N = 346)	19% (N = 84)	N = 450
6	3% (N = 10)	0% (N = 0)	73% (N = 240)	24% (N = 81)	N = 331

How Psychotherapy Is Different from Conversation

I propose a general model for differentiating psychotherapy from ordinary conversation, the so-called unmarked form of discourse. The model consists of seven dimensions on which psychotherapy or another form of discourse can be contrasted with conversation:

1. Parity
2. Reciprocality
3. Routine Recurrence
4. Bounded Time
5. Restricted Topic
6. Remuneration
7. Regulatory Responsibility

The *Parity* principle, which Good (1979) sees as underlying "unmarked" conversation, is suspended during therapy. The tacit agreement to share power and responsibility equally, which is presumed to characterize casual conversation in Western industrialized countries, does not underly therapeutic discourse. Whereas in Western-style conversations even people of relative inequality occasionally hold status in abeyance, the interactants in therapy, by mutual agreement, enter into a relationship that is not equal. By virtue of the client's need and the therapist's training, they mutually accept premises that automatically assign roles to each other. One is the helper, the other will be helped. Social situations of all types can usefully be regarded as implying an agreement about the power relationship they involve. In psychotherapy, this relationship is institutionalized. Therapists are responsible for initiating, regulating, and terminating therapy. They govern the situation.

Reciprocality is greatly reduced in therapy but presupposed in conversation. Conversations are by nature two-sided when there are two participants. Both partners share the floor by negotiation. In therapy, however, it is predetermined who will speak in which manner, and who will speak to what extent. (This varies, of course, by therapy style or theoretical orientation.) For example, it is unlikely that a client would ask a therapist about his or her emotions or how he or she felt about an event.

As originally conceived by Freud at the beginning of this century, therapy was to consist of minimal response by the doctor. In its modern forms, this tenet has evolved, but remnants of this planned asymmetry can still be seen. Unlike conversation, an underlying tenet of psychotherapy is that the therapist does not attempt to gratify any personal needs or make any personal emotional demands on the client.

Another major differentiating feature is the *Routine Recurrence* of therapy such that a client comes on a fixed schedule at a fixed time to the same quiet, private room. The frequency (once a week, twice a week, once every two weeks) and duration (usually 50 minutes) are negotiated according to need, ability, and means. In contrast, conversations can occur anytime, any place. They are by nature spontaneous, not routine. (In some instances, where appointments are kept, conversations may occur on a regular basis; for example, at the hairdresser, barber, chiropractor, dentist, or with a bartender, or in staff meetings, but these speech activities are distinguished on other dimensions.)

This third dimension plays a large role in differentiating therapy from such dyads as physician-patient, lawyer-client, loan officer-applicant, all of which also show lack of parity and lack of reciprocality. Crucially, such conversations do not recur on a preplanned schedule for a great length of time, although several consultations or visits may be involved.

A fourth dimension is that of *Bounded Time*. The time frame for therapy is at once both extended and bounded. In fact, the majority of conversations last less than 50 minutes, the typical duration of a therapy session, although conversations can continue longer. In addition, face-to-face conversations are rarely ever circumscribed from the outset as to time. (Long-distance telephone conversations occasionally are.) Like any "engrossable" [in Goffman's (1974) terms] in which participants can become absorbed, therapy has a time parameter preset. Beginning therapists are even trained in how to terminate sessions (Zaro, Barach, Nedelman, Dreiblatt 1977: 111). Most therapists' offices have a clock in full view and two of the therapists in the study have their watches set to beep five minutes before the end of the hour.

Therapeutic discourse is further differentiated from ordinary conversation by its *Restricted Topic*. Akin to the reciprocality dimension, it is assumed by both interactants in therapy that the topic of preference will revolve around the feelings, attitudes, and behavior of the client and will pertain to his or her mental and emotional health. It is assumed that such information about other people (including the therapist, in some styles) will be offered only if it is particularly relevant to the client. While some forms of conversation have restricted topics, such as shop talk (restricted to the world of work) and gossip (restricted to third parties' private lives), these are usually labeled by members of the community as different from general, unrestricted conversation.

Remuneration is yet another dimension on which therapy and conversation differ. While most conversations offer compensations or rewards (e.g., information, entertainment), there is seldom a monetary exchange unless a professional service has been rendered, as in legal, medical, or business consultations. Conversations are usually voluntary and not remunerated.

Therapy bears some striking resemblances to the medical consultation, but also some significant dissimilarities. As the research into doctor-patient communication continues to grow at a much faster pace than research into therapist-client communication, these are important differences to bear in mind.

Like therapy, the medical interview exhibits lack of parity. In both, a trained specialist, a health care giver, is "in charge." This power or status differential colors the interaction that is arrived at by mutual consent of the one in need of help and the helper. In both situations there is remuneration. On the time dimension there is minimal dissimilarity, with the allotted time for a medical consultation closer to 15 minutes than to 50. Likewise, the topic shifts from mental and emotional states to physical condition of the patient. Except in severe illness, visits are episodic, periodic rather than routinized.

Physicians ask mainly closed questions for which there is usually one correct answer (Did you have measles as a child? Does it hurt when I press here?). On the other hand, therapy consists of both open and closed questions, with open questions, for which there is no one correct answer, predominating (How did you feel about having to move? What are some of the alternatives you can think of?). Therapists are also active as receptive listeners, not just questioners.

The second major difference is in the dimension of reciprocality. Whereas both speech situations are basically one-sided, the balance in the medical interview is inverse to that of therapeutic discourse. It has been observed (West 1983) that in the medical interview the doctor does most of the talking and that the patient does not get an extended turn. Quite the opposite obtains in therapeutic discourse. There it is the client's responsibility to supply the majority of talk.

Intimate revelations to bartenders, hairdressers, or strangers on a plane do not involve a specialist trained to enhance mental health. For confession and for interrogation, what is missing is the nonjudgmental environment present in good psychotherapy. In seeking confession, a penitent knows that a penance will be levied. In interrogation, whether in chambers, court, or on the roadside, a judgment will follow. Obversely, a basic premise of therapy is nonjudgmental acceptance. Therapy also differs from counseling, because in counseling advice or guidance for a specific problem is expressly sought and frankly given (see Gaik 1992).

A seventh and final distinguishing dimension is the important factor of *Regulatory Responsibility* with which the therapist is empowered by mutual consent. By Regulatory Responsibility I mean to suggest that, unlike in casual conversation where two interactants jointly negotiate openings, closings, and turn taking, in therapeutic discourse, the therapist is empowered to initiate, regulate, and terminate the therapeutic portion of a therapy session.

I draw attention to the structural manner in which actual dialogue serves as boundaries to locate the literal or physical borders between the realms of therapy and conversation. Goffman's (1974) notion of frame is actualized in therapy in openings and closings, for, as Bateson (1972) observes, information about differences is stacked at the edges of events. I claim that therapeutic discourse lies framed within conversation. How then do participants in therapeutic discourse identify it as a different order of event from the conversation in which it is encased and signify that it differs from other contiguous contexts in the world at large, with conventions of its own?

In therapeutic discourse it is the therapist who attends to the role of framing the discourse, enclosing one realm in another or others, and specifying the relationship between them. We would like to know the moment at which conversation ceases to be conversation and becomes therapy, and conversely, how therapeutic discourse ceases to be therapeutic and returns to the world of ordinary conversation.

The openings and closings of the *conversations* that typically encase the therapy domain are drawn, it seems, from the details of mutual experience, events accessible to both therapist and client from the senses or from general human activities. In openings I observed, these include, for example, casual reference on entering to noise outside, weather, traffic, seasonal holidays, and political or athletic events of wide interest. Some examples in the corpus include:

1. Boy, it's cold outside.
2. Sorry I'm late. The traffic is really tied up.
3. What's all that commotion in the hall?

Both openings and closings can refer to time, as in 2 above and in the following exchange:

THERAPIST: Can you come at 5 instead next week?
CLIENT: Next Thursday? Yeah, sure. I'll be here.
THERAPIST: Okay. See you then. Bye
CLIENT: Byebye. Thanks.

These utterances reflect an equality between speakers that is not apparent within the therapeutic domain. Within therapy, asymmetry is noticeable. In the cases of therapy I observed, the therapist took responsibility for determining when conversation or chit-chat would end and "work" would begin. The characteristic use by therapists of the latter term is illustrative of professionals' attitude to one difference between conversation and therapeutic discourse, for few people would call conversation "work."

To mark the discontinuity, the end of chit-chat and the beginning of therapy or "work," some initiations of therapy are semi-formulaic. Recurrent references are to the time span between sessions, to "things," and the repeated use of the verb "go." The following are representative initiations of the therapy domain:

THERAPIST: How'd it go this week?

THERAPIST: How's it going?

THERAPIST: What's going on?

Some therapists focus attention on the task:

THERAPIST: How do you want to use your time today?

THERAPIST: What do you want to work on today?

Terminations, on the other hand, are achieved by pretermina-
tions whose very wording sometimes suggests the enclosed status
of the therapeutic domain, as shown by the words in boldface italics:

THERAPIST: How do you want to **wrap it up** for today?

THERAPIST: We need to **wind down** for today.

THERAPIST: We're going to have to **close up** this session.

These examples of pretermination suggest that there is an
enclosed status. The therapist, not the client, signals, prior to the
end of the session, that the engrossable activity is to be terminated
because the allotted time is nearly up. Actual termination of the
therapy domain before the realm of conversation is reentered may
take several forms, including but not restricted to an evaluation of
the quality of or the extent covered during that session, the content agenda for upcoming sessions, a reformulation of conclusions
or purposes, and the occasional use of aphorisms.

Another manifestation of this regulatory responsibility is the
extensive use by therapists of backchannel cues such as "Mmhmm"
and "Yeah" to regulate the flow of talk and perpetuate the institutionalized asymmetry. While these backchannel cues are common
in everyday conversation, their preponderance in therapy, accounting for, on average, in the corpus 19% to 35% of therapist utterances, is readily apparent.

Two questions of interest concerning the use of "Mmhmm" are
Does it constitute a turn? and If it has more than one function,
what is its primary function? I argue that use of "Mmhmm" does
constitute a turn in psychotherapy, yet an acceptable, most minimal turn, because interactants are sensitive to regulators if they
are removed, and the therapy transcripts I prepared show a wholly
regular alternation of turns if these are counted. I regard the primary function of such utterances as they are used in therapeutic
discourse as *reconfirmers of the asymmetry of therapy.* (This would
be consistent with Freud's early goal of minimizing the therapist's
physical or verbal presence.) Backchannel cues function on at least
three levels. They demonstrate to the client that the therapist is
really there, that the client is not just an object in a petrie dish,
and they display therapist empathy, implicitly signaling, "I see, I

understand." However, the central purpose of regulators or back-channel communication within the therapy domain, is to *reaffirm the right of the client to an extended turn.* Whereas in conversation, turn taking and length of turn are maneuvered by various means that are jointly negotiated (as shown by Sacks, Schegloff, Jefferson 1974), in therapy, I have argued, equity of length of turns is not presumed. Nonetheless, clients seem to "test" this context-specific rule of therapeutic discourse at repeated points in their utterances (with downward intonation, elongated syllables, uses of "you know") when they become self-conscious about "having the floor" or feel they have overused their turn at talk.

When clients display a turn-yielding signal, indicating a willingness to be relieved of a turn, therapists murmur "Mmhmm" as a signal that indeed they do not intend to interrupt or seize the turn and that it is correct for the client to continue. All this happens on the periphery of awareness but is illustrative of the regulative role of the therapist. Two other aspects of regulation are topic recycling and topic sifting. The therapist has the responsibility to reintroduce topics of import, those of ongoing interest, either from previous sessions, e.g.,

THERAPIST: Last time you talked about your relationship with your mother. She seems to be a central concern for you.

or those that may have been momentarily shoved aside, or skimmed over in the flow of talk:

THERAPIST: Let's go back to what you said about not wanting to let them down.

The therapist is also responsible for topic sifting, selecting from among the entirety of facts and ideas presented by a client those that bear further attention.

Overview of History and Development of Psychotherapy

The purpose of psychotherapy is to provide an accepting atmosphere in which to facilitate and effect change in behavior, emotions, and attitudes. The premise that change is possible underlies all of the over 200 types of psychotherapy that have been identified. It is beyond the scope of this study to detail each kind. As an outgrowth

of the first recognized form of psychotherapy, which was psychoanalysis, the creation of Sigmund Freud, psychotherapy has seen
rapid progress in the post–World War II era in general acceptance
and in the number of therapists. Concomitant with this growth has
been increasing federal, state, and local funding for facilities and
training of psychologists and a rapid increase in empirical research
on psychotherapy. Unfortunately little of this research has focused
on the actual words upon which interpretations are made by psychotherapists.

Psychotherapy differs from the once dominant psychoanalysis.
In psychoanalysis patients receive intensive treatment, sometimes
four or five times a week, often over four or five years. While lying
on a couch, patients speak to a trained analyst out of view. On the
other hand, psychotherapy, my focus here, is briefer, less frequent.
Clients meet usually once or twice a week, and speak in a more
conversational style while seated, face to face.

Psychotherapy is conducted in a variety of settings, including
mental health clinics, community clinics, hospitals, counseling
centers, and private offices. In a comparison of psychotherapy relationships in three different traditions, Fiedler (1950) found no difference in outcome, leading some to believe the underlying premises
are more influential than vagaries of setting or orientation.

Garfield and Bergin (1986) comment that "psychotherapy does
not constitute a distinctive profession but rather is an activity that
is performed by members of many different professions." Nonetheless, clinical psychologists, whose training includes an academic
degree (Ph.D. in psychology), clinical practicums, internships, and
a year of supervision, are perhaps the strongest voice identified with
psychotherapy in the American Psychological Association. Psychiatrists, whose credentials include a medical degree (M.D.) in addition to analytic training, also practice psychotherapy. Likewise,
counseling psychologists, educational psychologists, psychiatric
social workers, psychiatric nurses, pastoral counselors, and others
offer types of psychotherapy. Thus, the field is characterized by
heterogeneity of training, theoretical orientations, and disciplines.
This factor and the confidentiality of the relationships have perhaps contributed to the mystique that shrouds psychotherapy from
full public view.

In contrast, the origins of psychoanalysis and psychotherapy are
much more clear. It is possible to see the origination in the work
of Josef Breuer, but the traditionally recognized inception is with
the publication in 1900 of Sigmund Freud's *Interpretation of*

Dreams. Beginning with Freud's observation of Breuer, a Viennese physician, in his treatment from 1880 to 1882 of a 21-year-old hysterical woman, Anna O., and continuing until recently, psychoanalysis has been conducted chiefly by physicians and lay analysts trained at psychoanalytic institutes. The tension that once existed between psychoanalysts and psychotherapists has largely subsided. Collaboration on research and treatment of mental illness has replaced it. Because psychotherapists are not licensed to dispense medicine they frequently work in conjunction with psychiatrists when clients they are seeing require prescriptions (e.g., medication for depression). This type of cooperation was borne out several times in the current study, but equally obvious from client discourse was the fact that several clients were unaware that their psychotherapist could not dispense medicine directly.

In the last 20 years two major trends have affected psychotherapy, according to Garfield and Bergin (1986). More and more psychotherapists characterize their theoretical preferences as eclectic. One study claimed that 40% of clinical psychologists surveyed in 1961 reported that they preferred to use a combination of orientations and techniques rather than adhere strictly to any one dominant theoretical position. Four of the therapists who participated in the current study identify themselves as "eclectic." Apparently, their training is broad enough to expose them to a wide variety of procedures and they are able to select and tailor for individuals the unique combination that they deem most helpful.

The second trend has been toward briefer therapies. A study by Taube, Burns, and Kessler (1984), for example, reports that an average of 64% of those patients seeing psychiatrists and psychologists in private practice terminate before the tenth session. A study by Garfield (1986) reports six sessions as a median length of treatment in a VA Mental Hygiene Clinic. I have chosen to record six sessions per client for this study. This trend may have begun in the early 1950s following an influential article by Eysenck (1952) that seriously questioned the efficacy of long-term treatment and criticized the lack of conclusive empirical research on treatment effectiveness. As a result of a growing reticence of governmental agencies and private insurance companies to pay for extended individual treatment, there has been a public demand for briefer, presumably more cost-effective therapy. In conclusion, the conviction that psychotherapy is a process that can effect change is perhaps best expressed by the very people who have devoted their lives to acting out this belief. Two therapists in this study put it eloquently in the following short extracts taken from the corpus. In the first segment, Marian, an experienced therapist, is speaking with Shelly, a recent college graduate who has been in therapy for over a year and who has some difficulties in relations with her parents. Marian orients her to expect change:

MARIAN: Some of the issues that you're afraid of, in dealing with
           them [your parents], are going to come, you know. If our
           process here works
SHELLY: Mmhmm
MARIAN: you'll be shifting,
           changing, viewing the world in a different way, and they're
           going to have to deal with that.

In the next two short extracts, taken from the second session between Ralph, an experienced therapist, and Kurt, a new client, Ralph discusses the purpose of therapy and the rationale for talking to increase conscious awareness of past behavior patterns. In the first extract, Kurt has just abruptly revealed that he wants to relinquish all of the pornographic sketches he has made.

RALPH: Well, in one sense, this is a letting go for you; it's
          an emotional release
KURT: Yeah
RALPH: to share it. Well, I'm glad.
          I'm glad you did.
KURT: Uh-huh
RALPH: I think it will feel more comfortable for you and that's the
          main purpose of the therapy
KURT: Yeah.
RALPH: to (.) talk about anything that you have some lingering shame
          and guilt over.
KURT: Yeah.

The next extract illustrates the therapist's attitude toward talk as curative and shows the regulatory responsibility of the therapist as he attempts in the first line to recycle a previous topic ("Now let me go back to what you said...").

RALPH: Now let me go back to what you said about—You said you'd
          like to have a family uh but you were afraid that you'd repeat
          the cycle. You don't want to repeat the cycle.
KURT: Yeah.
RALPH: And you meant the cycle of of your own childhood?

KURT: (1) Uh. The cycle of alcoholism.

RALPH: Or alcoholism. Okay. Well I think it's good to be (.) to be concerned about the possibility but this is what the therapy is all about and your AA, is to <u>not</u> repeat the cycle. The cycle is more likely to be repeated if people <u>don't</u> talk about it. And don't increase their conscious awareness of it

KURT: Yeah. And I also know that when I <u>do</u> try to talk about it, I get a lot of hospitality

RALPH: A lot of hostility, yeah.

In the preceding segments, therapists show, through their talk *about* therapy, that they believe psychotherapy to be a "process" that depends on talking about "issues" or "anything that you have some lingering shame and guilt over."

Individual therapy is the focus here because I believe this dyad lies at the core of what psychotherapy has come to mean in the time since its inception. No less important in the lives of many, of course, are family and child therapy along with group therapy, but these are not my focus.

Advancements in linguistic science have provided clinical psychologists with techniques to study both the process and the outcome of their language-dependent medium. Labov and Fanshel's (1977) monumental work, *Therapeutic Discourse: Psychotherapy as Conversation*, set the stage for analysis of language in professional contexts. More than sixty years ago, Sapir (1927) advanced the notion that linguistics could provide valuable insights for psychological studies because of the objective nature of linguistics.

An interdisciplinary group at the Center for Advanced Study in the Behavioral Sciences also began work in the fifties. Bateson (1958) began applying the then recently developed tools of phonetic transcription and kinesics to video recordings of psychotherapy. Because therapists make interpretations and assess effectiveness of therapy largely on impressions gained through evanescent data (language interaction in real time), the prospect of an objective record with which to verify or modify their assessments was (and is) appealing. In order to produce a precise phonetic transcription, including paralinguistic phenomena, of a recorded psychotherapy session, Frieda Fromm-Reichmann worked in collaboration with linguists Charles Hockett and Norman McQuown. They were joined by the pioneer in kinesics, Ray Birdwhistell, and psychiatrist Henry Brosin. In 1957 a rationale for such work was proposed by Pittenger, a psychiatrist, and Smith, a linguist, in "A Basis for Some Contributions of Linguistics to Psychiatry" (Pittenger and Smith 1957). At the same time, a pilot attempt at linguistic description of the first half hour of a therapy session was offered by McQuown (1957).

The work of Pittenger, Hockett, and Danehy (1960), *The First Five Minutes: A Sample of Microscopic Interview Analysis,* is a careful phonetic transcription of the beginning minutes of an initial therapy session. Scheflen (1973) did research on the complex organization of kinesic behavior during psychotherapy. Turner (1972), an ethnomethodologist, describes the social-organizational features of group therapy, using segments of actual language to illustrate various properties of "therapy talk." Numerous psychologists have attempted to achieve an adequate categorization schema for encoding verbal behavior. Such coding devices are useful in quantitatively measuring verbal responses, increasing objectivity and reliability. Bales's (1950) work on small groups is an early and influential effort. Gottschalk and Gleser's (1969) coding scheme has been extended beyond the early measures of anxiety, hostility, and social alienation by international contributions in Gottschalk et al. (1986). Content analysis is similar to the extensive research carried out by psychologists on primary response modes. A number of important studies (e.g., Russell and Stiles 1979; Stiles 1978, 1979, 1981), Bieber, Patton and Fuhriman (1977) and Patton, Fuhriman and Bieber (1977) offer various proposals for categorizing response modes or discourse. However, different labels and definitional differences have hindered comparability. In recognition of this, Elliott et al. (1987) is a pioneering attempt by six psychologists to promote comparability across coding studies by synthesizing 7 of the over 20 category systems that have been developed to codify verbal action in psychotherapy. Russell (1987) is a compendium of contributions by noted analysts of language in psychotherapy, including Gottschalk, Stiles, Snyder, and others who have established coding systems. It includes work of Patton and Meara, pioneers in the computerized coding of verbs by case grammar.

Because of the similarity of therapist response modes to speech acts (Searle 1969, 1975), the pathbreaking work to codify language in a closed set of six or nine categories, however explicitly defined, is subject to criticism of oversimplification. As with speech acts, in coding systems it is often difficult to attribute a single function to a given utterance. Likewise, coding obscures insights to be gained from the particular context. The work of one psychiatrist interested in language use in psychotherapy, Havens, is especially attractive to linguists because it provides actual extracts to illustrate his points. Havens (1980:60) observes that "the selection of the language in which therapists work has been . . . largely neglected." This book thus fills a void in the literature by taking as its center the actual, situated use of discourse. Certainly no major studies of psychotherapy incorporating the perspective of the ethnography of communication or techniques of conversational analysis have emerged in the last 15 years, and this book is innovative in that respect.

With this orientation on the frameworks that guide the current study, background information on the general nature and history of psychotherapy, and awareness of the insights generated from previous research on language use in psychotherapy, I turn to detailing the idea that a strengthened and modified discourse-centered ethnographic approach is a valuable manner in which to examine this speech event.

3

Facets: Retellings in Therapeutic Discourse

An understanding of how narratives arise and function in psychotherapy is essential to a discourse-centered ethnography of communication of this speech event because narratives are a principal component of each and every therapy session. Clients tell from one to many stories in a given hour's session, and average four per session in the current corpus. These narratives are reconstructions of actual recent events, events of long ago, or childhood happenings in which the narrator was a participant. They are told in first person and belong to the genre of personal experience narrative.[1]

By and large, narratives in psychotherapy arise spontaneously; they are evoked and facilitated by the situation and its norms, rather than being elicited, as in speech events like the interview. They are thus of importance for analysts of natural speech because they would happen in the normal sequence of events anyway. The basic attitude of the therapist, "the set-to-listen-and-organize," silently activates stories in psychotherapy and induces their telling, according to Wyatt (1986:200–201). Narratives are tightly integrated into the ongoing talk of a therapeutic session, and this natural contextualization provides the ideal matrix from which to study narrative, not as a static product , but as a dynamic and creative interactive process.

While the early work of Labov and associates concentrated on determining the invariant part of narrative competence and devising a formal explication of narrative components in functional terms, the focus of this chapter is on narrative retellings, a prominent feature of therapeutic discourse that illustrates the variant aspect of narratives. That relatively little attention has been given to the study of the ongoing life of a narrative, despite the fact that even outside therapeutic discourse stories are often retold and have extended lives, is somewhat surprising. Renarration no less than narration is a universal phenomenon worthy of examination.

I emphasize that retellings occur naturally in therapeutic discourse. Therapists expect the recurrence of narratives, especially ones that are important to clients. In psychotherapy, if something has importance, it will resurface until it is noticed. Pittenger, Hockett, and Danehy (1960:235) observe that if a therapist misses some crucial sign from a patient, the very fact that it is crucial means that it will come again, perhaps in a more intelligible manner. Each retelling shows a different facet of the same thing.

The insights of two therapists I questioned about why narratives resurface are particularly helpful to interpret the role of retellings in therapy. According to one, the therapeutic technique operates partially by therapists listening on various levels to the clients' talk. Stories do resurface, not always as immediately as in the dramatic example to follow, but over time they reappear. Clients elaborate details of an event (perhaps as far back as childhood) that is relevant to them as they continue to "work through material" or process the meaning of an event. First, according to the therapist, clients must note that the event *has* importance, and then as more details become available to them, they become aware of the "affect" (emotional impact), and third come to experience the affect. From a therapist's point of view it is fully unsurprising that more and more details of an immediate sort such as inclusion of the emotion with which words are delivered would find their way into successive tellings. If storytelling in therapy becomes too ritualized, too pat, the therapist feels that progress is not being made. Therefore, retellings are a resource for both client and therapist to fully pursue. Retellings in therapy are indeed therapeutic. They indicate continuing growth of awareness.

It bears emphasizing that the making of associations between disparate elements, the work of interconnecting, drawing together isolated bits and pieces to "create sense," is what trained therapists are practiced in. When presented with multiple tellings, the therapist's role in interpreting narrative is to listen to stories on at least two levels, one called "content" and the other called by them "process." In explaining these two levels, one therapist said these two levels are somewhat analogous, in linguistic terms, to surface and deep structure. What matters primarily, he explained, is the underlying meaning, the "subtext" rather than the events.

In psychotherapy, clients offer stories or narratives with the knowledge that the giving of interpretation and the making of associations are two of the ways in which a therapist will receive them. A clinical trainer I questioned about the role of retellings in therapy observed that clients will go on telling the same story unless the therapist ties together the theme; that is, stories tend to reappear in therapy if their connections are not fully brought forward, sometimes weeks or even months or years later. One of the examples I provide shows the "same" story reappearing seven weeks later. Of course, therapists are selective about when they choose to draw the connections and it is not always the therapist who does this connecting work. Some clients are capable of doing this work themselves, as another example to follow will illustrate.

The goals of this chapter are to concentrate on the little studied act of retellings of personal experience narrative. The importance of such a study is that it can (1) provide insights on the nature of repeated tellings—how and why stories are retold, (2) elucidate some properties of narrative structure in general, (3) explicate the norms of interaction of this speech event, and (4) uncover the linguistic means of expansion available to narrators in subsequent tellings. I also comment on two issues that arise from comparison of previous research on retellings, the issues of narrative reportability and narrative expandability, in light of the new data from this study. I would point out that the data I collected differ from previous work on retellings, which deal with *elicited* recountings,[2] in that the present research focuses on spontaneous, *nonelicited* retellings that arise naturally in context. My inquiry is likewise restricted to retellings by the same narrator rather than encompassing multiple accounts of the so-called same event by different narrators.[3] This fresh source of data brings new evidence to bear and strongly points to narrative expandability.

I examine spontaneously arising, nonelicited retellings from the corpus of tape-recorded hours of psychotherapy sessions and give representative examples of narratives related by three different clients, pseudonymed Sharon, Shelly, and Kurt, to their psychotherapists during individual psychotherapy sessions. The procedure I followed of recording six consecutive sessions (and occasionally eight) per client facilitated the collection of recurrences from the same individuals.[4] The retellings are examined in both sequential and distributional terms, and based on these retellings by the same narrator to the same recipient in the same setting I propose a typology of retellings in psychotherapy. The three types of retellings that emerge in therapeutic discourse are

1. Same Event–Different Point
2. Different Events–Same Point
3. Similar Events–Same Theme

Examples of these three types follow, along with a discussion of the issues they bear upon.

Finally, I suggest a possible answer to the provocative question Can you tell the same story twice?[5] in the form of a Principle of Narrative Equivalency. In concrete terms, it is indisputable that each narration is essentially unique, but in more abstract terms it may be possible to see narrative equivalence. The discourse analysis here attempts to look at variation in tellings in order to discover a systematic basis for similarity.

Norms of the Speech Event and Issues of Reportability and Expandability

Consideration of the types of narratives that occur in psychotherapy, the things that are talked about, has considerable bearing on the notion of *reportability* of narratives, a concept put forward by Labov,[6] and underscores the importance of taking speech event into consideration. The norms of psychotherapy appear to offer fewer constraints on reportability than do the norms of speech events such as interviews or ordinary conversations. Unlike participants in conversations, client narrators in psychotherapy do not have to justify holding the listener's attention. They are paying for it. Clients are assured of having the listener's attention and therapists do not reject the many ordinary narratives given. Undoubtedly, what is reportable varies from context to context, from culture to culture.[7]

The conversational requirement to justify a relatively uninterrupted turn is loosened in therapeutic discourse. It is expected that clients will talk at length and the sole criterion is that their talk have relevance to them. Thus, all of the stories occurring in the corpus are "reportable" in that they are of sufficient interest to the people who have sought help with their problems to tell them to the therapist. This notion of even the quotidian being reportable in therapeutic discourse differs from the concept of reportability established for Western conversation. Some of the narratives collected in the current corpus do concern life events that the general public would consider unusual and therefore reportable in Labov's terms. In this corpus, clients narrate their experiences in such diverse, out-of-the-ordinary events as getting an abortion, taking a friend to an abortion clinic, seeing a man expose himself, nearly being raped, wanting to rape someone, being sexually and physically abused by relatives, and other events that are not widely experienced. Far more common than these unusual or shocking events, however, are stories about everyday events with conflict involved. For example, Lana gives a poignant narrative about wanting to prepare a birthday dinner and cake for her estranged husband to make amends, but not having time, and Norma narrates a story concerning her anguish over feeling it necessary to financially support her sister's marketing scheme for an unwanted vitamin product line for fear of rejection by her.

A common narrative event across clients is the reconstruction of being misunderstood or humiliated by parents or teachers. A large proportion of the over 150 narratives collected concern conversations with spouses, boyfriends, girlfriends, lovers, parents, teachers, employers, coworkers, or other people who figure significantly in the narrator's life. Instances of talk about talk are frequent. Some of these conversations happened recently in the client's lives, but some are reconstructed from long ago. It seems that the justification for taking an extended turn to narrate at length, in this speech event at least, does not require that the event be of general interest. The norms of the social situations, therapy and interview, clearly differ if ordinary, mundane events are relatable in therapy without the response "So what?" The criterion for reportability in therapeutic discourse is that the story have relevance for the client-narrator.[8]

There is some indication also that narratives in psychotherapy do not adhere to the same constraint for conversation proposed by Sacks (1970–1971) that a story be appropriately recipient-designed. In conversation a narrator must take into account whether or not those listening have heard the story before or even participated in the event themselves. The norms of interaction in psychotherapy do not so constrain the narrator, because narratives are sometimes renarrated without the usual check on prior listenership, as shown later.

Retellings give rise to questions of interest to discourse analysts, such as, What shape do subsequent tellings take? Do optional elements surface in successive narratives or are retellings pared down versions? There are conflicting claims regarding the issue of expandability, whether subsequent tellings are condensed or expanded. On the one hand, Chafe (1977) indicates that a second telling by the same speaker eight weeks apart is condensed. He bases his insight on elicited reports of a film scene. On the other hand, Hymes's (1985) analysis of the second telling of Cultee's Salmon myth by the same narrator three years later indicates expansion, with, among other things, the addition of direct speech.[9]

Bauman (1986) discusses three tellings of a tall tale, "The Bee Tree," by Texas storyteller Ed Bell, and discovers that later tellings are of greater length with all changes additive. The formal devices Bauman observes in expansion are addition of direct speech, parallelism (both syntactic and thematic), an increase in the number of exchanges and turns at talk, and addition of quoted interior speech.

Are retellings condensed or expanded? It is important to exercise caution in drawing parallels between different subtypes of narrative. Undoubtedly the discrepancy between these findings is due to the fact that narrative (whether first person or not) differs crucially from a report of vicarious visual experience. This critical difference between narrative and report, apparent also in Chafe (1980), is an important distinction for the analysis to follow. Narrative scholars have yet to define the core that all narratives share. We can conclude that the expandability issue is clouded by the comparability issue.

A fuller picture of the social relevance of a narration on a given occasion between particular participants in a certain setting can be obtained by keeping in mind that the meaning of a narrative is emergent and dependent on the conversational context in which it occurs.

The importance of the relatively few works on retellings, as contributions to the field of narratology, is great, but it is necessary to be cautious in drawing parallels between different subtypes of narrative. The telling of traditional tales (Cultee's "Salmon's Story"), tall tales (Bell's "The Bee Tree"), stories in conversation, and the various Kuna ways of telling and retelling described by Sherzer (1982c) all differ from narratives told in psychotherapy in some interesting ways, despite their many similarities.

At the forefront of any analysis of narrative, I claim here, is its placement in a sociocultural context. Context is taken here to include the purpose, norms of interaction and interpretation, social identities of the participants, and setting and scene, as provided for in Hymes's model (1964, 1972). The work of Sherzer (1982c) stands out as an example of a contextual approach to the centrality to naturally occurring tellings, retellings, and tellings within tellings among the Kuna. The analysis of retellings in psychotherapy additionally reveals the importance of yet another dimension of context: the passage of time, and the incumbent impact on subtly changing the relationship between individual participants. In the first of the three types of retelling in psychotherapy to be examined, for example, it is apparent that the same narrative, given by the same speaker to the same addressee, acting in the same roles, in the same setting, will still differ from week to week. Thus, a characterization of situation as setting and scene should be expanded to include elapse of time.[10]

The puzzling phenomenon that will be the first of three types of retellings in psychotherapy to be analyzed is a retelling by the same narrator of the same event to the same listener at different times. The analytical question that arises from the first type of retelling, identified above as "Same Event—Different Point" is Why would someone relate information that is not new to the same person? The answer, provided by observation of retellings in therapy sessions, confirms that narratives have both a referential/informative and evaluative purpose. That is, narratives are given to inform and illustrate a proposition, to make a point. Spontaneous retellings to the same person at weekly intervals (to a therapist by a client, here) indicate that the referential purpose of narrative is at times secondary to its power to make a point, and that *the point or general proposition illustrated, which can change each time, is not inherent in the narrative, but arises in the speech context.* Examination of spontaneous retellings shows that narratives are a *flexible* resource that can be shaped to serve varying purposes. This resource is universally available. In light of this plasticity of narrative, its retellability, a full theory of narrative that includes retellings needs to be offered.

First Type of Retelling

In the three extracts that follow, the client, Sharon, recounts the same events to Marian, her therapist, at three different sessions, each held a week apart. It will become evident that she uses the same events to make three different points (or general propositions) about herself. The points she makes are:

1. that she has not been treated as an equal at work, and that she is at the bottom of the ladder in her office
2. that although she was energetic her skills were underutilized
3. that she *was* assertive about her rights as an employee

The three extracts that illustrate the type of retelling called Same Event—Different Point I call "Part of the Management Team." The title is drawn from the thrice-repeated words of the narrator, Sharon. The recountings occur in three consecutive therapy sessions, beginning with the second week of my recording, and occurring in the third and fourth weeks also. Sharon has been in therapy with Marian, her therapist, for nearly two years, and they have established an excellent working relationship.

First, the texts of the three tellings of type 1 are given, and then discussion follows. Prior and succeeding discourse are included along with the narrative as a basis for understanding the propositions the narratives illustrate. The narrative is set off from the ongoing talk by boldface type.

As further background to the segments illustrating the first type, Sharon has recently been given the opportunity to move out of the central office of the property management firm where she has held an ill-defined apprentice position to assume the assistant manager's job on site at a new apartment complex. Despite some optimism for the new position, she is resentful that she is being moved out of the central office and feels that her aptitude and intelligence were never fully utilized by the two people who were her bosses (Tom and Mary), although they gave lip service to wanting to include her in decision making. In spite of holding a doctorate, Sharon has had a history of underemployment in the past and a series of unpleasant experiences with employers. For her, not being treated as an equal is a particularly sensitive issue.

Extract 1. *Kernel Narrative* "Part of the Management Team"
(Occurring in week 2)

SHARON: **We got there because of all the stuff that was**
thrown at <u>me</u> that I had no control over. He was mad!
He had his anger at other people but he can't lash out
(.) at people downtown. They're his bosses so he (.) kicks
it down the ladder

MARIAN: Mm

SHARON: **and I feel sometimes like I'm at**
the bottom of the ladder. Um.

MARIAN: Yes. Well, you were.
SHARON: That's probably true. That <u>is</u> true. **You know, they
            had <u>said</u> things lately about my being part of
            the management team, just like they are and I
            want to laugh in their face. I told Mary that**
MARIAN: So you feel like again, the bottom of (.) last last
SHARON: Yeah
MARIAN: in rank Mmhmm. (2) which does connect up with your
            dreams.
SHARON: (3) Connects up with the abuse and it connects up
            with some things in my family in that I felt <u>I</u> was the
            place that people played out their battles.

**Extract 2. *Narrative* "Part of the Management Team"
(Occurring in week 3)**

SHARON: . . . however long the job lasted and whatever it
            became later, I wanted to be involved in whatever
            was available there a:nd I was geared up, really up
            until the last month, maybe about the last five weeks,
            about what that job could become. I really thought I
            was gonna start learning more about the company
            a:nd and **even recently Mary was telling me that
            I was just as much a part of the management
            team as <u>they</u> were, and I said, you know,
            "That's a joke, don't <u>tell</u> me that" and she was
            astonished.** but uh (2) I thought all along especially
            after that conver—well not all along—after that
            conversation in December on that Tom began ignoring
            me
MARIAN: Yes=
SHARON: =that he had wiped his hands of me and that
            there was something wrong.

As background, the next extract occurs in a discussion of
employee's rights to be heard by their employers. Marian, the therapist, has asked Sharon, the client, challenging her (in Labov and
Fanshel's (1977:124) terms), "*Were* you speaking up?" implying that
Sharon had not been communicating her wishes regarding the types
of responsibilities she wanted at work. In the talk just prior to this
segment, Sharon has listed several ways in which she stood up to
her female employer, including telling her she would not take
staples out of papers. In this extract, Sharon is intent on retrieving
this narrative; she spends 11 seconds (rather a long time) in recall-
ing the events she wishes to narrate as support for her claim that

she is assertive. The narrative she tells is an expanded version of
that told in weeks 2 and 3 of the tape recording.

Extract 3. *Expanded Narrative* **"Part of the Management Team"**
(Occurring in Week 4)

SHARON: What else did I tell her? Ah (.) told Mary (3) I don't
                know. It'll come back to me. I forget now what else (.)
                I told her (3) You know, I've forgotten. It'll come back
                to me (5) hhh <u>Oh!</u> I know what it was. Uh (.) **She**
                said something to me three or four weeks ago,
                about be:ing uh as much a part of the
                management team as she and Tom were. A:nd
                I told her in no uncertain terms that that was
                a joke, I didn't even want her to tell me that,
                tha:t nobody on a management team would be
                expected to behave independently on hearsay.
                I said, "I don't even know—I hear—get
                everything third and fourth hand around
                here." She looked <u>horrified.</u> She said,
                ((gritted teeth)) "You <u>are</u> part of the
                management team!" And I just looked at her
                and said, "No I'm not." (l) But, see, funny things are
                going on with that. You know it's almost like (.) she can
                sit back and grin and sa:y "you know, I feel like I'm in
                a position now . . ."

It is clear that these three narratives, told in three successive
therapy sessions, relate the same event, yet they differ in several
interesting ways, both structurally and evaluatively. They also
reveal insights about the therapeutic process of narrative. Each
aspect is important. Note also that no mention is made of the story's
having been told in the week(s) prior.

The notion that the past is reconstructed rather than recovered
comes from Freud (1917 [1957]). The active listening of the therapist, including interjections, can make a tale gain momentum and
depth, can help "expand it toward plural contexts with which it
proves to be connected," according to Wyatt (1986:204). Psychotherapists and psychoanalysts are instructed in training, just like anthropologists and linguists, always to be alert to recurrences, similarities, and correspondences, and part of the active intervention of the
therapist is to help clients draw connections. The meaning of recurrent narratives is implicitly recognized by Pittenger, Hockett, and
Danehy, who observed in their seminal study of therapy that "any-

one will tell us over and over again in our dealings with him what sort of person he is" (Pittenger, Hockett, and Danehy 1960:235).

However, the client here, Sharon, uses the raw material of the narrative event to illustrate three propositions about herself. In Extract 1, she uses the kernel narrative to illustrate the point that she is not on a par with her supervisors and that the anger that is vented downward in a hierarchy falls on her because she ranks lowest. Her point, "and I feel sometimes like I'm at the bottom of the ladder," is reiterated by the therapist in her acceptance of the story. The therapist begins to use the same words ("So you feel like again, the bottom of," but switches to a paraphrase ("last last in rank"). Extract 1 is best seen as a kernel narrative,[11] an economical telling, similar to a report. It is a *potential* narrative. Extracts 2 and 3 show how this potential is realized.

In Extract 2, the client again presents herself in a certain light to the therapist, utilizing the raw material of the story to do so. Sharon still describes a two-party conversation between herself and her supervisor. She intends Marian to see her in a favorable light, as putting herself out more than her employers did. She presents herself as having tried ("I was geared up"), having been enthusiastic ("really up") and wanting "to be involved in whatever was available there" but as having been ignored ("he had wiped his hands of me").

The same material, the same events, as seen in Extracts 1 and 2, are used by the client in Extract 3 to support her contention that in fact she was assertive to her employers and did stand up for her rights as an employee. The realization that the point of this third telling, given in response to the therapist's question *"Were* you speaking up?"*, differs from the other two accounts also for several important linguistic changes from the second to the third tellings. There is a semantic upgrade of the adjectives. In Extract 2, the female employer is "astonished" but in Extract 3 "she looked horrified." The narrator is presented as more assertive in Extract 3, with the manner adverbial prepositional phrase addition "A:nd I told her *in no uncertain terms.*" The added element, not present in Extract 1 or 2, the new motif about the difficulty in acting autonomously without access to information, "I didn't even want her to tell me that, tha:t nobody on a management team would be expected to behave independently (.) on hearsay. I said, "I don't even know- I hear - get everything third and fourth hand around here," is also explainable in terms of the change in general proposition or point that Extract 3 is intended to illustrate. The addition of a new piece of reported speech and direct speech not previously included arises to support the narrator's claim to the therapist that she has acted assertively, counter to the therapist's question and implicit criticism that the client is not speaking up for herself. Note that this time, the claim that she is "part of the management team" does not arise on its own, but is given in response to Sharon's complaints, according to the retelling.

Examined next are the structural differences between these three extracts. Knowledge of how the tellings differ internally is interesting for a theory of how narratives are expandable and expanded and why, in psychotherapy, the same narrative is repeated voluntarily.

As seen, the first extract, like the other two, recounts a conversation between Sharon and one of her two bosses, a woman named Mary, about Sharon's status in the office. Mary claims that Sharon is "part of the management team." This extract is a rather sparse account containing three instances of reported speech ("they had said things," "Mary in particular had said things, " "I told Mary that") and the reaction of the narrator herself ("I want to laugh in their face") to the conversation. Entirely absent in Extract 1 is any direct speech or an account of Mary's reaction to the narrator's telling her that she wanted to laugh in their face. The story is perhaps cut short by the therapist in overlapped speech with her interpretation of the point of the narrative (:"So you feel like again, the bottom of (.) last last in rank").

As a kernel narrative it barely meets Labov's minimal criterion for narrative, that there be at least two clauses with time juncture so that reversal of clauses changes the meaning. A kernel narrative is similar to a report. It is a *potential* narrative, minus the so-called optional elements of abstract, orientation, evaluation, and coda.[12]

The potential to make from this kernel narrative or report a fuller narrative account *is* realized in Extract 2. Between Extracts 1 and 2, many of the elements are similar: The remark "had said things lately" becomes "recently Mary was telling me." The comparatives describing Sharon's status as part of the management team changes only slightly from "just like they are" to "as much . . . as they were." The account still describes a two-part conversation. In Extract 2, what Mary said is still reported speech but Sharon's reaction is transformed into a reply in direct speech, one of the hallmarks of narrative. Her reaction becomes "and then I said, you know, 'That's a joke. Don't tell me that.'" What is added is Mary's reaction to Sharon's direct speech, "she was astonished." Thus, Extract 2 contains one instance of reported speech, one of direct speech, and a reaction. It is still an economical accounting of events, scarcely notable individually for its narrative quality. The differences between Telling 1 and Telling 2 are not as great as are the differences to be seen between Telling 2 and Telling 3.

As the expansions in Telling 3 are examined, it will be helpful to keep in mind the puzzle of why this information is being relayed yet a third time to the therapist, who has heard the event related twice before, in the previous two weekly sessions. We suspect that it is not the referential aspect that is essential here. A significant fact of these retellings is that, in contrast to the elicited retellings of Cultee by Boas (Hymes 1985) or of Bell by Bauman (Bauman 1986), which occurred several years apart, they are not solicited; they arise spontaneously and occur not years apart but on the very next meeting between therapist and client. The narrator volunteers the retellings; no one has asked for them. More curiously still, the narrator makes no mention of her previous telling on subsequent retellings. She fails to 'recipient design.' In the absence of an introductory phrase such as "As I was saying last week" or "Like I told you before" it can be surmised that the events in the narratives are reconstructed each time. The lack of acknowledgment or apology that the story has been told before also indicates that the norms of interaction are different for conversation and therapy.

In Extract 3, occurring in the third taped session, one week after the second, the meager narrative is transformed into a full-blown narrative. The differences can perhaps be highlighted by viewing them in profile, blocked out as in Table 3. Extract 2 contained only three events: (1) Mary was telling me . . . ; (2) and then I said . . . ; (3) and she was astonished, whereas Extract 3 contains seven events, a greatly expanded inventory.

Extract 3 is thus seen to be more fully developed than Extract 2. It contains three instances of lively direct speech along with two instances of reported speech, one of which contains multiple dependent clauses showing three cases of reported speech. Viewed abstractly, the narrative is transformed upon the third telling into

Sequence of Events in Extract 3
1. Comment by Mary
2. Reply by Sharon
3. Mary's reaction to Sharon's reply
4. Mary's emphatic reiteration of comment
5. Sharon's reaction
6. Sharon's rebuttal

Table 3 Profile of Extract 3

Main Event Clause	Speech
1. She said something to me	3 or 4 weeks ago, about be:ing uh as much a part of the management team as she and Tom were.
2. A:nd I told her	in no uncertain terms that (a) that was a joke (b) I didn't even want her to tell me that (c) tha:t nobody on a management team would be expected to behave independently on hearsay.
3. I said	"I don't even know-I hear-get everything third and fourth hand around here."
4. She looked <u>horrified</u>	
5. She said	((gritted teeth)) "You <u>are</u> part of the management team!"
6. And I just looked at her	
7. and said	"No I'm not."

The first three elements were present in Tellings 1 and 2, but elements 4, 5, and 6 have been added in the expanded retelling of Extract 3. One other difference in the first three elements is that the narrator's remarks, "That's a joke. Don't tell me that" cited in direct speech in Extract 2 are given in reported speech in Extract 3. Also added to the same reported speech, "A:nd I told her . . . that that was a joke, I didn't even want her to tell me that" is a third dependent clause that buttresses the claim that Mary's remark is a joke, showing the cause or rationale behind Sharon's rejection of the assessment that she is part of the management team. The narrator adds the reported speech, "tha:t nobody on a management team would be expected to behave independently on hearsay," to the list of things "I told her." Sharon then elaborates on this added item by including the first of several new instances of direct speech to support the "hearsay" complaint and render the story more vivid.

> I said, "I don't even know- I hear- get everything third and fourth hand around here."

Delivered in an irritated tone, this direct speech contains a deictic demonstrative pronoun *here* in "around here," referring not to the therapy situation, of course, but to the situation at the central office, where the story events occur. In such a way narrators give immediacy to narratives.

As mentioned, Mary's reaction differs only in the escalation from "astonished" to "horrified." What is quite new is the direct speech attributed to Mary wherein Mary restates her assessment of Sharon's role as an equal. It is here that the narrative takes on the compelling qualities of engrossing storytelling because the narrator *performs* the words of her employer, through gritted teeth, rather than merely relating them:

> She said, ((gritted teeth)) "You <u>are</u> part of the management team!"

Increased amplitude in "You <u>are</u> . . ." also serves as a reenactment of the event. The calm and steely cold anger relayed by the narrator's deliberate vocal quality in her statement of rebuttal:

> And I just looked at her and said, "No I'm not."

is a dynamic juxtaposition that stands in sharp contrast to the excited direct speech or reiteration of her boss. This final direct speech (delivered staccato style) ends the narrative in a dramatic manner. By not engaging in a shouting match, delivering her comment in cool tones, the narrator presents herself as the victor in this argument about her status. The proposition or point the narrative is intended to illustrate is that she is able not only to "stand up to" her employer but also to contradict her.

The structural mutations of the three tellings of "Part of the Management Team," show that a narrative became successively more elaborated over time, that new episodes were added, and that additional direct speech was incorporated in later versions. These additions support the formulation of a general theory of narrative as expandable in retellings. Extract 1 contained no direct speech; Extract 2 contained one instance of direct speech. This same direct speech ("That's a joke. Don't tell me that.") was transformed into reported speech in Extract 3, where three new pieces of direct speech, two by the narrator and one by her conversant, emerged.

The newly added direct speech is performed with dramatic vocal quality. These additions changed a humdrum report and an ordinary telling into a narrative of some dynamism. While the foregoing is an individual sequential treatment of a retelling, as a representative of a larger corpus of retellings, it supports formulation of a general theory of narrative as expandable by addition of direct speech and dynamic elements inviting listener involvement, such as deictic reference to the event world (*here, this*) and unusual vocal quality.

From the therapist's and the discourse analyst's point of view, these three stories count as retellings. It is easy to see them as the same story; it is hard to miss their referential similarity. But is referential similarity the only qualifying characteristic for stipulating that two or more stories are "the same"? The next two types of retellings take up this question.

Second Type of Retelling

The second type of retelling I find in psychotherapy is the chained narrative told by the same narrator on the same occasion to the same participant. In chained narratives, narrators try to illustrate the same general proposition in several ways by narrating different events. Chained narratives, as so defined, differ from a series of narratives told by diverse persons in, for example, a group story-telling context where narration is a mutual activity.[13]

In the second type of retelling, which I refer to as Different Events—Same Point, chained narratives occur in quick succession, one after the other on the same occasion, here, in a single therapy hour. Because they are instances of personal experience narratives, the narrator, expressed as "I," remains the principal protagonist. Chained personal experience narratives are consecutively told narratives relating different events but the same point. The linguistic means by which they are linked are of interest.

In the extracts to follow, each illustrative of the second type of retelling, Different Events—Same Point, four short personal experience narratives are given in rapid succession in the first 20 minutes of a single therapy hour by Shelly, a recent college graduate with intense sexual curiosity. Each supports the same general proposition: that the narrator has trouble backing out after she has bitten off more than she can chew. Succinctly stated by the narrator at the end of the chained narratives, her point is:

> And just seems like sometimes I get my mind set on something that starts out to be something I want to do and I can't face the fact that I've changed my mind. You know, changing your mind is a sin to me, I think.

I have titled the story chain "Trouble Backing Out." The extracts to be examined come from a single session between Shelly, aged 21, and Marian, the same therapist who was the recipient of the previous narratives.

If these narratives are meaningfully related and chained together, that is, told one right after the other for a reason, rather than being just randomly occurring narratives about unconnected events that happen to follow in quick succession, then it is incumbent on the analyst to discover how they are interrelated and what the linguistic correlates of linking are. The role of the particles *like* and *just like* will be discussed.

As further background to the next extracts, Shelly has been seeing Marian for over a year. Shelly is an upper middle class only daughter of high achieving parents. She has recently graduated from college and has been taking beginning language courses in French and Italian in preparation during a "fun semester" for an intended trip to Europe. The conflict that she experiences is that she is not enjoying her study; she feels "on trial" during her Intensive French, her stomach churns during class, and she wishes she could drop the course but has strong feelings that she must continue with a course of action once initiated. She has trouble backing out, as each of the chained stories that follows illustrates.

I present the four chained stories illustrating "Trouble Backing Out" in two extracts. This grouping reflects their actual rapid succession in the therapy hour in which they arise. I have subtitled the four narratives "Dropping French," "Hating New York," "Dropping out of an MBA Program," and "Making Bread."

Extract 4. *Chained Narratives* 1 and 2, **"Trouble Backing Out: Dropping French; Hating New York"**

SHELLY: **At first I wanted to do it [take introductory French and Italian] to help myself. ((sniff)) and then I got into it, and everybody was saying "Oh, I'll really be impressed if you go through with this." "Isn't it hard to take two first year-two beginning languages at once?**

MARIAN: Uh-huh

SHELLY: **"My goodness." And now it's like I've gotten myself stuck and I can't back down cause that's too embarrassing you know, to say, "Oh gosh, I guess I can't do it after all." Well, it's just like. it was like when I went to New York, everybody said, "Oh wow, you're going to New York and you're only 19!" "Whoopee!" you know. And when I hated it I felt embarrassed**

> and stupid and when I came back and told
> people that I didn't like it and all, I felt like
> they were laughing at me behind my back.

MARIAN: Mmhmm.

SHELLY: [And]

MARIAN: [So] you were sort of betrayed by your own ambitions.

SHELLY: Right. . . .

Six minutes intervene in the therapy session between the preceding two narratives and the following two.

A point of interest here is that there is linguistic evidence of the narrator's planning for subsequent stories. This is seen in her correction of speech showing a reorganization of narrative resources, in the underlined words that introduce the second narrative, "Hating New York":

Well it's <u>just like</u>, it was <u>like</u> when I went to New York

The indications are that the narrator *plans* to add further narrative examples. She changes her words from "just like" to "it was like," which shows that she initially intends to compare the points of two narratives about her reluctance to back down, but quickly corrects herself to a less confining "it was like when . . . ," a strategic change by a narrator that allows for *a set* of instances to be given rather than a pair.[14] The status of these narratives as chained or linked resources that serve to bolster the same general proposition is thus linguistically signaled at their beginning by the adverbial particle *like*.

Narrators telling multiple stories in chainlike sequence, I claim, make use of the particle *like* to indicate in advance to their listener that the story is to be seen as one more instance of a previously offered proposition illustrated by a preceding narrative. In such subtle ways, narrators signal their recipients how narratives are to be interpreted and also make room for their upcoming turns at narration. By using "it was like" instead of "it's just like," Shelly reserves the right to call forth additional narration as support for her proposition. This future possibility is realized in the actual occurrence, six minutes later, of two further narratives, also chained, which support her proposition that she hates to back down and confess that she has undertaken too much. These two chained narratives are shown in Extract 5. They occur in rapid succession to one another. The first narrative in Extract 5, ("Dropping Out of an MBA Program") is introduced by " the way," a technique similar to the use of *like* ("That's <u>the way</u> I felt about that MBA bull-

shit") and the subsequent narrative ("Making Bread") is introduced
by *like*, showing the relevance as supporting material for a generalization: "<u>Like</u> right before school started, I got . . .) With such
linguistic signals the client narrators help the therapist to understand that the tellings are related.

**Extract 5 (occurring six minutes after Chained Narratives 1 and 2).
Chained Narratives 3 and 4, "Trouble Backing Out: Dropping Out of
an MBA Program; Making Bread"**

SHELLY: If I hadn't had this talk with you today, I probably
            would have (.) stuck with that French and just refused
            to think about it.

MARIAN: Now just a minute. Are you going to blame this on
            me? ((laugh))

SHELLY: No. I'm glad. I'll be glad that I dropped it after about,
            after about after about two weeks. I'll say, "Oh man,
            aren't you glad you got yourself out of that before it
            was too late?' **That's <u>the way</u> I felt about that
            MBA bullshit. You know, I was supposed to be
            in an MBA program last semester, and I just
            didn't want to. I wasn't ready for it. And
            Mark said, "Well, then why are you doing it?"
            And he made me think about it. He, you know,
            and I said, "Well, now that I really think about
            it I I don't want to so why should I. It's not
            like I have to do it.**

MARIAN: Mmhmm

SHELLY: **It's not like I have five starving children all
            waiting for me to make $30,000 a year so they
            can go to college.**

MARIAN: Hmm.

SHELLY: And, uh, I guess I just need somebody somebody
            who's sympathetic to to get me to to really look at
            what I'm doing. Usually there's no one like that
            around. And I when I'm going to do it for myself-

MARIAN: Hmm.

SHELLY: I get like this. **<u>Like</u> right before school started, I
            got, I wanted to make some bread. But that
            day, that, we were going to make bread and I
            thought, everything went wrong. It was a
            real bad day. And by the time it came time
            for us to go home and do it, I really didn't feel
            relaxed enough to do anything like that. But I
            said, 'No. I told Mark we were gonna do it and**

	I might not have time to do it tomorrow and I
	have to do it.' And it was terrible. We had a
	big fight that lasted like, the biggest fight we
	ever had, it lasted a day and a half. It wasn't
	really a fight, it was just I got real irritable
	and he put in 5 teaspoons of sugar instead of 5
	tablespoons or something and I got real snappy
MARIAN:	Hmm
SHELLY:	and I was pretty condescending to him and
	then I was in a real bad mood
MARIAN:	Yeah
SHELLY:	until about a

day and a half. After that I finally got over it.
And, just seems like sometimes I get my mind
set on something that starts out to be
something I want to do, and then I can't face
the fact that I've changed my mind. You know,
changing your mind is a sin to me, I think.

The client narrator, in this case, has sufficient self-awareness to explicitly state the point of her narratives following the narrative chaining, as shown in the two sentences immediately preceding. She has performed the connecting work so important in psychotherapy, for herself. Her therapist has modeled this type of behavior many times. Shelly is learning to be her own therapist.

These narratives are meaningfully related and chained together, for a reason; each illustrates the narrator's point that she has trouble backing out. How does a narrator signal that they are interrelated?.

In this case the narrator-client has given clues to their connectedness, by using *like* and a variant, *that's the way*, to introduce related narratives, and by distilling the generalization about her current attitude toward admitting her limitations. This client perhaps shows more self-awareness and more narrative skill than is usual. It can be noted that such interconnecting work is usually performed by the therapists, who are alert to regularities and repetitions and take pains to point them out to clients. Therapists are supposed to be "vigilant as to hints and recurrences to similarities and correspondences, ready to relate them," according to Wyatt (1986:199).

It may not be surprising to learn that Shelly, the narrator of the tightly sequenced chained stories, is, despite her youth, an accomplished short story writer who has sold several stories to leading magazines. This native ability may account for the fact that she is able to produce four stories back-to-back. People in general are natural storytellers, but it is widely recognized that some narrators have more facility than others. The ready and rapid production of the preceding connected stories is one means of retelling the same story.

Third Type of Retelling

The third type of retelling, which I term Similar Events—Same Theme, involves narration of different (though similar) events with the same underlying significance. In drawing connections, therapists make what some term *associative reflection* of content and or feeling. By this means, therapists comment overtly to the client about the interconnectedness of their accounts. This may be accomplished by comments on either the similarity, contrast, continuity, or distance among two or more related statements, narratives, or dreams told by the client but not previously overtly related by them. When therapists interconnect such discourse, the corpus shows, they often explicitly mention the word "theme." For purposes here, I characterize *theme* as the global proposition, the abstract or underlying communicative intent in contrast to local proposition, which is synonymous with *point*.

An analysis of the third type of retelling supports the claim that two or more narratives may be seen to function as the "same story" if they revolve around the same theme and illustrate the same global proposition, regardless of whether they recount the same events. Two much more highly developed and entertaining personal experience narratives form the basis for investigation of the third and final major type of retelling occurring in psychotherapy, Similar Events—Same Theme.

The extracts to be given involve a different dyad. A male client, Kurt, in sessions with Ralph, his therapist, seven weeks apart, gives two narratives that bear a special relationship to one another. They are retellings, I claim, in terms of the Narrative Equivalency Principle to be given later. Not everyone, it is acknowledged, would be prepared to admit that the two examples to be examined are the same story, despite some surface structural similarities, which will also be pointed out. Unlike the previous type of retelling, these do not involve sequential adjacency nor do they relate the same events.

It is claimed that within the therapeutic context the two narratives that follow function as retellings primarily because they revolve around the same theme and illustrate the same global proposition. I have titled the two narratives "Albatross I-Motorcycle" and "Albatross II-Rifle." They illustrate the global proposition about the client that he is capable of cleaning up his life. The twin tales both show the client as able to cast off the remnants of a former lifestyle, specifically, to "get rid of" an unwanted item of some value and considerable attachment. These remnants are, on the surface, a motorcycle that is sold for $100 and a rifle that is sold for $225 despite Kurt's personal mixed feelings about parting with them.

On a more abstract level, the client may also be alluding to his ability to give up cigarettes and whiskey and other relics of his former ways including some pornographic sketches that he recently discarded; in short, to sort out and clean up his life. The connection between drinking and smoking is indicated by the very next comment that the therapist initiates following the narrative.

The two narratives, occurring seven weeks apart, are drawn from the second and ninth weeks of Kurt's individual therapy with Ralph. Through narrative, Kurt is trying to present himself to his therapist as able to change. Emphasis on change is a primary value evident in therapy. It is also the case that narratives are a form of self-presentation. In them, narrators make claims to a particular personal-social identity, and everything said functions to express, confirm, and validate this claimed identity, according to Mishler (1986).

Both Albatross narratives told by Kurt to Ralph are given at this point and discussion follows. Surrounding context is provided and the narratives themselves are presented in boldface type.

Extract 6. *Narrative 1* **"Albatross I-Motorcycle"**

KURT: Yeah. I read a (charming) book not too long ago called
         (*Cloak*) *of the Last Band*. It was written by a president of a
         uh cleaning company and he talks about the uh how to clean
         up, declutter your life.
RALPH: Declutter your life?
KURT: Uh-huh. He tells you stuff like, you need-shouldn't- uh
         Throw out everything that you-he makes things clear, you
         know, that there are material (.) possessions that (.) hold you
         down.
RALPH: Mmhmm.
KURT: I don't know, like uh, Christmas greeting card that
         goes back 20 years, you know and stuff like tha:t. He says,
         "If you can't stand the sight of it, you know, don't keep it.
         You know, don't feel like you have to keep it cause your

aunt you haven't seen for 15 years gave it to you. Don't
keep it."

RALPH: Mm<u>hmm</u>. Mmhmm. Uh (1) you told me that you had been
actually cleaning <u>out</u> your apartment

KURT: Yeah

RALPH: of a lot of
things. [What]

KURT: [And] I do this quite periodically. I: go through my
apartment and (.) look through all my uh stuff (1) a:nd (.) I try
to decide, "Do I need that?" and "Do I need this?" If not,
you know, I just throw 'em out.

RALPH: Mmhmm.

KURT: Sometimes I get - I can't get rid of an item fast enough. I
just put a note on it

RALPH: Hmm, so that's a little bit different then than your attitude in
throwing the cigarettes away.

KURT: Yeah.

RALPH: Because on the one hand you seem to get nervous if you-if
you hang onto (.) odds and ends and (.) cards and (.) stuff like
that.

KURT: Well, too (two of em's) cheap. That's the problem with
throwing away but (1) I do ( ) mind if it's for a hunderd
dollar. I just can't seem to throw 'em away.

RALPH: No, of course not (.) yeah. Hm

KURT: **It's the uh (.) and I- one time (.) one of the hardest
things I ever tried to get rid of was my (.) first
motorcycle.**

RALPH: **Hmm.**

KURT: **Hard for me to get rid of.**

RALPH: **That had a lot of (.) emotional meaning to you,
hunh.**

KURT: **Yeah. Uh, actually yeah. I keep thinking about
that motorcycle system. It was a (Ed
Greenhough) It was a good piece of machine but
nobody wanted to buy it.**

RALPH: **What did you finally do:?**

KURT: **Well, finally got my brother-in-law, who was
an ex-Bandido**

RALPH: **((laugh))**

KURT: **who knew who knew
quite a few friends in those Bandidos, he was (.)
one of his buddies got it, bought it off (.) of me:
for a hundred dollars.**

RALPH: **Really? Hmm.**

KURT: **He was gonna fix it up. He was also legally**

	blind, too. In California you can't drive. Not that he was blind-nearly, legally blind in California (.) where he came from.
RALPH:	Hmm.
KURT:	So he got a motorcycle. Well, you can't drive (it) in California.
RALPH:	Well! (3) Interesting story.
KURT:	(2) But that was the hardest thing. It was very emotional
RALPH:	Yeah
KURT:	to try to get rid of it. Cause I felt like it was just hanging around my neck like an albatross.
RALPH:	Yeah, the albatross (.) around your neck. Yeah. Hmm. Well, you know, the thing is (1) last time when I saw you (.) individually you had told me you had had a slip with your drinking and smoking.
KURT:	Yeah.

Kurt "retells" the same story, although the events in the second telling are merely similar, not identical, in a session seven weeks later. Explicit comparisons of the two tellings are made following the narrative. The second narrative (shown in boldface) has a short embedded conversation within it.

Extract 7. *Narrative 2 "Albatross II-Rifle"*

KURT:	You know, I'm trying to look out for pitfalls.
RALPH:	Mmhmm.
KURT:	For pitfalls. (2) And uh the more I looked at it, the more it seemed there're plenty of pitfalls. You know, like you can get, just a fixation on money.
RALPH:	Mmhmm.
KURT:	And I believe there was this other part of the New Testament. I remember reading it years ago, about this rich man that came up to Jesus. You know, Jesus said, "Give up all your worldly goods." He couldn't do it, or wouldn't do it, that is. And he was supposedly=
RALPH:	=Then he says it's easier for, what is it now? for a camel to get through the eye of a needle
KURT:	Uh-huh
RALPH:	than for the rich man to part with his money.
KURT:	Right. (I tried to go) **One thing uh I uh (1) I got rid**

	of (.) I finally sold that old rifle of mine. I just [took it down]
RALPH:	[Did you, uh-huh?]
KURT:	to this garage . I:
RALPH:	Mmhmm.
KURT:	A:nd I felt so good after I finally got rid of it. You know, it had been a dead weight to me
RALPH:	Hm
KURT:	for about the last year or so. I never shoot it, you know.
RALPH:	Mmhmm.
KURT:	I wanted (.) to get rid of it you know but I felt (.) like I had to get value for it and uh I tried to offer it to Teddy. He got about 30 gun now. Now he's crazy. And he said, "Oh, no::. Don't sell that gun. You can give it to your grandson."
RALPH:	((laugh))
KURT:	But in the meantime I got to keep that thing, take care of it and I-I don't shoot it.
RALPH:	Well, you know, Kurt, you could go and <u>buy</u> a gun for your grandson some day.
KURT:	Right.
RALPH:	At (.) that point. If you really want to do that.
KURT:	Yeah.
RALPH:	[Well]
KURT:	[A:nd] probably my grandson wouldn't be interested in guns anyway. You know, I'm the only one in my family that has been interested in guns.
RALPH:	Mmhmm
KURT:	Nobody else in my family.
RALPH:	Mmhmm (.) mmhmm.
KURT:	*Anyway,* **Monday, I just took a look at my gun. Uh and I finally decided, "Ah, I'm just gonna get rid of it." And I took it down to this guy and sold it for whatever he's willing to give me.**
RALPH:	Mmhmm.
KURT:	I asked him $250. He gave me $225. [I was]
RALPH:	[Hm. Not bad.]
KURT:	Yeah.
RALPH:	That's not bad.
KURT:	No, when I walked out of there you know I just felt so relieved (1) just getting rid of that thing.
RALPH:	Really? Good.

KURT: **That's one of the pitfalls I need to work out.** Uh
          (3) and I'm stuck and I need to hold on to something uh
          take care of something.
RALPH: Umhm. Umhm
KURT: Well a: not the material things but ideas as well, too.
RALPH: Uh-huh. Holding onto ideas too long.
KURT: Hm
RALPH: ((louder)) Holding onto ideas too long.
KURT: Right (.) that's for sure.
RALPH: (2) Well, Kurt, you know, I think that (2) that uh (2) in
          terms of my understanding of your philosophy, you are
          really (.) going through and sorting things out now, as an
          adult, into what you want to keep and what you want to let
          go of
KURT: Um-hm. Right.

It is obvious that there are many surface similarities between the two personal experience narratives told by Kurt, beyond the facts that they are both told by the same narrator to the same recipient in the same setting, albeit nearly two months apart, and that they involve the same central character, the narrator Kurt. The reported events are similar despite differences; they involve the sale of an unwanted male-oriented luxury item with sentimental and monetary value. Each narrative makes metaphorical reference to the albatross: "it was just hanging around my neck like an albatross" and "it had been a dead weight." The same lexical choice is made; "get rid of" occurs three times in the first of the two narratives and five times in the second story. A distinguishing characteristic of the narrator's style is that in both narratives the coda appears quite early. Each has a literary allusion prefacing the story. Reference is made to *The (Cloak) of the Last Band* and the New Testament. Both contain colorful secondary characters: the potential buyers, Crazy Teddy with 30 guns, and the blind member of the motorcycle gang, the Bandidos.

Nonetheless, the narratives differ in many interesting ways. The first narrative contains irony. That the narrator is able to interest a member of a motorcycle gang, a presumed connoisseur, in a motorcycle no longer of use to him is unusual or reportable. In both narratives the recipient (the therapist) plays a part in the telling; however, in the first narrative the therapist plays a more active role in the conjoint achievement of a narrative. The therapist's role includes expressing surprise ("Really?"), laughing at appropriate points in the telling, giving both External (relating to the narrative as a whole) Evaluation ("Well! (3) Interesting story") and Internal (relating to the narrative events) Evaluation ("Hm. Not bad" in response to the sale price). In the first narrative, "Albatross I-Motorcycle," there are fewer paralinguistic shows of appreciation (Hmm, Mmhmm) than in Narrative 2, "Albatross II-Rifle." Examples of the active role and questioning of the therapist-narrative recipient are the Elaboration of Internal Conflict (in Labov's terms) after the client's statement of Internal Conflict, "That had a lot of emotional meaning to you, hunh?" and what is likely a Request for the Resolution, "What did you finally do?", given after the client's statement of External Conflict ("It was a good piece of machine but nobody wanted to buy it.").

On the other hand, although the recipient is more active in the first, the second of these two narratives is more fully developed by the narrator. Whereas the first narrative about the albatross has no dialogue, the second contains a wealth of dialogue. It includes both direct speech ("And he said, 'Oh no::. Don't sell that gun. You can give it to your grandson.") and internal speech ("And I finally decided, 'Ah. I'm just gonna get rid of it.'"). In addition, the second albatross narrative contains an embedded conversation of five turns between the narrator and story recipient (shown in plain face as opposed to boldface type). This conversation is nested in the middle of the narration, and involves spontaneously arising side talk on the same topic, talk that does not advance the story.

Despite their noncontiguous occurrences, the two narratives are closely matched in structural elements. Nine classic components of narrative, as isolated and defined by Labov (1972a, 1982) are present in both. These include abstract, internal and external conflict, narrative events, resolution, coda, character development, description, and evaluation. (For full descriptions of these classic elements see Labov 1972a, 1982; Labov & Fanshell 1977; Labov & Waletsky 1967.)

Examples are labeled and given in profile in Table 4, which presents a comparison of narrative structural elements in the two narratives being compared. Table 5 profiles a contrast between the two narratives. Both of these outlines detail the narrator's structuring of the narrative. The recipient's role in the two tellings is reserved for Table 6.

After a look at the localized similarities and differences in the two narratives as shown in Tables 4–6, the claim that the two narratives are at some level "the same story" can be viewed more independently of the vagaries of internal structure. Despite the

Table 4 Comparison of Narrative Structural Elements
Given by the Narrator in Two Therapeutic Narratives

Structural Elements	First Narrative Albatross I-Motorcycle	Second Narrative Albatross II-Rifle
Abstract	One time (.) one of the hardest things I ever tried to get rid of was my (.) first motorcycle.	One thing uh I uh (1) I got rid of. I finally sold that old rifle of mine.
Narrative events	—	I just took it down to this garage I:
Internal conflict	Hard for me to get rid of	I wanted to get rid of it you know but I felt (.) like I had to get value for it.
Coda	I keep thinking about that motorcycle system	I: A:nd I felt so good after I finally got rid of it.
External conflict	It was a good piece of machine but nobody wanted to buy it.	And uh I tried to offer it to Teddy. And he said, "Oh no::. Don't sell that gun. You can give it to your grandson." But in the meantime I got to keep that thing, take care of it and I I don't shoot it.
Resolution	Well, finally got my brother-in-law, who was an ex-Bandido, who knew quite a few friends in those Bandidos, he was, one of his buddies got it, bought it off (.) of me: for a hundred dollars.	Anyway, Monday, I just took a look at my gun (.) uh and I finally decided, "Ah, I'm just gonna get rid of it." And I took it down to this guy and sold it for whatever he's willing to give me. I asked him $250. He gave me $225. [I was]
Description/ item development	It was a (Ed Greenhough)	You know, it had been a dead weight to me for about the last year or so. I never shoot it.
Description/ character development	He [the Bandido who bought the motorcycle] was gonna fix it up. He was also legally blind too. In California you can't drive. Not that he was blind - nearly legally blind in	He [Teddy] got about 30 gun now. Now he's crazy.

(continued)

Table 4 Comparison of Narrative Structural Elements
Given by the Narrator in Two Therapeutic Narratives (*continued*)

Structural Elements	First Narrative Albatross I-Motorcycle	Second Narrative Albatross II-Rifle
	California where he came from. So he got a motorcycle. Well you can't drive (it) in California.	
Evaluation	But that was the hardest thing. It was very emotional to try to to get rid of it. Cause I felt like it was just hanging around my neck like an albatross.	No, when I walked out of there I just felt so relieved (1) just getting rid of that thing.

obvious importance of the narrative's *structure*, narrative *structuring* in the ongoing discourse is also of concern. In psychotherapy, with its ample referencing of talk in previous session, this includes discourse from prior hours of therapy. A particular narrative is given at a certain point, and how it relates to the talk that precedes and may follow is also important. Connections are usually made.

The two narratives here are related to each other because they are about the same thing. Not that the sale of motorcycles and rifles is similar, but that the narrator is portraying himself as a central character in a personal experience narrative in the same light each time. There is a recurrent theme; the client maintains that he is capable of cleaning up his life and discarding remnants of his former lifestyle: old items, material possessions, habits, and attitudes. In this way, his twin Albatross narratives can be regarded as retellings, although structurally speaking they relate different events.

In summary, the analysis of the three types of retellings in psychotherapy has elucidated some of the norms of the speech event, thus contributing to the ethnography of communication, and has expanded the field of discourse analysis of narrative by claiming that narrative retellings, as frequent, natural and spontaneous occurrences, deserve an integral place in any adequate theory of narrative. To overlook the fact that, even in ordinary conversation, the successful story gets retold is to ignore the insights that can be gained on possible structural expansions and the significance this

Table 5 Contrast of Narrative Structural Elements
in Two Therapeutic Narratives

Structural Elements	First Narrative Albatross I-Motorcycle	Second Narrative Albatross II-Rifle
Direct speech	—	C: And he said, "Oh, no:: Don't sell that gun. You can give it to your grandson."
Direct internal speech	—	C: And I finally decided, "Ah, I'm just gonna get rid of it."
Embedded conversation within the narrative	—	T: Well, you know, Kurt, you can go and buy a gun for your grandson some day.
		C:. Right
		T: At (.) that point. If you really want to do that.
		C: Yeah.
		T: [Well]
		C: [And] probably my grandson wouldn't be interested in guns anyway. You know, I'm the only one in my family that has been interested in guns
		T: Mmhmm
		C: Nobody else in my family.
		T: Mmhmm (.) mmhmm.

C = Client
T = Therapist

has for determining, in a given culture or subgroup, what are the optional and what are the essential structural components of narrative.

Inquiry into the invariant aspects of repeated tellings makes it possible to see the three types of retellings as permutations of the three elements: event, point, and theme, with variation only in the degree of similarity between each element in the three types.

Table 6 Comparison of Therapist's Role as Narrative Recipient in Two Therapeutic Narratives

First Narrative Albatross I-Motorcycle		Second Narrative Albatross II-Rifle	
Response by Recipient	Trigger	Response by Recipient	Trigger
1. Appreciation (Hmm)	After abstract	1. Appreciation (Did you? Uh-huh)	After abstract
2. Elaboration of internal conflict (That had a lot of emotional meaning to you, hunh?)	After internal conflict	2. Appreciation (Mmhmm)	After (presumed) resolution
3. Request for resolution (What did you finally do?)	After external conflict	3. Appreciation (Hmm)	After internal evaluation and description
4. Appreciation ((laugh))	After introduction of colorful character	4. Appreciation (Mmhmm)	After description
5. Surprise, appreciation (Really, Hmm)	After ironic resolution	5. Appreciation ((laugh))	After direct speech in external conflict
6. Appreciation (Hmm)	After character development	6. Embedded conversation with 5 turns	After external conflict
7. External evaluation of narrative (Well! Interesting Story)	After character development	7. Appreciation (Mmhmm)	After resolution
8. Agreement with repetition of evaluation (Yeah)	After repetition of evaluation	8. Internal evaluation (Hm. Not bad.)	After elaboration of resolution
9. Appreciation of theme (Yeah the albatross around your neck)	After evaluation	9. Repetition of internal evaluation (That's not bad)	After agreement with internal evaluation
		10. Surprise, appreciation (Really? Good.)	After repetition of evaluation

These insights lead to a proposal of the Narrative Equivalency Principle:

Two or more narratives can be viewed as a retelling or as the same if one or more of the narrative elements: event, point, or theme, is the same.

This principle shows what counts as a retelling in psychotherapy, but it is possible that the generalization is not confined to a single speech event.

In contrast, inquiry into the *variant* aspects of repeated tellings highlights the notions that meaning always depends on context and the manner in which narratives are delivered, and that individuals create anew or reconstruct past events in narrating personal experiences.

The focus on the nature of personal experience narrative as it arises spontaneously in psychotherapy allows a unique glimpse at the situated institutionalized utilization for interpretive purposes of a universally occurring phenomenon–telling and retelling. Much work remains to be done to comprehend narrative from a sociocultural point of view, not only as a product, but as an interactive process accomplished within a social context. An ethnographically enriched approach to discourse analysis can assist in achieving this goal.

The analysis demonstrates that retellings, as frequent, natural, and spontaneous occurrences, deserve an integral place in an adequate theory of narrative. A complete theory of narrative must account not only for the plasticity and expandability of narrative over time but also for how and why and where stories are told and retold and how retellings are to be interpreted in a given speech event.

4

Visions Through a Prism: Dream Telling and Interpretation

A fundamental premise of psychotherapy is that perceptions can be mediated through the filter of words and that talking to another about those perceptions can bring about an enhancement in mental health. Nowhere is the essence of this belief more activated than in the telling and interpretation of dreams, for dreams are a highly personal, quasi-visual experience, which can only occur to an individual. When they occur, they do so in a medium that is little understood. In order to be transmitted to another at all, dreams must be framed in language. Language thus serves as the prism through which the light shed by dreams is directed onto a new ground. When a psychotherapy client relates a dream, he or she transforms the experience into a new medium. The process of transforming a dream into a relatable narrative is similar to that of catching a ray of sun and redirecting it through a prism. As an example of the prismlike distortions that can occur when this process is followed, one therapist who makes a practice of recording his own dreams in writing remarked to me that a short dream can take pages of writing to capture.

In psychotherapy, and even more so in traditional psychoanalysis, the recounting of dreams, and, in some cases, even the recording of them in journals, is actively encouraged as a prelude to discussion of their presumed meaning. Dreams as a topic occurred in the majority of the clients' sessions in this corpus. Since dream telling and dream interpretation are speech acts that occur quite frequently within the speech event of psychotherapy, a discussion of these practices should be part of an ethnography of communication of psychotherapy, and in this respect this chapter complements the work of Labov and Fanshel (1977) who do not discuss the phenomenon in their pioneering analysis of therapeutic discourse but elaborate on the structure of personal experience narratives, a related phenomenon that will be drawn upon here.

In this chapter I focus on two aspects of dream telling. I wish to stress first the social uses of dream telling and interpretation, that is, the socioculturally appropriate ways in which dream telling and dream interpretation (talk about a dream telling) are used in the specialized context here as compared with the uses to which dreams are put in other contexts and other cultures. While the sensation of having a dream is universally recognized as a common experience, not every culture and not every segment of a given society encourage the remembering or reconstruction of dreams. Some regard dreams as ephemeral or frivolous while others such as psychotherapists encourage their telling and interpretation. Exploring the attitudes toward dream telling in psychotherapy is a contribution to the ethnography of communication. How dreams are dealt with in waking life by individuals often reflects the cultural beliefs of a people. Likewise, it is of interest to analyze how meaning is jointly constructed in the attempts by participants in psychotherapy to interpret their dreams.

Second, I explore the question of the relationship between structural elements of dream tellings and personal experience narrative. It is evident that the recounting of an experience one has had while in an altered state, such as in a drug trance, under hypnosis, while inebriated, in intense pain, or in a sleep state, is not identical to the reconstruction of a personal experience in which all of one's senses and faculties are active. Nonetheless, the recountings are linguistically presented, and there appear to be similarities between the syntax of dream tellings and that of personal experience narrative such that a comparison of the two is of theoretical interest to discourse analysts. I suggest that a complete theory of narrative will have to recognize dream tellings as a subtype of personal experience narrative. A study of dream tellings can increase our understanding of the structure of personal experience narratives. To paraphrase the title of one of Labov's (1972a) most influential and compelling studies, we might consider dream telling as the transformation of unconscious experience in narrative syntax.

The Social Uses of Dream Telling

While dream telling, and the subsequent talk about the possible meanings of a dream, called "drawing of associations" or dream interpretation, are characteristic of therapeutic discourse, the informal recounting of dreams is also an infrequent, but not uncommon aspect of Western conversation in general, particularly among intimates and associates. The social use of dreams discussed in casual, everyday conversation is frequently for amusement, or to express feelings that would not otherwise be acceptable outside of the dream. Some persons express sexual attraction obliquely by saying enigmatically to someone, "I had a dream about you last night." Some innovations can only be tolerated if couched in the language of dreams of visions, and charismatic or religious movements have frequently derived their authority from dreams. (See, for example, Martin Luther King's "I Have a Dream" speech; see Bourgignon 1972.) In any examination of the social uses of dream telling, it is important to consider the social setting of the dream telling. Whether in a particular culture dreams are reconstructed informally at breakfast the next day, in ceremonial or institutionalized settings, to family, to certain elders, only to women, to professional dream interpreters, or to no one are contextual determiners of the social meaning of dreams. The types of dream telling and interpretation that occur in individual psychotherapy, for example, take place in a small private office. The participants are never standing, always seated. The interpreters have undergone years rather than months of rigorous training, and are licensed by their peers after strenuous examination. A brief comparison of the cultural attitudes of several diverse peoples can serve as a relief against which dream telling and dream interpretation in the psychotherapy of Western industrialized society can be more easily seen.

It is important to emphasize that the having of dreams is a worldwide phenomenon, but the telling of dreams is not necessarily universal. Nor do recipients of dream tellings behave in identical ways. The basic distinction to be recognized is that, whereas dreaming is undoubtedly both a physiological and psychological phenomenon, and best studied by the relevant disciplines, the relating of dreams to others is a social and linguistic phenomenon. Because the relating of dreams is a linguistic activity that takes place in a sociocultural context, dream telling (as distinguished from dreaming) is properly an important sociolinguistic phenomenon. In this section I consider how dreams are related and talked *about* in therapeutic discourse. Such an examination highlights the social and linguistic aspects of dream telling and interpretation and can yield insights on the sociocultural attitudes toward the role of dreams in Western industrialized societies. A number of anthropologists (e.g., Hallowell 1966) have also seen the attitudes toward and beliefs about dreams held by a people as constituting a direct clue to the basic premises of the world view of various peoples.

A number of important ethnographies of dreams have been published for individual groups.[1] Several excellent review articles have also appeared.[2] These studies acknowledge that dreams can be both projections of the personality of the dreamer and reflections of the culture. Thus they invite a cross-cultural perspective on the social significance of dreams and further point to the need to distinguish between the dream as (1) experienced, (2) remembered, (3) reported or reconstructed, and (4) interpreted. I am concerned primarily with the last two.

In many cultures dreams are considered prophetic. For some groups, such as the Kenyan Gusii or the Pokomam,[3] dreams portend the opposite. That is, if a person dreams that his friend who is sick will die, his friend will in fact recover. In other cultures, including Judeo-Christian biblical accounts, dreams (such as those of Noah or Sarah) are believed to constitute divine messages. Dream interpretation functions as a form of divination for Haitians and a large number of Afro-American groups.[4] Whether the origin is divine or from the individual, in the current corpus dreams are treated as messages whose content is potentially valuable. How dreams are dealt with in waking life by an individual often reflects the cultural beliefs of a people. In Fiji, on the island of Fulaga, there is a strong cultural prescription that erotic dreams are evil and that young girls must immediately confess them to older women.[5] In the current corpus, Shannon, Shelly, Kurt, and Sharon all express discomfort about the erotic dreams they have.

The act of seeking assistance in interpreting dreams attests to the underlying belief by an individual or a people that dreams have meaning or carry hidden messages. An interesting area of cross-cultural research arises in examining what types of people are allocated the special role of dream interpreters in a particular culture. How interpreters are chosen, what special training, sex limitations, or accoutrements they require, and the social settings in which they act are all variables of interest. In Tedlock's (1981) ethnographic work among the Quiché Mayans of Guatemala, there are nearly 10,000 dream interpreters (*ajk'ij* "day (sun or time) keepers") out of a total population of 45,000, and they are recruited to a branch of the Momostenago medical secret society by divine election through birth, illness, and dreams. As part of their training, the novice reports any dreams of the previous week, which the lineage head or "mother-father" (*chuchkajaw*) will interpret in great detail, sometimes telling the novice any of his own past dreams that may have had similar symbolism.[6]

This practice of reciprocal dream telling is not unlike Freud's own practice of sharing his dream about a patient in order to teach about dream interpretation. Freud reported 50 of his own dreams and offered interpretations.[7]

In Morocco, where both dream books and popular knowledge of the codes of symbolic equivalences are widespread, people rarely attempt to interpret their own dreams, but seek the help of a *fqih*, a local Koranic schoolmaster.[8]

In contrast to dream interpretation in Morocco and Guatemala, clients in Western cultural tradition do not seek out therapists or analysts solely to have their dreams interpreted. They come to the therapy setting for a variety of reasons. Dream telling and dream interpretation are but one possible component of the therapy session, and not all therapists engage in dream interpretation. Nevertheless, dream interpreters in each of these cultures share the same assumption. There is a tacit acceptance of the belief that dream symbols constitute a form of inner communication, that the elements are a decipherable code,[9] and that specialized individuals are equipped to assist in interpreting them or discovering their meaning.

Even the differences between Jungian analysis of dreams[10] and Freudian analysis of dreams,[11] stemming from whether dreams arise from infantile sexual drives or are the result of the unconscious rising into the conscious, are subsumed by the fundamental belief of both approaches that dreams are meaningful and that deciphering their symbolic messages can provide valuable insight.

Consider the discussion between the therapist Marian and her client Shannon over the benefits to be derived from coming to one's own analysis of the meaning of dreams. Marian refers to not wanting to give Shannon an interpretation that is formulated for her ("a big package with a bow on it, all tied up"), and states that she recognizes that Shannon would prefer to make her own analysis of what her dreams mean.

SHANNON: . . . I mean, I think in a way I would like you to say
             the dreams mean this, and this and this.
MARIAN: But you've already told me that you think sometimes
             that's all bullshit.
SHANNON: I know, if you did say that I would (.) I wouldn't
             believe it.
MARIAN: So along with the dreams, there's a great deal of
             skepticism, and (.) dare I use the technical term? I
             usually try so often not to. Resistance.
             Resistance to what it is they're supposed to do. It's
             like you've dumped them there almost daring me to
SHANNON: ((laugh))
MARIAN: You laughed, why do you laugh?
SHANNON: I think it's funny.
MARIAN: Is it true?
SHANNON: I think so. Yeah it is true. It's like I'm not gonna be
             put in a box. Any kinda box. Even my own.
MARIAN: So there is some sense that when you give,
             something like that, here, there's an irritable side of it
             too, like "All right, so what bullshit are you gonna
             shove around, make of this one."
SHANNON: Kinda. But I think one of the things I like about you
             is that you really don't do that. You (.) uh (.) make
             me say what it is, most of the time.
             Which is harder.
MARIAN: Which sometimes makes people feel like they're
             doing it alone. On the other hand, if I gave you a
             great big package with a bow on it, all tied
             up, you've already said you wouldn't take it. This
             does have to be your way.
SHANNON: Yeah, it really does, and I think I know that, but
             sometimes it really is hard . . .

   In discussing the benefits and techniques of Western approaches
to dream interpretation, psychoanalysts are also often initially
puzzled by the hidden meaning of dreams. What is meant by "associations" is the probing of any meaningful connections in terms
of the dreamer's past experience, present situation, or future expectations. For both Jung and Freud, associations provided the key to
decoding dreams for both dreamer and therapist. (For example, the
associations of "a slab of beef" would mean something different to
a vegetarian than to a cattle rancher.) In psychotherapy, "associations" are given by the client at the request (spoken or implied) of
the therapist. An instance from the current corpus involves the

therapist Ralph's asking Kurt for his associations to a strange dream recorded in a journal.

RK(8)25

RALPH: ((Looking through journal)) Let's see what else I found in
there. There were one or two other things. (3) I think
there's a dream that I read here that was interesting. Yeah
(1) It was a- this is rather strange a:nd uh **I want just to
read it to you and see what your associations are
now.** It is the dream you had (1) dated uh the 25th of of
May. Said "Had a strange erotic dream last night. There
were about three dozen gymnasts walk- working out in a
field in a pastoral scenery of rolling green
hills. . . . It was obvious early spring for there were patches
of snow everywhere and the appearance of the overall scene
was chilly but it wasn't winter because green buds were
appearing on a few trees and green grass was appearing
through the snow. It was a Russian country scene and the
gymnasts were Russians." 'Member?

KURT: Yeah.

RALPH: "Half of them were boys and half of them were girls and
they were naked. The boys were dressed in blue and white
gymnasts' suits and the girls were bending over while the
boys had their thumbs up the girls' asses."

The verbal drawing out of client's "associations" can be handled in a variety of less direct ways; for example, by asking what a dream element brings to mind. Observe the therapist's three queries (in bold face) in the following extract from a session between Marian and Shannon. Marian tries several times to get Shannon to make "associations." She is probing the connections.

In the following extract, Shannon, a 30-year-old woman whose father has recently died, reports that she still feels "pretty bad" about an abortion she had some time ago, that she feels she "killed a baby" and that she has recently begun dreaming about babies.

MShan(43)6

MARIAN: And the dreams with all the babies tell us babies are
something important for you, and that this comes up for the
first time tells us that too. There's something important
about that, that it connects up with a dream. Which dream?

SHANNON: The, the one with the empty picture frame.

MARIAN: **What do picture frames do?**

SHANNON: Well, it was a little tiny picture frame, that was like a picture frame that should've had a picture of a baby in it, but it was empty.

MARIAN: **Like any you've ever seen?**

SHANNON: Uh, no, in fact it was, it was weird looking; it was made out of wood and looked homemade.

MARIAN: Homemade ( ) Made at home. So the empty picture frame was made at home?

SHANNON: I guess ((throat clear)).

MARIAN: **What do baby pictures bring to mind?**

SHANNON: Babies, just thinking about pictures makes me think about home. I've been wondering lately where my father's scrapbooks are.

MARIAN: Yeah? Are there things you want to look at?

SHANNON: I just want to have 'em, you know, would like to look through 'em, you know.

Later in the same session, associations are referred to by a lay term equivalent, *connections*. Marian reports that she prefers not to use technical terms with clients. (Noticeably, all of the therapists here avoided "jargon" and carefully defined any terms (e.g., "depression") from psychology. In the next example it is the client, Sharon, who has been in therapy for two years, who uses the technical term *associations*.

MS4

SHARON: I've had some real interesting dreams but I've been caught up primarily in what's going on there.

MARIAN: Okay.

SHARON: One of the dreams that I want to tell you about is just (.) so obvious to me, what it means (.) that I'm really amused by it. (1) I dreamt one night late last week tha:t I was either manager or an assistant manager of an apartment complex. I'm about to be an assistant. And Tom was calling me on the carpet for having not exterminated (.) for bugs for two months.

MARIAN: ((lip noise))

SHARON: A:nd ((smile)) we walked through a park ((laugh)).

MARIAN: ((laugh))

SHARON: You pick up some associations already?

MARIAN: Mmhm

SHARON: We walked through a park and sat on a bench (1) a:nd can't remember exactly how he brought up this question, but it boiled down basically to uh asking me (.) if I knew what D-category people thought about me. And I said, "You mean

people that choose D?" thinking of a multiple choice test.
And he said, "No, D-category people." And he said, "They
don't find you attractive at all." And he did like that
((gesture)).

MARIAN: Mmm.

SHARON: And that was the end of the dream. Thank goodness. I
didn't get any more out of that discussion.

MARIAN: Um.

SHARON: The thing about bugs (.) calls to mind debugging a program,
like you would on a computer. I've done a lot of computer
work.

In the following extract, Marian comments to Shannon about
the process of interpreting dreams that it is really the client who,
with the therapist's assistance, must discover for herself the personal message contained in dreams, rather than relying on a formulaic symbolic interpretation. She appears to position the therapist as a facilitator of personal interpretation rather than as a seer.
In this segment Marian alludes to arbitrary analytic categories as
"little boxes that everybody fits into," and seems to suggest that
the best interpretations are those that the client herself is able to
formulate.

MShan(43)13

SHANNON: Yeah, I've had this picture of myself lately that, little fighter,
standing behind the wall throwing rocks at people ((laugh)).

MARIAN: Yes, indeed, scrappy little one too. What flashed through
my mind was, and sometimes throwing dreams at them.

SHANNON: [((laugh))]

MARIAN: [((laugh))]

SHANNON: You really think like that? I mean, that that's that those that
dreams are like rocks, those dreams are like rocks?

MARIAN: Mmhmm, and then again, they're dreams. ( )

SHANNON: Same here ((laugh)).

MARIAN: No, no I'm not. I'm not turning from them at all. Don't let
that sound as if I was discounting them.

SHANNON: Treading on thin ice ((laugh)). No.

MARIAN: Who?

SHANNON: Just a joke. You. Treading on thin ice to discount my
dreams.

MARIAN: Oh gracious no.

SHANNON: ((laugh)) No, I think I'd want you to read mine. Say, okay,
let's see what you can figure out. ((laugh))

MARIAN: Mmhmm.

SHANNON: That kind of=

MARIAN: =Does it frustrate you some when I turn back
             to you and say, "What do you make of that?"

SHANNON: Oh yeah.

MARIAN: It does?

SHANNON: ((laugh))

MARIAN: So you really want me to DO it. There's a part of you, your
             head says, "I know, I want this, I'VE got to find **the
             connections**. They're **MY connections**. There aren't
             any little boxes that everybody fits into, that she can add."

SHANNON: Not just my head, too, though. It, it is frustrating, but I
             don't want to do it any other way. I mean, not just my
             hea:d, but=

MARIAN: =your feelings too.

In addition to the references to associations as "connections,"
the foregoing extract is particularly useful to examine because it
attests to both client and therapist's belief in the importance of
dreams as Shannon jokingly warns Marian not to take her dreams
lightly ("treading on thin ice to discount my dreams"). Marian
appears quick to confirm that she would not devalue dreams ("Oh
gracious no"). Shannon's belief that dreams are puzzles ("see what
you can figure out") is revealed, as is Marian's position that it is
the client who should make the ultimate connections ("... when I
turn back to you and say, 'What do you make of that?'").

It is useful to note that different schools of therapy place greater
or lesser emphasis on interpreting dreams. While Gestalt or object
relations therapists might actively elicit them, a primarily Rogerian
therapist, for example, who is not principally interested in dreams,
might merely listen attentively. What matters is that no therapist,
regardless of orientation, would dismiss a client's voluntary telling
of a dream as inappropriate in the therapeutic session. Dreams are
considered valuable and apropos in the psychotherapy setting. As
two psychologists I interviewed noted, it is remarkable that clients
persist in wanting to relate dreams, despite the great difficulty they
have in reconstructing them.

The factor of repetition is apparent in dream telling because
many people, including the clients here, report that significant or
troubling dreams tend to reoccur. There is also thematic repetition
throughout dreams. For example, Marian, the therapist, remarks to
Sharon:

MARIAN: And uh in the last several dreams you've told me there is a
            the theme of uncovering. The one you told me last time
            about not, you know, not thinking you had much on out,
            you know, out in the parking lot.
SHARON: Yeah.
MARIAN: And here the wedding dress (.) you have many layers. We've
            talked a lot recently about your guardedness too. And uh,
            and taking off layers.

In another segment, themes are also sought.

MARIAN: Hmm. What you thinking?
SHARON: Just going back over my dreams.
MARIAN: Picked up any themes?
SHARON: (4) Well, violence. Um
MARIAN: Violence?

Among psychotherapists there is disagreement about dream
interpretation, but even those with different orientations consider
repetition of dreams significant and pay particular attention to
recurrent dreams (e.g., Perls 1969:89–90) and themes.

There are many competing theories about the origins of dreams.
Certainly physiologists' approach to their genesis is slightly different from that of Freudian or Jungian analysts. It is not my intent
here to review the various theories or methods of interpretation,
although this is a fascinating area. Instead, I invite the reader to
consider dreams as an intriguing puzzle, to reflect on their social
use and structural resemblance to personal experience narrative, and
to observe that meaning is jointly produced in attempts at dream
interpretation.

Dream Telling as a Type
of Personal Experience Narrative

An intriguing aspect of dream tellings is that they appear to be
couched in narrative syntax. There are several unmistakable parallels between the syntax of dream telling and that of narratives told
about waking life. As distinguished from legends, myths, and tall
tales told about third persons, both dream and personal experiences
are narrated in the first person ("I") and reconstruct the feelings
and sensations of the teller. An examination of both the similarities and differences between narratives and dream tellings can con-

tribute to knowledge about the genre of personal experience narrative in general. Much of what is known about the internal structure of personal experience narratives has been contributed by William Labov,[12] and the observations here continue that tradition, as well as taking into consideration work by discourse analysts.[13]

Dream tellings begin in a manner that is similar to but slightly different from that of typical personal experience narratives. While the latter begin with reference to time, place, persons, and behavior characteristic of the situation, the initial statement of a dream telling presupposes the place (usually in bed) where the dream occurred; tellers make no reference to place in the opening utterance. However, the time of occurrence of the dream (e.g., last night, two weeks ago) is characteristically referenced in every initiation of a dream telling observed in the corpus, suggesting that this is an invariant component. The topic (what the dream is about) is optionally added in the first utterance as a type of abstract.

Three typical formats and some example initiations of dreams from the corpus below illustrate how important dream tellers presume the date on which they had the dream to be.

Form of Initial Utterances in Dream Tellings

I had	a dream	(about X)	[time]
There was	a dream	(where)	[time]
I dreamed		about X	[time]

Examples of Initial Utterances in Dream Tellings

1. There was a dream about a week ago (.) where I was talking to two or three guys that were (1) laughing and (.) being very lighthearted about thinking they needed to hide from the police force.
2. There was another dream that I had about a week or two ago about (2) ((turning pages of dream journal)).
3. There was a dream I had at the end of January or early February that (.) I uh hadn't told you about. Just never thought about it the times that I was here (.) but you were in it and this is one time you played yourself.
4. I dreamed about you the other night and now I've forgotten.
5. I dreamt one night late last week that- I was (.) either manager or an assistant manager of a bank.
6. Two nights ago I dreamt about (2) working in an office.

A difference between dream tellings and personal experience narratives is that the orientation elements of time and place are considered optional for personal experience narratives but in dream tellings, only place is optional. Time is not.

Dream tellers, like narrators of personal experience, also employ a type of evaluation device I call narrative *singularizers* to initiate their telling. Singularizers single out the realm of events as tellable and point to the story or dream's uniqueness as an indicator that it is reportable. The three principal means of singularizing are (1) use of numerical quantifier *one* followed by a noun , (2) use of the frequency adverbial *once*, or (3) use of the superlative morpheme *-est* (or bound morpheme variants of *-est* such as *most, worst, least, first*)[14] to individuate a narrative. The similarity in initiating devices for both dreams and narratives in the following examples suggests that the syntax of dream telling is similar to that of personal experience narrative.

Sample Dream Initiations

1. And last night I had the strang<u>est</u> dream . . .
2. Uh a couple of dreams lately about libraries (4) In <u>one</u> of them I had gone back to a library.
3. <u>One</u> of the mo<u>st</u> violent dreams I've had lately was about Randy.

Sample Personal Experience Narrative Initiations

1. It's the uh (.) and I-one time (.) one of the hard<u>est</u> things I ever tried to get rid of was my first motorcycle.
2. <u>One time</u> (.) I was just about 16 years, 17 years old. I was just sitting in the bathroom taking a crap.
3. Martín and I got to talking <u>one night</u> and he said he-something like some time I was (.) like two people.

Similarly, the tense/aspect choices employed in dream tellings are the same as the four choices frequently used in English narrative: preterite (e.g., I went), past progressive (e.g., I was shopping), past perfect (e.g., I had driven), and historical present (e.g., He comes in). However, in dream tellings and the discussion *of* dreams another tense, the present progressive, is also utilized. Consider the surprising tense-aspect choice of the present progressive to discuss a past event in the following extract, where the therapist, Marian, questions her client, Sharon, after Sharon has recounted a dream about hearing her therapist have a conversation with a man regarding where she [the therapist] slept the night before.

MARIAN: Who is it I'm talking to?
SHARON: I had. It's a man that you're talking to but I don't know who you're talking to.
MARIAN: And you're?
SHARON: I'm listening to the conversation. I'm in a chair and you're at a desk.
MARIAN: Mmhmm

The ongoing nature of dreams, their ability to be replayed in the mind (and even redreamed in the case of persistent dreams) may account for the overt similarities that talk about dreams has with talk about drama. When people discuss plays they have seen, they also employ the present progressive to describe events they have "seen." The playlike nature of dreams is observed by Sharon in the following extract as she introduces another dream about her therapist. She says, "but you were in it and this is one time you played yourself." What follows is a complete citing of the dream in question, reconstructed by Sharon for Marian. Note that this example also illustrates a strategic type of repetition termed *narrative enveloping*, which is a technique to bound the unit. It can also be seen that the parallel usage of

"but you were in it"

and

"But anyway you were in that dream"

shown in boldface in the opening and closing utterances of the dream serves to bound the discourse unit and bracket or frame it.[15]

MS(1)4

SHARON: (5) There was a dream I had at the end of January or early February that (.) I uh hadn't told you about. Just never thought about it the times that I was here (.) **but you were in it** and this is one time you played yourself. This one, I mean I knew who you were uh and it had to do with going to take an exam of some sort (2) and so (2) what what made me think about it was uh the GRE. It was a big exam and

there were a lot of people that were going to it. And I had
gotten to a building and I was trying to find the place to go.
Found I was in the wrong building, but uh before I headed
to the right place I was in a large open area that reminded me
of a cafeteria. There were rows of tables and there were a lot
of people there. I think I remember having a meal in the
dream too (.) or finishing a meal. And as we all got up to
leave (.) I was one of the last ones to get out and I happened
to look at one person sitting over at the table by herself and
it was you. And you were eating soup and looked up and
kinda grinned a little bit and uh I don't- we didn't speak and
(1) I recognized you but I don't think I really (3) this wasn't
any big friendly greeting. I (.) just turned and went but I
knew that you were there. (1) As I was leaving the building
I ran into this tall (1) uh (.) rather masculine, deep-voiced,
sombre woman that told me where I needed to go to take this
test. And I headed out. Headed out of the building toward
my car to drive to another building that was close by on
campus. And that part of the dream interested me because
(1.5) I was leaving a building, walking into a parking lot that
reminded me of a dream that I had had earlier. It reminds me
a lot of one of the parking lots. (1)

MARIAN: The one you told me about last week? (1) That was sort of
            a (.) circular thing. And you=

SHARON: =No=

MARIAN: =were pulling out of the
            parking lot.

SHARON: No, I remember telling you about that one but it was a
            different kind. It was kind of a wall that is long in front of
            me. It reminds me a lot of the parking lot at Wilmington,
            the apartment complex I live in. Maybe I haven't told you
            about that dream. (2) I think I told you about the one that
            had that parking lot in it. I'm not sure. Um. **But anyway,
            you were in that dream.** (1)

MARIAN: Hm

SHARON: I had a lot of dreams the last week or two. And I brought
            my journal. I'm gonna think about leaving it with you. Um
            (1) a lot of dreams that have been very violent, not only to
            me, but to other people, for example, my aunt and my
            family.

Like personal experience narratives, many but not all dream
tellings contain direct speech. Quoted speech from what is presumed by many to be a quasi-visual event raises an interesting
question: Where does the dialogue of others come from? Is it imag-

ined or remembered?[16] The answer bears upon the fictive versus
(re)constructed qualities of dreams and hence upon the status of
dreams as subtypes of personal experience narrative. Just as in typical narratives, speech in dreams is often expressively given, during
dream tellings, in dialects or with vocal quality (such as a higher
or deeper pitched voice) differing from the teller's own.

Freud treats the subject of speech in dreams extensively in *The
Interpretation of Dreams* (1900) and briefly in "Metapsychological
Supplement to the Theory of Dreams" (1917). Freud's notion of "day
residue" as the raw material of dreams held that fragments from
the happenings of the previous day were interwoven into a tapes-
try by means of what he calls "condensation and displacement."
Akin to this, Fleiss (1973:137) asserts that the raw material of speech
in dreams is speech in waking life that was "either spoken, heard,
read or thought on the day before it is reproduced as a dream speech."
This tacit assumption is reflected in Marian's comments to Sharon
after she tells a dream about getting married in Russia.

SHARON: ... That's what comes to mind right now but I just don't
            know. I don't know if we were planning to get out of
            Russia.
MARIAN: Hmm. Mhm. (1) And again you thought this was last
            night.
SHARON: Mmhm.
MARIAN: Anything come to you from yesterday that connects up?
SHARON: (12) Nothing specifically.

Nearly everyone has had the experience at one time or another
of hearing a person who is sleeping speak aloud, occasionally shouting, prompting the possibility of aural imagery.

The blurred quality of images in dreams is apparent in the following complete dream telling of "Getting Married in Russia." In
the underlined portion, Sharon describes her difficulty in reconstructing the words of her aunt although she makes two attempts.
This particular dream illustrates the problematic nature of quoted
speech in dream telling. (I will comment later on the interpretation of this dream.)

MS(1)7 "Getting Married in Russia"

SHARON: (2) And last night I had the strangest dream. I was
            i:n: Russia (1) ((tsk)) about to be married (.) and my mother
            was there and some of my other relatives were there too I

think. My aunt was there and I think one of my cousins, although my cousin was much younger. And (.) I was very upset in the dream that I was having a white wedding dress with (.) black (.) pumps. I wanted different color shoes. I was mad at my mother for not having gotten the right colored shoes. A:nd for some reason I left the church, ((swallow)) left this room where the wedding was gonna be (.) and went back to a smaller room (.) where my mother was and (2) took some clothes off. I- I realized that I had a lot more on than just my wedding dress and at one point I took off a brown jacket and underneath this brown jacket I found long red sleeves on. So I I think I took that off too (.) a:nd <u>I told my aunt that I was mad about the shoes and she said, "Well" (1) um, I can't quote what she said. I was mad about the shoes and I said, "I don't want to wear these shoes" and she said, "Sometimes you have to do things you don't want to do," something to that effect.</u> And then I was out of the church. Walking around I remember seeing, looking out over a distance there was a lot of uh, there were some cars in the distance, and and there were a few small hills, a lot of dirt and almost like a perimeter that cars were going around, could go around (4) and I wound up really yelling at my mother about two or three things that she had done. Uh one thing was the shoes. I don't know what else I was mad at her about, but I wound up telling her that uh (2) she hadn't had to deal with much as far as I was concerned, over the years. (1) And it was (.) something to that effect. There's more <u>to</u> it than just that too. There's more <u>to</u> it than just the wedding. There was something else that wasn't even concerned with the wedding. (2)

MARIAN: A couple [of dreams ( ) something (.) else that] doesn't quite come to you now.

SHARON: [Maybe it'll come to me.] It probably will later (.) I (.) yeah I haven't had time today to write it down. Sometimes things come back to me when I write them but not (.) now.

It is characteristic of dream tellings that the tellers have difficulty remembering aspects of the dreams. Nearly every dream telling observed contains commentary on the difficulty of recapturing the experience. This is exemplified in the preceding exchange, and in the former example, with the statement, "I think I remember having a meal in the dream too (.) or finishing a meal."

In another previous segment Sharon says, "I can't remember exactly how he brought up this question, but it boiled down basically to uh asking me (.) if I knew what D-category people thought about me."

Often during the course of a dream telling, tellers comment upon the illogic of dream world actions or their inappropriateness for daily life. They make comparison between the logic of the two worlds (waking and sleeping) as if they expected dream worlds to adhere to the same cultural norms governing the pattern of their waking world. An example occurs in the following extract taken from Sharon's account of a dream where she talks with two men who are hiding out from the police. She comments that their choice of a hideout, "back at their home" seems illogical: "Sure doesn't sound like a very good place to hide out but (.) but that's what they were gonna do." In waking life, as a young girl, Sharon was raped by her brother and his friends.

MS(1)6

SHARON: Um, there was a dream about a week ago (.) where I was talking to two or three guys that were (1) laughing and (.) being very lighthearted about thinking they needed to hide from the police force. And I was being lighthearted too, but I knew I was playing along with them. I didn't want them to know that I was listening to what they said (1) because it was information I might use at a later point. Uh (1) and they wound up saying that one of the places they might hide out was back at their home. <u>Sure doesn't sound like a very good place to hide out but (.) but that's what they were gonna do.</u> And then later in the dream the police and my aunt went to that house. I don't know why but they went there and (.) these young men were there and my aunt was raped in this house. And I felt very guilty in the dream because I thought I had information that could have protected her. But (.) I talked myself out of the guilt because I didn't know that they were going there and I hadn't seen her and I hadn't seen the police and I didn't know anybody else was going to that house. So I finally convinced myself in the dream that I wasn't responsible because I really I didn't know what they were going to do.

MARIAN: Mmhmm

SHARON: I had been listening (.) to find out where they were going (.) I think with the idea of telling the police, but (1) um (1) I didn't really have a chance to tell them before my aunt went over there with them. And then later in the dream, I I, it was like I was standing in the (.) kitchen of my grandmother's house. She was sitting at the table talking about what had happened (.) and (.) I went to this house (.) also (.) and they were still there and I knew they were gonna rape me if I didn't get away from 'em, but I got away. I ran from the house. I remember struggling with them, getting away.

Another client, Wilma, comments on the illogic of her dream about a coat, "this kinda sounds weird."

GW2(31)

WILMA: I I think toda:y the biggest thing I talked about was uh (3) the feeling (.) that I was lettin' myself in for somethin' you know like comin' down here and, the vulnerability (.) and- I had a I I don't know if I dreamt it at times or what, but I, it seems I'm by myself and scared and there's just like, this kinda sounds weird but it's just like opening a coat up and seeing everything inside, you know.

GERALD: Opening a coat up? (4) I I guess that sounds like it would be sort of (.) frightening and exciting at the same time.

WILMA: But I mean it wasn't like seeing my physical self, it's just like, it was my feelings, everything.

GERALD: Oh. (3) We:ll, you know, I think people, some people (2) you know wear their heart on their sleeve too much and really let themselves open (.) for a lot of things. Some people keep stuff uh locked in a closet and lose the key. (8) I I don't guess that either extreme is uh (.) of much benefit when you do it all the time.

WILMA: Yeah, I feel like I kinda wore, like you said, wore my heart on my sleeve too much. ((crying))

Further evidence that dream tellers expect dreamworld characters to adhere to the same sociocultural norms as are observed in waking life lies in the embarrassment dream tellers express about dreams involving nudity. An example is given below. Freud has described such dreams of nudity or partial undress as "typical dreams," in that they are experienced by many Western people. In fact, Freud's own dream of "Going up the Stairs"[17] is one such example.

The blurred visual quality of dreams is also metalinguistically commented upon in many cases with expressions like "it seems like"; "it looks somewhat like." An example of this blurred visual quality is apparent in a short dream involving nudity, told by Sharon.

MS(1)9

SHARON: There was another dream that I had about a week or two ago about (2) ((turning pages of dream journal)). I don't think I was fully dressed, but I don't know what I was doing. I seemed to be working. I was in (.) it seemed to be a business

of some sort ((turning pages)) um and I was leered at by
these by three or four guys a:nd

MARIAN: So: sexual violence
SHARON: But nobo- yeah=
MARIAN: =sexual violence=
SHARON: =quite a bit of sexual
violence. Really, more of that than any other kind.(11)

Dreams, like drama, appear to be segmented into scenes. In the
dream cited earlier, "Getting Married in Russia," Sharon says, "And
that part of the dream interested me because (1.5) I was leaving a
building, walking into a parking lot that reminded me of a dream
that I had had earlier."

Because therapists interested in dreams often ask clients to keep
a dream log or journal in which they write down their dreams (as
several of the clients here did), one interesting prospect for future
research is a comparison of written dreams with oral versions. In
both, the transformation of a quasi-visual experience into narrative
syntax is a fascinating and little understood process.

In the present corpus, the manner in which dreams were treated
differed. Some therapists encouraged dream telling, some allowed
it. Several of the clients in the corpus were keeping dream logs or
journals, some like Wilma and Kurt on their own initiative, and
others, like Sharon, at the request of their therapist. Their attitudes
toward showing these logs to their therapists differed. In the first
example that follows Wilma initiates keeping a log, while in the
second the therapist tries to elicit further discussion of a dream
recorded by Kurt quite some time ago by alluding to "associations."

GW2(2)

WILMA: I do have bad dreams sometimes that get me up but I I go
back to sleep shortly. I'll lay there for a while, thinking that
if I (.) pound it into my head what I just dreamt that I can
remember things in the next morning, which most of the
time I don't, so that's- I'm gonna keep this pencil and
pad by my bed so I can write 'em down.

RK(8)13

RALPH: Well, you're getting more in touch with a whole range (.) of
sever- how shall I say, several gradations of feelings
KURT: Uh-huh.
RALPH: Really good. (1) Let's see what else I found in there. There
were one or two other things. (3) I think there's a dream

that I read here that was interesting. Yeah. (1) It was a -
this is rather strange a:nd uh I want just to read it to you and
see what your associations are now. It is the dream you had
(1) dated uh the 25th of May. Said, "Had a strange
erotic dream last night. There were about three dozen
gymnasts walk- working out in a field in a pastoral scenery
of rolling green hills. It was obvious early spring for there
were patches of snow everywhere and the appearance of the
overall scene was chilly but it wasn't winter because
green buds were appearing on a few trees and green grass
was appearing through the snow. It was a Russian country
scene and the gymnasts were Russians." 'Member?

KURT: Yeah.

RALPH: "Half of them were boys and half of them were girls and
they were naked. The boys were dressed in blue and white
gymnasts' suits and the girls were bending over while the
boys had their thumbs up the girls' asses."

One very noticeable difference between dream tellings and personal experience narratives is that during dream tellings, recipients
of the dream tellings play a much more minimal verbal role than
do recipients of typical personal experience narratives, who often
shape the course of a telling or negotiate its point. The therapists
here restrict the number of backchannel cues and remain silent
almost throughout the dream tellings. There can be no doubt that
they are attentive despite the lack of typical backchannel cues. In
contrast, *after* dreams have been told, therapists often assume a very
active role in discussing their presumed meaning.

Dream Interpretation

Just as in many aspects of language use, dream interpretations in
this corpus are jointly negotiated by speaker and hearer, and judg-
ments are either confirmed or changed by the reactions they evoke.
Therapist and client mutually contribute to the search for meaning. The role of the therapist is to hear the dream telling and then
to draw out the client in exploring possible interpretations together.
Unlike cultures in which people refer to dream books that contain
the answer, or in which seers are empowered with the correct
vision, in the psychotherapy context, the sociocultural assumption
prevailing, as we have seen, is that the client and therapist will work
together to personalize an interpretation that will be relevant for
the client. In this jointly constructed meaning, or verbal working

through, the therapist takes the lead in evoking, suggesting, and probing, while the client searches within for connections or associations to help reveal what both consider is the inherent meaning. The following example illustrates a jointly produced interpretation following Sharon's dream telling of "Getting Married in Russia." The therapist probes with several pointed questions:

What do you make of that?

What does that mean to you? The Taj Mahal?

Yes and dangerous.

Seems to me you've told me that the last couple of times it was right before you come to see me that (3) . . .

Anything come to you from yesterday that connects up?

In citing the following discussion I emphasize that dreaming, a process, is largely involuntary and physiological. On the other hand, dream telling is voluntary and social. Further, dream interpretation, as evidenced in psychotherapy, is an exercise in jointly constructing meaning through language.

On the heels of Sharon's telling her dream about the strange wedding in Russia, Marian initiates the exercise in interpretation with the question, "What do you make of that?"

Dream Interpretation MS(1)8

MARIAN: What do you make of that?

SHARON: (5) Some things I can make sense of. Ah, the anger at my mother (.) and telling her at the end that I thought she had gotten by pretty easy with me cause I think in some ways she has. There have been very few responsibilities that she has taken (.) with me as far as I'm concerned, and I guess I thought in the dream that (.) you know <u>at least</u> she could have gotten the right color shoes for my wedding day. I don't know why it was her responsibility to get the shoes. I don't know, but um (3) I can imagine why I would tell her that because she'd gotten by pretty easy as far as I was concerned. And Russia. I've heard about being in Russia before. Russia is a very repressive (.) country. I can imagine why I would be there.

MARIAN: Mmhm.

SHARON: Um ( )

MARIAN: Yes and dangerous.

SHARON: And dangerous. (2) There was something else I was planning with some other people. I don't know whether it was- whether it was planning an escape (2) That's what comes to mind right now but I just don't know. I don't know if we were planning to get out of Russia.

MARIAN: Hmm. Mhmm. (1) And again you thought this was last night.

SHARON: Mmhmm.

MARIAN: Anything come to you from yesterday that connects up?

SHARON: (12) Nothing specifically. (3)

MARIAN: Seems to me you've told me that the last couple of times it was right before you come to see me that (3) Hunh?

SHARON: Yeah, breaking out of Russia? Um (.) yeah (.) I I didn't go through that this week. I didn't (.) my Monday night this week was not characterized by thinking about quitting therapy.

MARIAN: Hm.

SHARON: Hmm. I hadn't thought about that but that's true. I didn't think about quitting last night. Also in the dream, um, recollection of an article of a headline, really. I didn't even bother to read the short article in the paper. There was something about the Taj Mahal. Somebody was gonna do something with the Taj Mahal,. or to it (.) or something. I didn't even read the article. And that that article crossed my mind=

MARIAN: =Mmhmm=

SHARON: =So I don't know.

MARIAN: What does that mean to you? The Taj Mahal?

SHARON: (4) Very ornate building in a foreign country. I- I don't even know what the article was about. I didn't even - obviously I can't even remember the headline. I didn't take time to go ahead and read that.

MARIAN: Mm. (7) So (.) very rich detailed (.) complicated dreams.

SHARON: Yeah.

MARIAN: Many themes. (3) Are you feeling okay? I mean it sounds to me as though something is (.) stirring.

SHARON: Something is stirring.

Together Marian and Sharon explore the significance of, among other things, the locus of the dream: Russia. For example, Sharon suggests that Russia is repressive, hinting that it is like the stifling environment of her grandmother's house. Marian agrees, and proffers another dimension "Yes and dangerous." "And dangerous," Sharon ratifies. Marian continues to probe the significance of the dream's site in Russia, offering that it might be related to the client's chronic presession wishes to quit therapy, to "escape." The therapist says, "Seems to me you've told me that the last couple of times it was right before you come to see me. . . ." Sharon agrees, "Yeah, breaking out of Russia?" implying that quitting therapy is similar. She admits that that interpretation had not occurred to her but that it might be accurate, "Hmm. I hadn't thought about that but that's true."

With this give and take, of mutual exploration of proposals and counterproposals by both client and therapist for interpretation, the typical dream interpretation proceeds. Client and therapist share the creation of meaning in talk about dreams, through the prism of language.

In summary, in light of the fact that most of the dreams people experience (estimated by psychologists to be three to four per night) are forgotten, those few that are remembered and reported, or offered to a specialist as a basis for interpretation, provide a unique glimpse into a person's innermost thoughts. When dreams are reconstructed, tellers of necessity utilize language to convert their quasi-visual dream images into a form surprisingly like that of personal experience narrative. I have considered here two aspects of dream tellings. First, dream telling and dream interpretation as sociocultural events were viewed in cross-cultural perspective, and the attitudes of the participants in therapeutic dream interpretation were investigated. Both therapists and clients treat dreams as valuable resources with covert meanings. A dream is a deeply personal experience, one that can be experienced only singly. However, in the telling, a dream becomes a shared experience, part of the social fabric. When clients and therapists, using language, make an attempt at dream interpretation, they jointly negotiate meaning. A second aspect I investigate is the relationship of dream tellings to narrative structure. Because dream telling is framed in narrative format, yet differs somewhat in tense choice, optional elements, and listener's role, the comparison of the structure of dream telling to that of personal experience narrative is a fruitful area to pursue. Although dream telling has previously escaped notice by discourse analysts, a complete theory of narrative must take dream telling into consideration because a full understanding of the relationship of this universally available resource to personal experience narrative can offer valuable insight into a pervasive genre.

5

Reflections: The Role of Repetition

The focus of this chapter is on a type of repetition that lies at the heart of therapeutic discourse and resoundingly confirms the essence of the social interaction as a search for insight or self-understanding. The type of language resource I concentrate on here is the dyadic use of immediately contiguous full and partial repetition employed as rejoinders to statements. I differentiate two types of rejoinders to statements, termed here *echoing* and *mirroring* (to be defined), and contrast them with a third type of repetition found in psychotherapy, called *(urged) repeating*, in order to highlight the fact that speakers can and often do use repetition as a discourse strategy. This repetition of the words of others in turn shows that people often construct their discourse out of bits and pieces of others' talk, that is, they speak interactively, jointly building discourse.

The focus on contiguous full and partial repetition is particularly useful in highlighting differences between therapist and client speech and in comparing therapeutic discourse to other types of professional discourse, such as classroom uses of repetition. The analysis also makes apparent the role of the speech event in determining the interpretation of discourse. I propose that there are two principal types of repetition of another's statement in therapeutic discourse, echoing and mirroring, which will be defined, and that these differ along three dimensions: (1) syntactic form, (2) function, and (3) originator, and that both types can be strategic resources in discourse.

One important point to note is that the cohesive use of repetition focused on in this chapter is dyadic and dialogic; it is the second speaker's rejoinder to a first speaker. Thus, this treatment differs from that in other studies touching upon repetition in discourse that examine a single speaker's repetition of his or her own words. I am emphasizing that dyadic, dialogic repetition is a means of mutually creating worlds through words.

Far more is known about self-repetition or monologic iteration[1] than dyadic repetition, with the important exceptions of Tannen (1987a,b; 1989) and Norrick (1987), who study the functions of repetition in everyday conversation. Tannen's (1989) focus on repetition in oral discourse and my own grow out of Jakobson's observations about the ubiquity of parallelism and may be seen as part of a larger move to analyze the poetics of oral discourse. In the past scholarly work tended to deal with single writer or speaker repetition of his or her own words.

Although universally available as a discourse resource, repetition has not received extensive examination by linguists, possibly for two reasons. One is that repetition has been considered syntactically unchallenging. However, even given precise copying of syntactic form, dialogic repetition involves overlays of prosodic patterns of pitch, amplitude, and timing as the examples that follow illustrate. In fact, variation abounds in repetition. Johnstone (1987b:211) observes that "repetition is never exact." Where variation exists, it is the task of sociolinguistics to discover the reason for such variation. Another reason that repetition has only recently begun to draw attention is that linguistics has for a long time considered the referential function of grammar to be paramount, in effect, overlooking the expressive, poetic, and pragmatic functions of language. Precisely because repetition offers little referential novelty, analysts must look to its interactional functions for understanding.[2]

As a preface to the discussion to follow, it is necessary to point out several crucial distinctions between types of repetition.[3] Attention needs to be paid especially to intonational contours (rising, falling, level), and a distinction between self- and other-repetition is crucial for an understanding of the different uses of repetition by client and therapist in therapeutic discourse. Another distinction of value is the difference between whole and partial repetition, that is, whether an entire utterance is repeated, or only a portion. Degree of exactness or paraphrase also needs to be distinguished, as does whether repetition is adjacent or delayed, contiguous or noncontiguous.

Regarding intonational contours, many crucial differences in types of repetition have been glossed over in the literature and these need to be clarified. Intonation contours are central in differentiating response. In (1a), a standard upward/downward pairing (indicated by arrows) is shown.

(1a) Q: Do you have a preference for chocolate? ↗
      A: I have a preference for chocolate.   ↘

This typical response (rather than rejoinder) format will *not* be the focus here. The example in (1b), however, contains a matching upward intonation that is associated with stalling and is familiar to many classroom teachers and parents.

(1b) Q: Do you have a solution to the problem? ↗
      Q: Do I have a solution to the problem?   ↗

The example in (1c) from the data shows a statement followed by a clarification question. This involves a downward intonation on the part of the first speaker, and an upward intonational pattern on the part of the second speaker. Quirk et al. (1980) call this "recapitulatory echo question." (In this example, Kurt, the client, has remarked that he feels he must smoke two packs a day, his quota, but his therapist, Ralph, does not understand the use of the word *quota*.)

(1c) KURT: I didn't meet my quota.   ↘
      RALPH: Didn't meet your QUOTA? ↗

However, the most intriguing type is (1d), in which downward intonation by the first speaker is matched with downward intonation from the second speaker. A sample from the corpus is the therapist Marian's empathic statement about the client Sharon followed by the repetition below:

(1d) MARIAN: You're scared of men. ↘
      SHARON: I'm scared of men.   ↘

The focus of this chapter is restricted to this type, a statement followed by a rejoinder to the statement exemplified in (1d), because it is characteristic of therapeutic discourse, and, as Tannen (1987a) says, this type is the most puzzling. Echoing, as the type in (1d) will be called, is germane to therapy because it is an instance of insight and empathy, two key values in psychotherapy. If empathy is the ability to take the other's point of view, then being able to formulate a statement about another which that other takes up as his or her own demonstrates empathy. If insight is the ability to see inside, then therapists' formulations are models of insight for clients. Later, clients will become adept at making insightful statements, such as "I'm scared of men" on their own, without assistance.

To explain two types of rejoinder to a statement frequently found in therapy, I draw on Halliday and Hasan's (1976:206–215) terminological distinction between response and rejoinder. Their distinction rests on the fact that "not all answers have a question" (Halliday and Hasan 1976:206). I am concerned with rejoinder.[4] A rejoinder is a general category of sentence sequel. A rejoinder that follows a question is a response, but no less fundamental are the sequences involving rejoinders to the other near-universal utterance types, command and statement (or imperative and declarative).

I argue that a complete theory of repetition in discourse needs to take into consideration spontaneous, nonspontaneous, involuntary, and strategic uses of repetition. A second general claim I make here is that because languages provide substitution, paraphrase, and ellipsis as alternatives to repetition, the occurrence of repetition as immediate rejoinder indicates a discourse strategy. For example, there are several alternative rejoinders available to the statement: "Your uncle is very good with kids," as shown in (2).

(2a)	ELLIPSIS:	Yes, he is.
(2b)	PARAPHRASE:	My uncle is very patient with children.
(2c)	SUBSTITUTION:	He's very patient with them.
(2d)	REPETITION:	My uncle is very good with kids.

Given these alternatives, the occurrence of repetition as immediate rejoinder to a statement suggests that a choice has been made, that some social meaning is being conveyed. I argue that the choice can be deliberate, in the psychotherapy setting, as elsewhere.

The third general claim is that the range of functions of repetition have not yet been exhaustively researched, and that contextual considerations or comparison of different speech contexts, such as classroom discourse, conversation, and therapeutic discourse, show the importance of speech event for interpretation. The study of repetition has much to offer analysts of oral discourse.

A number of functions have been proposed in the literature. Weiner and Goodenough (1977:217–220) investigated "repetition passing turns" in order to discover why "a speaker spends his turn adding nothing new to the conversational content" in three types of speaker situations: teacher-student interaction, peer interaction, and doctor-patient interaction. They conclude that the function of such repetitions is a temporizing or stalling one, buying time for the speaker to finish planning the next move without relinquishing the floor. Tannen (1987a) also comments on repetition as a stalling device, but I point out that this type involves matching upward intonation (as in 1b), which will not be my focus here.

Repetition with downward intonation in therapeutic discourse will be seen to differ. I argue that repetition can serve other functions besides stalling and that these functions are determined by the culture that provides the options, by the speech event or setting in which they occur, and by the interlocutors who chose among discourse options. Because classroom uses of repetition[5] do not have the same purpose as does dyadic repetition in therapeutic discourse, the concept of speech event is relevant.

In contrast to classroom uses of repetition, in therapist-client discourse, therapists, unlike teachers, regularly ask patients or clients questions to which only the latter know the answer. They do not usually comment on the correctness of the other's response, but may make comments like, "I see."

Sacks (Fall 1967, Lecture 12) has commented on the clarification function that repetition can perform (as in 1c) in his discussion of "doing tying," which serves to locate something that one didn't hear. Each of the functions proposed in the literature (e.g., temporizing, rebroadcasting, clarification) seems accurate, yet I claim the inventory is incomplete and that intonation needs to be taken into consideration. The two types to be examined shortly, echoing and mirroring, are very different from repetition that is interrogative or exclamatory in function.

I make use of "sound slices" to illustrate, among other things, the precise time junctures between repetitions because the feature of timing bears on claims for the strategic nature of repetition. I base the discussion that follows on instances from actual speakers in psychotherapy sessions, drawing extracts from four different dyads. First I take up a client-generated type of repetition, termed here echoing, and then deal with a therapist-generated type of repetition, called mirroring.

Echoing

Echoing, I propose, involves the contiguous repetition of another's utterance or statement using the same downward intonation in an adjacency pair, as in this example.

THERAPIST: You're scared of men. ↘
CLIENT: I'm scared of men. ↘

Echoing is a client-generated verbal behavior, typically clausal rather than phrasal, and ranges from four to nine words in length.[6] Echoing constitutes *emphatic agreement* in the therapy setting. The very basic distinction between echoing and mirroring, that echoing is client-generated while mirroring is usually therapist-generated, will prove to be revealing about the speech event. Likewise important are the distinctions of syntactic form and purpose.

The most common responses to a statement are the ordinary confirming utterances such as *yes, yeah, I know, You're right.* However, by choosing to repeat the statement of another using the same word choice and basic intonation pattern, a speaker signals acceptance of and agreement with a statement. This echoed acceptance is even more emphatic than agreement with the words *yes* or *exactly* and may be a colloquial discourse level equivalent of *Indeed.* In psychotherapy I have noted that the phenomenon can occur frequently in a short stretch of discourse, as often as one every minute and a quarter. Repetition of an entire utterance is the most common type of echo, and these are typically of four to five words in length, although echoes appear as long as nine words in length (as in the example that follows).

In the following samples of echoing in discourse the echoed portions are in bold face. The following two extracts illustrating echoing are taken from hour-long sessions between Sharon, a client, and Marian, an experienced therapist in her early fifties. Recall that Sharon has been in therapy for about two years. She has until recently been unable to keep a job for long, although she is well educated and holds a doctoral degree. She has difficulty in relationships with men, stemming, her therapist reports, from childhood sexual abuse.

In this first example of echoing, Sharon is discussing how her boss Tom, a sort of father-figure in her life, is both paternalistic and neglectful of his employees.

MS(1)28

SHARON:	((angry tone)) He thinks he's doing me a favor, I'm afraid, by letting me get on my feet financially, and as long as I'm doing $10 a month better than I was doing before, they don't have to consider anything else.
MARIAN:	(4) So this father is not a real good father.
SHARON:	(1) Well, he's helpin' his kids out.
MARIAN:	(2) **You don't want to be one of his kids.**
SHARON:	(1.9) **I don't want to be one of his kids.** I would never have told him some of those things if he hadn't asked me something about (.) "what did he use" (3) had to do with the word "mistake" or whatever. I don't know what it is.

In this example, the echo Sharon makes stands out from a more usual reply, "No, I don't" and appears more emphatic. This echo of an entire proposition is nine words in length.

In the second example, Marian and Sharon are discussing how her previous male employer, like the present one, offered her a sympathetic ear, and then later seemingly turned on Sharon, in her opinion.

MS(1)35

SHARON:	But (2) you know, I've been in his office too when I was real upset and he stood up and put his arms around me, and I know he felt supportive at the time ((upset tone)) and for the support I got my feet tied to the floor.
MARIAN:	**You were run over.**
SHARON:	(1.0) **I was run over.** I refused to tell him as much as he wanted to know. I- he said that I agreed to check in with him every week. That's why I got fired. I didn't check in with him. I missed two class meetings at the end of the semester.

In both of these examples, the pause between the therapist's utterance and the echoing by the client meets or exceeds one second, which in itself is a rather lengthy pause in discourse. These samples suggest that repetition here is not "split second" or "automatic" as in the examples from conversation of Tannen (1987a). The increased length of time between utterances in psychotherapy suggests that repetition here may be a discourse strategy.

Consider next an extract from the second recorded session between the therapist, Ralph, and the client, Kurt, who is hearing-impaired. In this segment Kurt states that he feels to blame because his hearing impairment required that his mother devote the majority of her concern to him, leaving his older sister less well attended.

RK(2)30

KURT: . . . and when they discovered that I was hard of hearing, well, you know, she just had to push her [the sister] away
RALPH: **and gave you all of her attention.**
KURT: **and gave me all of her attention.** Well, when- my sister has never forgiven me.
RALPH: Okay. Okay. I hear you. Yeah.
KURT: (5) But that's just pure speculation on my part.
RALPH: (1)Well, that's interesting. It- because, you know, when you told me a while back that you (.) had a lot of shame and felt a lot of ridicule over being (.) hearing impaired. People in school had called you retarded. There's a lot of I think value for you telling me that. Um it seems like in some sense you could even blame yourself for being born (.) hearing impaired.

In this example from Ralph and Kurt, the strength of the tendency to echo is evident in that the client responds with the verb tense that matches the utterance of the therapist, "gave" rather than with the uninflected form "give," which would normally follow "had to," as in "She just had to push her away and give me all of her attention."

Echoes occur when the therapist makes an interpretive summary about the client's experience, based on previous discourse by the client, and when the client wishes to signal emphatic agreement. There is a minimal pronominal shift from "you" to "I." These echoings represent very important moments in therapy, when the therapist has made an insightful interpretation that is "spot on" and reflects the client's situation to such an extent that the client agrees, claiming the statement as his or her own. It is in fact therapeutic to be understood so thoroughly by another that you can emphatically agree with statements they make about your life. Thus repetition is a crux of the interactive nature of discourse in psychotherapy.

When a first speaker, A, makes a statement about events or conditions in the biography of the second speaker, B, [called B-events by Labov and Fanshel (1977)], echoing can be expected if the second speaker wishes to signal agreement.

In other words, the sequence of discourse that favors use of echoing in therapeutic discourse is:

1. Speaker B's description of prior events (or conditions)
2. Speaker A's statement about those B-events (or conditions)
3. Speaker B's emphatic agreement with A's statement

Stated in Labovian speech interaction terms as a regularity or "Rule" of discourse: Emphatic Agreement - Echoing: If B repeats (with downward intonation) a statement A has made about a B-event, then the repetition is heard as emphatic agreement. This regularity is formulated for therapeutic discourse but appears to be extendable to other types of speech events in Western industrialized societies. Whether it is in fact extendable even to other cultures is a question for future ethnographies of communication.

The claim that echoing represents not simply agreement but emphatic agreement receives support from two observations that can be made by "looking" at sound through an analog to digital sound capture application for the Macintosh computer called Sound Cap (Fractal Software 1986). The echoing I observed is typically produced with (1) greater amplitude or (2) longer duration than the utterance being repeated. These increases are iconic indications of emphasis.

The following visual representations of echoings that were produced by Sharon as a repetition of Marian's utterances have the advantage of allowing accurate time measurement in fractions of seconds as well as graphically representing wave forms, and giving some idea of amplitude.

From the wave form in Figure 1, where amplitude is seen in height and duration in length, and hatch marks represent tenths of seconds, it appears that Sharon's repetition is both louder and longer than Marian's. Marian's insightful statement about Sharon and her patronizing boss, "You don't want to be one of his kids" takes 1.15 seconds to produce. After a pause of 1.9 seconds, Sharon's iteration, "I don't want to be one of his kids" lasts slightly longer, about 0.2 second more.

The same louder, longer pattern is perhaps shown more dramatically in Figure 2, where Sharon echoes Marian's statement about

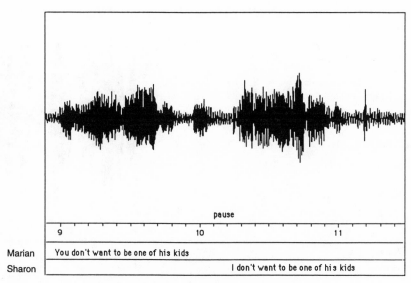

Figure 1 An example of echoing in Sound Cap notation.

her boss' treatment of her, "You were run over," with considerably more amplitude, seen here in height, and more than double the time: seven and a half seconds compared to 1.8 seconds. This stretching out is particularly noticeable.

That therapists can make such "interpretive summaries" indicates not only a high degree of attentiveness by the therapist to the client's descriptions of events and conditions, but also depends on an empathic assessment by the therapist of the client's internal (e.g., emotional, mental, psychological) reactions to a life experience. The interpretive summaries made by therapists involve taking the client's descriptions and commenting on the events or conditions from the client's point of view. The ready agreement signaled by the client's repetition or echoing is evidence of the success of the therapist's interpretive summary. Thus, these echoings represent powerful moments in psychotherapeutic discourse. The echoed acceptance, I claim, is even more emphatic than agreement with the words *yes* or *exactly*. The repetition of the words of another seen in echoing appears to be one more linguistic resource available to speakers to signal strong agreement and acceptance. Double echoing was also noted and seems to indicate even stronger agreement than does one echo alone.

Echoing occurs frequently in therapeutic discourse but is not confined to this type of speech event. Echoing can be expected to

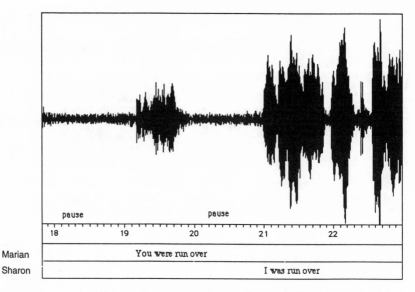

Figure 2   An example of a longer and louder echoing in Sound Cap notation.

occur in situations in which one speaker takes the other's point of view following the recounting of experience and where the second speaker wishes to signal agreement and acceptance of the summary. The frequent empathic statements of many therapists (e.g., "You felt betrayed," "You were too young to be able to handle it") make echoing a likely occurrence in therapeutic discourse.

In the following discussion I contrast echoing with mirroring (to be defined) and show how both are best viewed in context within a body of speech (or text). Neither echoing nor mirroring is fully comprehended from a sentence level analysis. The role of subsequent speech will be emphasized in the analysis of mirroring. While both involve repetition of the statement of another and are characteristic of therapeutic discourse, echoing and mirroring will be seen to differ in fundamental ways.

Mirroring

Mirroring is most frequently a partial repetition by the therapist of a client's statement. Thus the speaker origin is directly counter to what was observed with client echo. The two types are complementary. In echoing the client repeats the therapist's speech, whereas in mirroring, the *therapist* repeats a key portion of the *client's* utterance. An example of mirroring by a therapist is seen in the following example from Sharon and Marian. Notice that the intonation is falling, not rising.

SHARON: When I went home last week I made a discovery. ↘

MARIAN: A discovery.   ↘

In contrast to echoing, mirroring is strategic word or phrase iteration using the same downward intonation. It serves, I claim, as an *indirect request for elaboration*. Typically in mirroring, a salient phrase (noun phrase, verb phrase, prepositional phrase), not a clause, is picked up from the preceding discourse and uttered with downward intonation. Audiences for whom I have played tape-recorded samples say the tone of voice is even and thoughtful. Whereas in echoing the whole phrase is repeated, in mirroring only a key portion is highlighted by repetition. In both types, speakers weave discourse out of bits and pieces of each other's talk.

The difference between echoing and mirroring is especially clear in the next discourse segment where both occur. The segment is again from a session between Marian and Sharon. They are discussing Sharon's persistent anger, her pent-up bitterness, and the prospects of containing her anger within the therapy setting. Marian suggests that it would be preferable for Sharon to restrict her angry feelings to the therapy session but that this may not be possible. It appears that the therapist uses this mirroring strategy to draw the client out, to get her to expand. For clarity, the echoed portion is shown in boldface type while the mirroring is in boldface italic.

MS(5)23

MARIAN: ... You have much to be angry about. It'd probably be better you know, if we can keep it here (.) for the time being, but you know, **it doesn't always (.) work that way.**

SHARON: **No, it doesn't always work that way.** (11) But I don't feel *in danger of exploding* at Larson Management.
I'm hardly in the office anymore.

MARIAN: (1.7) *In danger of exploding*. ((thoughtful, even tone)

SHARON: Yeah. I don't feel that way. There aren't gonna be any more outbursts like there were with that (.) neurologist I worked for.

MARIAN: Oh, yeah! Boy! Wasn't <u>that</u> some time ...

Echoed speech is the repetition by the *client* of an independent clause in agreement with the therapist's statement. Mirroring, on the other hand, is repetition by the *therapist* of a phrase uttered by the client, a portion that the therapist feels is worth further expansion and that the therapist singles out for elaboration. Notice that neither echoing nor mirroring involves rising intonation. Thus both echoing and mirroring, as defined here, are distinct from the type of speech characterized by Quirk et al. (1980) as echo utterances.

Because the mirrored speech is pulled out from previous discourse, the phrase or word in question is not always that which immediately precedes. Other words may intervene. In contrast, echoing is always of the immediately prior discourse. For mirroring there is a tendency to add nonprimary vocal quality. These dramatic characteristics help highlight the phrase or word and bring it into focus. I claim that mirroring functions as *an indirect request for elaboration*. It serves a discourse function similar to the imperatives, "Tell me more" or "Go on," but is less overt. At the same time, it is designed to increase the clients' awareness by inviting them to actually listen to their own words and consider their meaning as they expand on the semantic content.

If we examine the talk subsequent to mirroring we find that it is elaboration. Mirroring serves to return the "turn at talk" quickly to the prior speaker. It also signals attentiveness and invites continuation of a topic, like a backchannel cue. In the next extract, Bonnie, the therapist, and Jake, the client, are talking in their fourth session together. Jake's uptake following Bonnie's mirroring ("Everything.") consists of elaboration.

As a brief background to this segment, Jake, an engineer, has recently separated from his abusive wife, although he is considering a reconciliation. He complains that his wife has no regard for order and that life with her is chaos. Notice that Jake reacts to Bonnie's mirroring ("Everything") by elaborating.

BJ(4)13

JAKE: But uh, you know, it just seemed like (.) if you were gonna try to sit down and plan to do something, like planning on moving the trailer, uh she would jump into the middle of it.

BONNIE: Are you unsure that she would do that? Did it just seem like she did that? or [was that every time?]

JAKE: [*She did that about*] *everything.*

BONNIE: *Everything.* ↘

JAKE:	Very- she was very disorganized, you know. Uh ((throat clear)) you'd come home and try to find the mail, try to find the bills. Uh, you may find them in the yard

JAKE: Very- she was very disorganized, you know. Uh ((throat clear)) you'd come home and try to find the mail, try to find the bills. Uh, you may find them in the yard
BONNIE: ((laugh))
JAKE: You may find them anywhere in the trailer
BONNIE: Mmhmm
JAKE: You may find them in the trash.
BONNIE: How did you feel about that?

The regularity or "Rule"of Indirect Request for Elaboration-Mirroring stated in Labovian speech interaction terms is: If A makes a partial repetition (with downward intonation) of a statement B has made about a B-event, the repetition is heard as an indirect request for elaboration.

In Figure 3, the wave form representation is given for the client Sharon's utterance, discussed previously, "in danger of exploding" and the subsequent mirroring by the therapist Marian.

Sharon's utterance, with a wave form in white, takes 1.5 seconds to utter, but Marian stretches out the phrase in a thoughtful manner, to 1.8 seconds, after deliberating in a pause of 1.7 seconds. It is important to note that a pause of 1.7 seconds is rather lengthy in discourse and suggests that this case of repetition and others like it are strategic and deliberate. One advantage of this type of computer-generated visual display of sound is that it provides accurate time measurements so that analysts do not have to rely on intuitions about "split seconds."

To summarize the differences between echoing and mirroring so far, echoing is a client response to a therapist's statement about the client's conditions or events. Echoing constitutes emphatic agreement and acceptance by the client of an assessment made by the therapist about the conditions or events best known to the client. The form taken is full repetition of the immediately previous utterance of another, spoken with the same downward intonation. On the other hand, mirroring is a therapist repetition of a portion of the client's speech, a phrase picked out from the preceding discourse for the purpose of drawing out an elaboration or further comment on a topic that the therapist feels is of particular value to pursue. Mirroring indicates the therapist's willingness to hear more; it invites expansion from the client.

The mirroring in the next example is taken from a session between the therapist, Gerald, and his client, Wilma, an ambitious

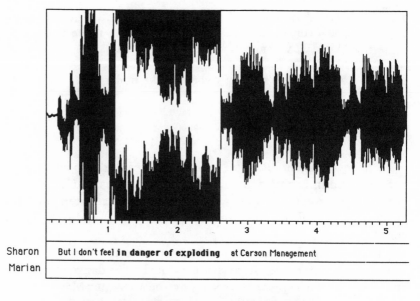

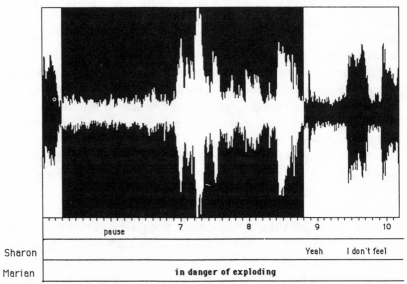

Figure 3 An example of mirroring in Sound Cap notation.

woman who nonetheless has low self-esteem. Wilma is discussing the feeling that she has two warring sides to her self, a weak side and a strong one.

WILMA: I never knew for a long time what it WAS. I always felt like there was *kind of a turmoil.*

GERALD: *Turmoil.* ↘

WILMA: Within myself. And I didn't know what it WAS (.) until this one night Martín and I was talkin' (2) and (.) and uh (3) I forgot what that was. I had (.) I wrote it down (.) in a book. And I've got the book out in the car. I should have brought it up. (1) How I'z feelin' that night.

This example of the selective highlighting called mirroring (in the therapist's repetition of "Turmoil") follows the typical pattern in that the topic is continued by the client after the therapist's short mirroring.

In addition to the differences discussed previously regarding initiator and purpose of the two types of repetition, a further difference between client echoing and therapist mirroring is that mirrored speech tends to replicate shorter segments, usually salient phrases or key words rather than clauses or entire utterances. Mirroring, like backchannel cues such as "Mmhmm," is a most minimal response intended to insure that the previous speaker continues an extended turn with little interruption. Mirroring serves to quickly return the "turn at talk" to the prior speaker and has the added advantage that it signals attentiveness and invites continuation of a topic. By selecting a key word or phrase for repetition, and by delivering it either in a monotone or with downward intonation, therapists indicate that they are in fact actively listening. The data indicate that the technique of mirroring appears to foster rapid resumption by the prior speaker and a continuation or elaboration of topic. Examination of discourse segments throughout the corpus indicates that the result of a minimal speech unit produced by the therapist is client continuation or elaboration of the previously initiated topic.

I have emphasized that mirroring, like echoing, involves downward or level intonation. It is necessary to point out that repetition of another's utterance that involves merely matching intonation of the previous speaker such as matching rising question intonation serves quite different purposes. In the case of matching rising intonation, these purposes may include stalling for time while an answer is being formulated in response. Thus my definition of mirroring must state not only that the second speaker matches the intonation in the prior speaker's utterance but that the intonation is falling, never rising. The example that follows illustrates a partial repetition which does *not* constitute a case of mirroring, as I have defined it. This case of partial repetition is also strategic. However, the instance is calculated not to encourage the prior speaker to continue, but apparently to provide planning time for the current speaker, as discussed by Tannen (1987a) and Weiner and Goodenough (1977). The example is taken from Jake and Bonnie's first recorded session. Bonnie, the therapist, is asking Jake to describe the moment during a fight with his wife when he lost control and struck her. He appears reluctant to talk about it.

BONNIE: *What happened to her* when you hit her?
JAKE: *What happened to her?*
BONNIE: Yeah, was she hurt?
JAKE: Yeah. I broke a nose. If I would have TRIED to hit her and
            TRIED to break her nose, there would have been no way to
            do it.

This example is offered as a contrast to mirroring. It typifies a type of repetition described in the literature. However, an examination of the talk subsequent to an utterance reveals that repetition with rising intonation is followed by a very different type of discourse from that which follows repetition with downward intonation such as mirroring or echoing. Here, the therapist rephrases the question after the repetition, apparently providing time.

Although my focus is on repetition in therapeutic discourse, and the data are event-specific, it is useful to see that echoing and mirroring are not restricted to psychotherapy. Echoing and mirroring undoubtedly occur in everyday conversations and in personal service encounters such as consultations. Mirroring can be observed in many types of consultations where a thoughtful or attentive listener is actively pursuing the listener's role rather than demanding a next turn. Priests hearing confessions, lawyers hearing first-hand accounts, supervisors sounding out advisees, chiefs or commanders hearing news from the battlefront, detectives interested in keeping a detainee talking, and many others can utilize the technique. Echoing, likewise, occurs in ordinary conversation, although because it requires and emphatically signals speaker B's agreement with the interlocutor about conditions or events pertinent to her, it may be rarer. On the other hand, because therapists frequently make assessments or interpretive summaries about clients, echoing arises frequently in therapeutic discourse.

Other Forms of Repetition

I have stressed the voluntary and spontaneous nature of echoing and mirroring, and these characteristics can be clearly seen in relief against divergent forms of repetition such as involuntary and nonspontaneous types. The contrast afforded supports the argument that repetition can be used strategically in discourse.

Two pathological or involuntary forms of repetition thought to be a result of a cerebral lesion, a form of aphasia, or a motor disorder such as Parkinson's disease are echolalia[7] and palilalia,[8] in which patients senselessly repeat a verbal stimulus. They stand in sharp contrast to the deliberate exploitation of repetition for social purposes. While they occur in clinical situations, they are not characteristic of psychotherapy.

Finally, I discuss a nonspontaneous yet dyadic type of repetition that sometimes occurs in therapy: (urged) repeating. It, too, provides a contrast to the voluntary repetition that constitutes the discourse strategies of echoing and mirroring.

As discussed, mirroring appears to elicit elaboration of previous discourse without actually being so direct as to state, "Keep talking," "Go on," or even "Please elaborate." Mirroring is non-imperative, indirect (what therapists call *nondirective*). However, a decidedly directive technique employed by Gestalt and other therapists is a clinical technique, called *repeating* [described by Passons (1975:64–65), where a therapist singles out a client's words and overtly asks the client to repeat them. Mirroring is declarative while "(urged) repeating" is imperative.

While the speech examined earlier was *spontaneous* repetition of *another's* words, the activity called "repeating" is *nonspontaneous self*-repetition of one's own previous words at the instigation/ urging of the therapist. In this case, the material repeated, the doer of the verbal action, and the impetus for the repetition all differ. This final type is other-instigated self-repetition, not spontaneous other-repetition, and I find this distinction crucial. In addition, both mirroring and echoing can be seen as what Sacks calls "local operations" (Sacks, Lecture 11, Fall 1967) in that they occur in the next utterance. That is, they are contiguous. On the other hand, urged repetition ("repeating" technique) has the intervening request for repetition and does not immediately succeed the utterance being repeated. Contiguity is not total. Therapists urge self-repetition by using the imperative form, "Say that again." The underlying assumption of therapists is that a seemingly inadvertent remark made by a client may contain a message that is missed but is nonetheless important and should be explored.

The following extract from the data contains an example of this nonspontaneous urged repeating. Sharon is discussing who is responsible for the general chaos in the central office of the firm where she works. Sharon feels guilty and accepts all the responsibility for what her therapist, Marian, sees as the basic incompetence and disorganization of Sharon's two supervisors, Tom and Mary. In telling Sharon to "Say that again" she wants her to realize that the fault lies not with her, but with the disorganized people at work.

MS(3)19-20

SHARON: . . . if I had presented my case more strongly (.) somehow it would have gotten across that- somehow I didn't try hard enough to make them see. They hired- they can always throw this back at me (.) and whether they will or won't is something else. They can always say we hired you to get us organized. And I see all sorts of things around them that are <u>not</u> organized, but they reflect their personalities. They don't reflect little things they haven't thought about.

MARIAN: That's right. You should.

SHARON: You know I can't go in and tell Mary.

MARIAN: *Say that again. So you're sure you hear it.* They reflect THEIR personality.

To explore and expand awareness of one's own actions, a therapist urges a client to repeat a behavior. It should be noted that the behavior in question can be verbal or nonverbal. A therapist may request repetition of a body movement, gesture, or utterance. Urged repeating allows a client to experience a behavior, to explore, accept, and integrate it, according to Passons (1975:65). The technique is designed to clarify and illuminate meaning by bringing the behavior into focus; it is designed to foster self-examination by the client. It embodies the goal of learning to listen to your self.

In summary, the principal focus of this chapter has been the definition and explication of two instances of repetition that frequently occur in psychotherapy but are not confined to it: echoing and mirroring. These types differ on three dimensions: (1) syntactic form—whether phrasal or clausal, (2) function, and (3) originator. Their functional regularities go beyond temporizing, interrogation, or exclamation. One form of repetition, echoing, signals emphatic agreement, and the other form, mirroring, serves as an indirect request for elaboration. Two rules were formulated to capture the functional regularity of both types of discourse strategies. Because echoing is client-generated and mirroring is typically therapist-generated, the analysis provides insight into differing forms of talk by the participants in the speech event therapeutic discourse. The discovery of their form and function is also an important advance in discourse analysis because it illustrates the strategic use of dyadic or conversational repetition for institutional purposes.

The differences between spontaneous, nonspontaneous, involuntary, and strategic repetition need to be considered to obtain a complete picture of dyadic repetition. I briefly contrasted these spontaneous and strategic uses of repetition with involuntary and urged repeating to show that speakers can and often deliberately do use repetition in socioculturally provided ways. Finally, the analysis shows that a comprehensive understanding of discourse repetition is dependent on a study of context and speech event for interpretation and underscores the fact that discourse is jointly constructed out of selected elements of the talk of interlocutors.

6

Glimmers: Therapeutic Uses of Metaphor

In this chapter I focus on the actual and situated use of metaphor in therapeutic discourse from a discourse-centered perspective. This differs from the approaches taken in the vast literature on metaphor from various disciplines such as philosophy, psychology, anthropology, and linguistics.[1] Often, in other approaches to metaphor, actual language tends to be set aside once codings are made, and extracts showing language in use are a rarity. Here, actual language is the centerpiece of my analysis, and the orientation is to the functional and interactional aspects of language in use.

I address the functional aspect by asking: How are metaphors therapeutic? Why are they used in this speech event, who uses them, and how do therapists receive them? I address the interactional aspect by seeing metaphor not as static but as emergent in context, creatively offered in apt and well-timed moments. I show particular cases of negotiated meaning between client and therapist and offer instances of the discourse strategy of deliberate prolonging of metaphor in chains of collocational cohesion (a type of dense layering of semantic associations).[2] In line with my thesis that discourse is interactively constructed, I pay particular attention to two-party, jointly achieved, extended metaphor and the manner in which entailments are proposed, considered, and accepted or rejected by the interlocutors and the therapeutic consequences. In this respect I acknowledge indebtedness to an important book by

Sapir and Crocker (1977) called *The Social Uses of Metaphor*, which illustrates many of the social ends that metaphors serve and advocates viewing figurative language in the context of a particular social moment. In highlighting an example of collocational cohesion, I continue a tradition of work on verbal art and speech play and the poetic nature of everyday language.[3] To accomplish the purposes of showing how metaphors are therapeutic and how they are received in psychotherapy I use both distributional and sequential techniques of discourse analysis.

Previous interest by psychologists in metaphor has principally been in the realm of comprehension or processing. Only a handful of research targets the therapeutic uses of metaphor.[4] A claim by Lenrow (1966:145) that discussion of the role of metaphors in individual therapy is rare is still true over a quarter of a century later.[5] Nonetheless, most experienced therapists know that figurative language is frequent and plays a significant role in the therapeutic process. One study, for example, found an average of three metaphors per 100 words in a single hour of therapy.[6] Such frequent use of metaphor requires serious attention for any full understanding of the speech event in which it is embedded.

I see three basic ways in which creating metaphor contributes to the therapeutic nature of the speech event. First, in the therapeutic setting use of metaphor constitutes a nonthreatening way of talking obliquely about problems. Speech play of all sorts allows participants to communicate ostensibly about one thing, while targeting an entirely different, usually more serious, area. In psychotherapy, this is sometimes termed communicating with the client in an "area of displacement."[7] For example, in the illustrations I give, metaphor enables the troubled people in this study to talk about such problematic aspects of life as anger, insanity, marital difficulties, being fired, and not living up to potential.

Second, metaphor distills and compresses thoughts and feelings, and allows for an economical condensation of themes. Metaphors provide a glimmer of understanding by summing up and generalizing global insights. One study hypothesized on the basis of independent coders' assessments of instances that "insight" occurs simultaneously with or adjacent to novel metaphorical utterances and that metaphors come in clusters.[8] Corroborating this assumption is the remarkable redundancy of metaphoric themes across the sessions I studied. Clients consistently tend to favor a particular domain for metaphor selection. For example, the client Wilma throughout six sessions uses metaphor to speak of aridness, suffocation, drying up, and the stifling aspects of the isolated hometown she has fled. Likewise, two-thirds of the clients refer to erecting "walls" or barriers to communication in their relationships.

Third, metaphor is therapeutic when the mutual effort involved in creating and interpreting a metaphor leads to the development of rapport between therapist and client. The sucessful working out, for example, of the meaning of elaborate extensions of a metaphor fosters an atmosphere where participants come to trust that language can be used to advance mutual understanding. This rapport is in turn the basis for future mutual endeavors. I emphasize the interactive nature of metaphor when I point out that client and therapist together create meaning and that this joint accomplishment sets the stage for other collaborative work.

Therapists constantly refer to therapy as work. We can ask: Why is therapy called work? What is so laborious about it? Two characteristics of metaphor in general can reveal a partial answer to this question and are relevant to the claim that working together can serve as a means of creating rapport.

I refer to the aspect called indeterminacy of metaphor, an aspect that Martinich (1984:284) calls special attention to. When one speaker declares to another that X is Y or X is like Y the extent of the overlap (or similitude) is not declared. The first speaker merely asserts *that* two things are related; the second is charged with figuring *how* the two things are related. Calling this the "inexhaustibility of implications," Martinich states that this indeterminateness is what makes metaphor salient. It is often to the advantage of both speaker and hearer to leave the major premise vague.

The vibrancy of a metaphor's unresolved tension lies in the reverberations of the similarities to be resolved by individual hearers, as they must interpret, if possible, the extent of similarity. For example, in a metaphor proposed by the client Jake, "marriage is a cocoon," it is up to both the recipient and the creator to negotiate if he means that it is (1) a safe place, (2) a place to develop and grow, (3) a place of confinement, (4) a place to escape from, (5) all of these or others.

The interpretation of metaphor is work because the reverberations are not finite but open-ended. Even long after utterance of a metaphor, new reverberations can be felt, new connections can be seen. Both clients and therapists must be alert to this ongoing nature of meaning.

Metaphor is also work because it is an *invitation* to an audience to resolve its apparent anomaly or nonrelevance to the ongo-

ing speech. Basso and Selby (1976:111) note that makers of metaphor speak in semantic contradictions and extend to their audiences
an invitation to resolve them, and that when the invitation is
accepted and efforts to resolve the contradiction are successful, the
result is the acquisition of a concept that is in a very real sense
unspeakable.

It is this *inviting quality* that makes of metaphor a sociolinguistic concern, especially in how people accept or reject the
invitation. Just as Ervin-Tripp (1976, 1984) has noted the force that
questions have, metaphors require problem-solving skills of a listener and provide a mental challenge. Metaphors command
attention and thus are work. Listeners cannot be passive if they are
to "get" the point of a metaphor, and perhaps it is this pricking of
consciousness, this external stimulation to assume a more active
than usual role in listenership, that fosters an increased participation by hearers. In short, metaphoric invitations, no less than questions, command attention. This aspect of metaphor has special
bearing on the interactive focus on the mutual construction of
extended metaphor and helps answer: Why is extended metaphor
the engaging activity it appears to be? What makes it interactive?
How does metaphor captivate and command audience participation
as in the following example, rather than receiving mere appreciation? What is the essence that compels hearers to contribute further to an apt metaphor, to "go along" with, to engage in playful
extensions?

Another pertinent aspect of metaphor is that it paradoxically,
by presumably running counter to established truth values in
asserting that something abstract is something concrete, establishes
a special relationship to truth: it *approximates* the truth. Metaphor
approaches truth obliquely. For this reason, because the dimensions
established only touch upon but do not coincide with the truth,
often several metaphors for a concept jointly contribute to forming a
coherent picture. One is seldom enough. For example, one very angry
client who was abused as a child and is "in danger of exploding" in
the current corpus formulates three different metaphors for anger:[9]

(1a) Anger is poison
(1b) Anger is fire
(1c) Anger is a weapon

No one metaphor alone captures the magnitude of the concept
for the client, but the overlapping edges help define it. Each in turn

is taken up by her therapist in subsequent discourse. These examples illustrate my point:

Re (1a) Anger is poison

SHARON: It's just a lot of *pus* and *poison* getting over everything.

. . .

MARIAN: You let your guard down and what came *squirting* out?
SHARON: (2) Anger. ((laugh))
MARIAN: Yeah.

Re (1b) Anger is fire

SHARON: Yesterday afternoon *reignited* it. I don't like how much *fire* there is in me.
MARIAN: See that's what I think you're afraid of finding in you is all (.) [that *fire*] all the anger and the *flames* . . .
SHARON: [that *fire*]

. . .

MARIAN: No one would ever <u>dream</u> that beneath that calm, cool exterior (1) there raged *a fire*.

Re (1c) Anger is a weapon

(explaining why she doesn't often express anger to her mother)
SHARON: ((laugh)) You don't like to *bludgeon* people either. I don't do that very often.

. . .

MARIAN: It could be that she see::s your anger. or senses it and keeps you know a ((laugh)) bo:dy between the two of you so (.) to deflect the *missiles* (.) or it could be that she needs the distance too (.) to protect herself.

Consideration of other properties will frame the analysis of metaphoric use in individual cases. It is possible to see metaphorical expressions as ranging along two continua: the creativity continuum and the explicitness continuum. Like food, metaphors can be fresh, frozen, or even precooked. Thus, dead or frozen metaphors can become idioms in a language. "Down the road," once metaphorical, is now considered an idiom, as is "over the hill." Both of these expressions are discussed further. Conventional metaphors are those preestablished within a culture, still viable but preformulated. "She's a butterfly," offered by the client Jake, or "the chief is a tree" in Kuna are conventional metaphors, although they may be used creatively to fit a situation. At the opposite end from idiom are novel, newly arising metaphors such as "Courtship is a ski ride" or the formulation of an eight-year-old boy after a snowfall, "Look, the garage is a package, just waiting to be opened."

Likewise, metaphors can vary on an explicitness continuum. They may be implicit, as when Jake says of his troubled relationship with his wife, "She's wanting to lead and I'm wanting to lead, and we're both stumbling over each other," implying that "marriage is a dance." Metaphors can either be of the prototypical form X is Y (e.g., "People are corn," said in Hopi) or X is like Y (as in the Apache saying, "Friendship is like a deerskin."). The latter is traditionally called simile.

With this general appreciation of the important characteristics of metaphors, their indeterminacy, their inviting nature, their approximateness, and their range of creativity and explicitness, the role of metaphor in therapeutic discourse can be approached.

To illustrate various ways in which metaphors can be received, a sequential approach to metaphor in discourse will be used. However, it is also informative to study metaphor from a distributional approach. In the therapy sessions I recorded, both metaphors *for* and *in* therapy are revealing. For example, when I interviewed the client Norma about what therapy was like, she resorted to metaphor, stating, *"Therapy is a dance. First my therapist takes a step, then I take a step and then we're moving together. It's beautiful."* To express the unfamiliar she used the familiar.

Lakoff and Johnson (1980:47) comment that a pervasive structural metaphor is *"ideas are food."* All of the therapists who participated describe therapy as a process. One suggests, by means of numerous cooking metaphors, that the process is similar to the creative process of food preparation.

Session initial

What you got cooking today?

(speaking of a lengthy string of dreams)
That does suggest that *something's on the front burner.*

Well, I'm struck, not so much with the details of the themes, although I hear the sexual violence in that, but uh, but with the fact that they're coming and they're *perking up* lots of rich detail, lots of complications . . .

Sometimes so much *perks up, bubbles to the surface.*

With this distributional account of metaphor in mind, I turn now to
a sequential analysis of actual short samples of interaction involving
therapeutic metaphor. My purpose is to explore the four basic ways
in which metaphors can be received in therapeutic discourse:

Ways in Which Metaphors Can be Received in Psychotherapy

1. Comprehension without comment
2. Misunderstanding, failure to comprehend or get the point
3. Ratification by comment, repetition, or use of associated
   word in later discourse
4. Extending the metaphor jointly, corroborating by helping to
   construct a chain of collocational cohesion

First, therapists can comprehend a client-proffered metaphor but
let it pass uncommented upon, without further attention. Second,
therapists can fail to comprehend a metaphor and miss the point.
Such misunderstandings can be costly. If the misunderstanding itself
becomes noticeable, attempts to rectify it can ensue.[10] An example
of a misunderstanding is given later. Third, mental health specialists can show appreciation or otherwise "reward" the client by rati-
fying the metaphor. Ratification can take several forms, ranging
from a comment (e.g., "That's right") to repetition of the client
metaphor, to use of a semantically entailed or associated word or
phrase in later discourse. Therapists can also take up another similarity or dimension of a metaphor, one not brought out by the client.
This is illustrated later. A fourth way in which therapists can cor-
roborate the aptness of a metaphor is to help construct a chain, to
assist in weaving an elaborate web of correspondences that tease
out additional ramifications and add new dimensions. Rather than
presenting metaphors of *their* choosing, therapists can try to emphasize the raw material presented by *clients*, and, if possible, use the
lead established by them to spin out further connections. In this
fourth manner, they can exploit a natural aspect of language, lexico-
semantic cohesion, as a strategy to densely layer semantic associations in jointly constructed extended metaphor. They can use what
Halliday and Hasan (1976) designate as collocational cohesion, the
cohesion that results from the co-occurrence of lexical items that
are in some way or other typically associated with one another, such
as synonyms, antonyms, superordinates, synechdoche (part-whole),
hyponyms or cohyponyms of the same superordinate term (i.e., both

members of the same more general class, such as *chair ... table*—both hyponyms of *furniture*). An example of an extended case will follow.

Analysis of Metaphor Misunderstanding

The first sample I provide is a microanalysis of a Misunderstanding. Despite the fact that therapy is considered an appropriate place for expressive language, not every excursion into metaphor is successful. There is considerable risk of misunderstanding with figurative language. The extract below contains an apparent misunderstanding of an intended metaphor. The segment is from a session between the client, Jake, and the therapist, Bonnie. The misunderstanding arises from confusion over Jake's metaphoric use of *hill* in the statement, "Well, it's not going to be much longer and I'm going to be *over the hill* ((mumble)) and it's gonna be *downhill*." As background, Jake is a 36-year-old computer salesman with an engineering degree whose abusive wife has recently filed for divorce. His therapist, Bonnie, is a 26-year-old clinical psychologist in training. The discrepancy in their ages may be a key to the misunderstanding in their interaction.

JAKE: It's always when I've sold and I'm having you know a bad month in sales or maybe a bad two or three months on sales.

BONNIE: Mmhmm

JAKE: Uh the only way I could ever get out of that was just to work twice as hard at it.

BONNIE: ( )

JAKE: I think I'm trying to use the same thing again.

BONNIE: So you're having bad times so you're going to work extra hard and maybe make up for it.

JAKE: Mmhmm. ((laugh)) It's not looking good! I've had a bad first quarter as far as sales

BONNIE: Yeah

JAKE: and it's going into the second quarter. Uh, you know, it's all looking real bad and I'm saying, "Well, it's not going to be much longer and I'm going to be *over the hill* (((mumble)) °and it's gonna be *downhill*.° I don't know. I'm just trying to hang on till that time.

→BONNIE: When you say "*over the hill*," what do you, what do you mean?

JAKE: Oh, probably feeling sorry for myself. You know, just
             thinking, everything is happening, everything is going
             wrong with me.
BONNIE: Mm
JAKE: Well, I think there's good things if you can-
→BONNIE: So *the hill* really is not ba:d ( ) [but good.]
JAKE: [Yeah.]   About
             the time you think you're at *the peak of it*, well, some
             drunk Indian backed into my car door and caved it in.
BONNIE: Oh.
JAKE: So uh I don't know if I told you (.) and I didn't want to
             turn him in, you know and call the police at that time,
             didn't wanna give any trouble . . .

The therapist appears to realize there is a mismatch in interpretations
when she says, at the first arrow, "When you say *'over the hill'* what
do you, what do you mean?" The client responds as if she had said,
"Why do you say that?" rather than "In what sense do you mean
that?" The indication that her interpretation of *over the hill* is
pejorative and does not match that of the client is in the question, at
the second arrow, "So *the hill* is really not ba:d ( ) but good?"

Based on his connections with the italicized portions, *peak* and
downhill, the client appears to use *hill* metaphorically to signify
life's struggles, as in the myth of Sisyphus, seized by Camus as a
metaphor for the existential predicament and its solution, because
he makes reference to how he has worked hard, expected success,
but has encountered repeated setbacks at work (and in the marriage,
in previous discourse). This example of miscommunication is
caused by faulty uptake of the *hill* metaphor. There are two different interpretations. One is the client's use of the metaphor; the
other is the therapist's idiomatic reading. Jake's understanding is
that "Life is a hill. Uphill is hard, but downhill is easy. You need
to try to get to the peak. Like Sisyphus, you may experience setbacks, but you keep trying." On the other hand, Bonnie's interpretation is centered on the idiom *over the hill*, meaning "past one's
prime, near 40, on the wane." Psychologists argue that processing
of idioms is more rapid than that for metaphor.[11] In terms of the
difference betwen idiom and metaphor,[12] the therapist here has
approached *over the hill* as requiring the retrieval of institutionalized meaning (idiom), whereas the client has generated meaning,
inviting figuration (metaphor). Rather than occurring interactively,
the figuration is one-sided here; the metaphor is unsuccessful. Cru-

cially, in this example, the two interlocutors never do resolve their misunderstanding.

Analysis of Ratification

Far more typical of the successful therapeutic encounters that I recorded, however, is the frequent occurrence in which therapists, moments or minutes after a client's initial metaphor, bring that metaphor back into focus, either by repetition, synonym, or with semantically associated terms. This form I call *ratification*. What is communicated by such ratifications is that the client's word choice has been attended to and is deemed potent. When a client's own figurative language is held in consciousness for a while and then reemployed by a therapist, the message to the client is that metaphor is a valuable resource for understanding or insight.

An extract that illustrates this pattern is taken from the second session between the therapist, Ralph, and Lana, a recovering alcoholic who is separated from her husband and has two teenagers at home. She has been sober for one year but is subject to moods where she feels overwhelmed, out of control. She describes how, after one bout, she had a blow-up with her children but is now developing a new coping strategy for mood changes or what she refers to as "the crazies."

RL(2)32

LANA: And the next time *I felt it coming I could feel it
        coming* and I just kinda (3) did anything I could
        to get the pressure off. You know, I called people, I
        got my body out of the house and you know I figure,
        I hope, *if I can see it coming,* I can look at it and just
        go, *"There is an insanity tidal wave coming.* I'm going
        to take this and myself out of your [the kids'] face so
        you won't get it, because you don't deserve it but *it's
        coming."* ((laugh))

RALPH: Mmhmm

LANA: I want to do that.

RALPH: Yeah, anything that you can do

LANA: Mmm

RALPH: that's active (.)
        to cope with that. That means calling your friends,
        turning to an enjoyable, uh, diversionary activities,
        going to a movie.

In the intervening two minutes Lana continues, describing another such "attack" after the buildup of pressure in which she felt out of control.

RALPH: but you're getting overwhelmed with it
LANA: Uh-huh
RALPH: to be perfect. And you've finally caught yourself and
          realized, "Wait a minute. This is crazy. This is
          insanity." You called first one-
LANA: And it's gonna make everything craz*ier*.
RALPH: Right. *It, the tidal wave, it just grows bigger and
          bigger and bigger. It keeps growing.* Uh, this ( ) part,
          the thing about the guardian angel
LANA: Oh
RALPH: can you
          tell me a little bit more about that?

In the preceding segment Ralph ratifies Lana's metaphor for insanity, *the tidal wave,* by referring to *the tidal wave* two and a half minutes later. He also uses one other ratification device. The indeterminacy feature of metaphor discussed previously, its virtually inexhaustible reverberations, comes into play in this example. Lana emphasizes five times (in italics) that *the tidal wave "is coming."* Lana figuratively conveys the natural, overpowering force she experiences at times. Her phrasing, *"feel it coming"* makes prominent both the inexorable and the unpredictable qualities of her emotions. She can't stop them but she can get out of the way. However, the aspect that the therapist chooses to emphasize is different. He points out that *the wave* gathers size and momentum as it approaches. *"It just grows bigger and bigger and bigger,"* he says. These slightly different aspects are nonetheless complementary, and, of course, there are other aspects waiting to be taken up in subsequent discourse. By such acceptance and extension of clients' original uses of language, therapists can build rapport, facilitate further client self-expression, and foster insight.

Analysis of Joint Construction of Extended Metaphor

Nonetheless, even greater degrees of ratification are possible. The final example, shown in (2) and schematized in (1) and (3), illustrates how client and therapist can jointly enhance meaning and collaboratively construct an extended metaphor with unusual power and relevance for the client. The exercise in developing insight and subsequently gaining understanding from another is therapeutic. I claim that collocational cohesion, an inherent characteristic of language, is purposely stretched out and exploited in this discourse segment. In the example that follows the play aspects of lexico-semantic repetition are very noticeable. The jewellike nature of this extract illustrates the verbal art and the poetics of everyday discourse. It is the cohesiveness of the various semantic extensions that become the focus of interaction.

As background to the segment in (2), Howard is a client in his midthirties who is talking with Judy, his therapist, in their third session. It is relevant to note that Howard has a college degree, has served in Vietnam, but for a while has been underemployed, working as an orderly in a hospital. Crucial to this segment, a month prior to the session he was fired from the hospital because he was suspected of stealing drugs that were missing. He maintained that he did not steal the drugs and has since been reinstated in his job, with apologies. It is true that he has experimented with several drugs. He considers the period in which he fought for reinstatement as a challenging period. In this segment a structural metaphor is proposed by the client.

> *Floating   down the River   in a Great Ole Big Barge*
>
> represents
>
> Drifting   through Life   in a Low Level Job.

Both client and therapist weave an elaborate web of extensions. The cohesive items are shown in italics.

(2)
1. JUDY: When you have a problem, what do you do with it?
2. HOWARD: I usually let it be a problem. I don't usually do any-
3.   thing much or I (.) I was thinking about that the other
4.   day.
5. JUDY: Does the problem go away if you don't do anything
6.   about it?
7. HOWARD: No, it gets worse (.) or it just complicates things as you
8.   go on further **down the road**.
9. JUDY: Can you look at your own life, kind of on a continuum?
10.   **Look down the road** of that line and see what that's
11.   gonna do (.) in your own life?
12. HOWARD: S- look on [**down the road?**]

13. JUDY: [Yeah] Kinda visualize what um (.) your own
14.   life will be like if you- you don't deal with some of it
15.   ( ) your problems (1.5) Can you see how it might
16.   complicate (.) [your life?]
17. HOWARD: [It will] just continue the way it is.
18. JUDY: Kind of like *a snowball*? (.) [effect]
19. HOWARD: [No, no] *not a snowball*.
20.   Just kinda *floating, floating down the river*.
21. JUDY: *Floating down the river*.
22. HOWARD: That's what I'm doing now. That's what I was afraid I
23.   was gonna go back into after this. I said something
24.   the first time I talked to you about
25. JUDY: Yeah
26.   *floating*
27.   and being afraid of going back into *floating*. That's
28.   just, you know, *floating, drifting* . . .
29. JUDY: So you're *adrift* right now?
30. HOWARD: Yeah. And I feel dead and I feel and I'm-I drink to
31.   feel a little bit deader. No, that's not true.
32. JUDY: Feel depressed (.) or numb?
33. HOWARD: Yeah.
34. JUDY: Numb, you feel?
35. HOWARD: Yeah. (.) Yeah.
36. JUDY: What's it like to be *floating down the river*? Tell me
37.   more.
38. HOWARD: (2) It's (1) comfortable. It's safe. (.) Everything just
39.   *keeps on an even keel*, you know.
40. JUDY: Mmhmm.
41. HOWARD: You're just kinda *floating* . . .
42. JUDY: Kind of *in a canoe*? (.) *going down the river*, or-
43. HOWARD: No, more like *a great ole big barge* (.) *on a great old
44.   big [river.]*
45. JUDY: *[barge]* very stable, kinda.
46. HOWARD: Yeah. *Plenty of room to spread out* and (.) *sit in the
47.   sun*. Yeah, and you don't have to worry about
48.   *falling off the edge*.
49. JUDY: Mmhmm.
50. HOWARD: And sun, you know, it's *kinda hazy*. It's *not really
51.   clear sun. It's kinda hazy*.
52. JUDY: Mmhmm.
53. HOWARD: Kinda *half asleep*, that's what it's like.
54. JUDY: What happens when you kind of come to *the* (.) *falls*,
55.   *the falls that are down there, about two miles*
56.   *[down the river?]*

57. HOWARD: [Get the hell off] *the river*
58. JUDY: That's certainly one way to handle it. Get out.
59. HOWARD: I feel a lot of discomfort. That's what happened last
60.   month. *I hit those falls* last month.
                ((noise))
61. JUDY: I don't know why it did that. So that's what happened
62.   (.) um this (.) last time there was kind of um (.) an external
63.   (.) situation that sort of *forced you out of your boat* . . .
64. HOWARD: It was uncomfortable but I was, I was pretty, I was
65.   enjoying it too. And I didn't want to go back to just
66.   *floating*. It was uncomfortable and I was (1) out, I
67.   don't, I been *floating* a long time.
68. JUDY: Mmhmm (.) Well, you've found that it works for you (.)
69.   in a sense.
70. HOWARD: What works for me?
71. JUDY: *Floating.*
72. HOWARD: Because I'm (.) stay (.) comfortable and
73. JUDY: In a sense, but it may (.) now be inappropriate. It may
74.   not be working as well (.) as it did in the past.
75. HOWARD: Mm. (.) Yeah, I'd like to have a little excitement now
76.   and then.
77. JUDY: *Some rapids.*
78. HOWARD: Yeah. ((laugh)) Something I can s- keep in control of
79.   maybe and *not drown.* But (.) yeah, I think I am
80.   bored.

The discourse begins prosaically, but when the client uses a dead metaphor **down the road**, in line 8, the therapist seizes upon the client's own words. She picks up **road** as signifying the future, and asks, "Can you visualize your future, look down the road?" In line 12 the client has not yet shifted into figurative language. He questions what it is he is supposed to do: "Look down the road?" In line 13 the therapist specifically asks him to visualize, but in line 17 he makes a prosaic response that if he doesn't deal with his problems his life will just continue in the same manner. In line 18 the therapist offers an alternative interpretation. Using a conventional metaphor, *snowball*, she asserts that, if left unattended, his problems will increase in size until they are gargantuan. So far their discourse is ordinary.

However, in lines 19–20 the client rejects the therapist's formulation. He says, "No, no, *not a snowball*," and prefers to create his own metaphor. The metaphor he offers is, "*Just kinda floating, floating down the river.*" In line 22 the client has a flash of insight.

He claims the metaphor, *floating down the river*, is pertinent to describe his present situation. "That's what I'm doing now." It is notable that by line 21 the client has used the words *floating* or *drifting* six times.

In line 29 the therapist ratifies his metaphor with a semantically related term, the synonym *adrift*. I draw attention to line 36, in which the therapist makes an open request for more information, using the client's metaphor and asking him to describe what *floating down the river* is like. There is a significant pause of two seconds while the client formulates a response. In line 39 he uses the phrase, *on an even keel*. This boating term allows for collocational cohesion with the *river* metaphor and is the first indication that the metaphor may be extended. At this point we have the start of a language game. An invitation to speech play has been extended and accepted.

The game continues. In line 42 the therapist broaches an extension, "Kind of *in a canoe?*" Although the client rejects the specific choice of a boat offered, he indicates his willingness to continue playing with language by offering his preference for a type of boat. He seizes upon "*barge, a great ole big barge*" in lines 43–44 to symbolize, perhaps, the unglamorous but serviceable job as an orderly in a hospital. Observers can be certain that the participants are speaking obliquely.

The therapist confirms that she accepts the client's choice of *barge* in line 45 when she repeats the word and comments that she comprehends that a barge is stable. In lines 46–48 the client continues describing the barge (job), saying it allows room to spread out. (In a previous session he had commented that his job allows him to roam all over and that he doesn't like to feel confined to sitting at a desk all day.)

A very interesting point arises in line 54 when the therapist uses an entailment of *river*, "*the falls.*" She asks, "What happens when you kind of come to *the falls?*" This question appears to probe the client's understanding of his life course. The therapist gently prods him into taking notice that his current behavior (*floating on a barge*) could prove dangerous or disastrous if there are *falls*. The client's response in line 57 that he would avoid a dangerous situation (*the falls*) by getting "the hell off the river" indicates that the client has not fully equated *the river* with life. The therapist in line 58 indicates that she feels this is not the most appropriate approach to a dilemma. There are indications that the client and therapist do not have equally isomorphic understandings of what they have constructed so far.

However, audiences who have listened to this segment can hear a change of tone in the client's voice in line 59. There is a quickened tempo, an air of excitement, which may correspond with a flash of understanding. The client says, "That's what happened last month. I hit *those falls* last month."

In lines 59–60 the client states his realization that he has already experienced the falls last month (in being suspended from his job as an orderly at the hospital for suspicion of drug theft). This traumatic and unforeseen experience of being "set up" is like the falls.

In line 61 the therapist explicitly confirms that she understands that *the falls* is equivalent to his being fired last month. She gives an explicit paraphrase of *the falls*, "an external situation that . . . forced you out of *your boat*." She again ratifies his metaphorical extension of *barge* with her use of *boat*. In lines 64–67 the client comments that although "it," his firing, was uncomfortable, he enjoyed the situation (of fighting for reinstatement), and it provided a diversion from his continual aimless "floating." In line 75 the client states his need for a change. "I'd like to have a little excitement now and then." He would prefer a less monotonous existence than *floating*.

The crowning achievement of this jointly constructed extended metaphor is in the therapist's two-word metaphorical interpretation of the client's literal statement (lines 75–76) that he would like some excitement. She offers the metaphorical interpretation (line 77) of *some rapids*. (Both *rapids* and *falls* are cohyponyms of *river*.) Her formulation *some rapids* is apt, cohesive, surprising, and playful. It brings both delight and satisfaction to the client. He laughs and agrees in line 78. The client accepts the therapist's metaphor ("Yeah") and further contributes to the joint construction of extended metaphor by adding to the elaborate web of extensions they have both been engaged in weaving with the metaphorical assertion that he'd like something he can keep in control of and *not drown* in line 79. (Note *drown* as an antonym of *floating*.)

To summarize this interaction, we find that three major metaphors, *floating, river, barge*, are chosen by the client to represent his attitude toward life and his current work. As shown in (3), between the client (C) and therapist (T), 15 extensions revolving around these three metaphors are introduced.

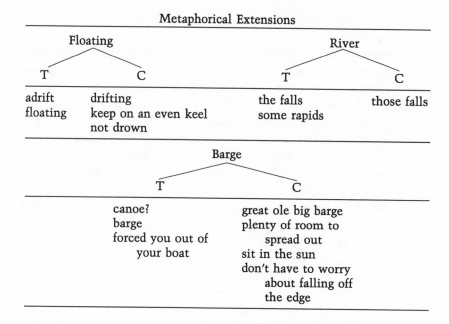

Metaphorical Extensions

Some metaphors are accepted and some are rejected. The point is that they are all negotiated. Their meaning is not static but interactive. The discourse here is not by accident. The speech play emerges as interlocutors talk. The discourse participants have seized upon an inherent property of language, collocational cohesion, and have exploited it, magnifying the effects. In jointly accomplishing what the reader can see is a piece of verbal art, the client and therapist have experienced working together through language. The client is spurred to regard metaphor as an appropriate mode of expression and to contribute to an elaborately structured extended metaphor that is highly personalized.

The previous samples indicate that metaphor is a discourse strategy that enables people to talk about troubling and important aspects of life. Metaphor is not always successful, but when it is, therapists and clients find in metaphor a useful means of learning about and talking through the client's concerns in an oblique and less threatening way. These examples illustrate that serious messages can be communicated in speech play[13] and that speech play is an important aspect of psychotherapy. I conclude that in psychotherapy, when metaphor is apt, and jointly constructed, it builds rapport between therapist and client and helps develop insight, a core goal of psychotherapy. Collaborative work on a common goal is an opportunity to build rapport, and good therapy flourishes in such a situation.

With its focus on dyadic verbal exchanges, this study goes beyond previous systematic observations of textual cohesion that have largely been based on written material. The study illustrates the various manners in which metaphor can be received in psychotherapy and demonstrates that collocational cohesion of metaphorical entailments can be a resource, a discourse strategy in dyadic oral interchanges. A study such as this with its emphasis on the interactional rather than static nature of metaphor advances understanding of one of the many social uses of metaphor and illustrates the poetics of everyday language.

7

Double Vision: Aligned Speech in Joint Productions

How do therapists and clients exhibit a high degree of attention to the talk of the other in the focused setting of psychotherapy? In this chapter strategic use of cohesion in discourse, the Joint Production, is examined. Joint Productions are interlocked utterances that are the result of one speaker's initiating a proposition and a second speaker's completing or extending it in a syntactically and semantically consistent manner, as in the following example:

SHARON: I'm gonna have to find some way=
MARIAN: =to tell her.

In this discourse strategy, it is the proximity aspect of cohesion that is the resource exploited for social purposes. In a seemingly seamless way, speakers manipulate contiguity by contributing to the utterance of another close on the heels of the prior person's talk. Speakers appear to splice sentences. The linguistic evidence offered by such jointly achieved constructions points to a fine tuning of thoughts and words between discourse participants.

This surprising type of synchronicity in therapeutic discourse prompts the questions: What is it about therapeutic discourse that gives rise to such a phenomenon? What makes Joint Productions especially pertinent to therapeutic discourse? Havens (1978:344), a professor of psychiatry interested in language use, has observed that "conversations between persons who are deeply empathic with each other, is, above all, spontaneous, and each often completes the sentences of the other." My analysis shows this to be true. I have found Joint Productions as infrequently as once per hour in early contact situations and as often as seven times per hour for dyads who have been meeting over a period of several months.

Joint Productions* are a type of *attuned talk*, defined as talk by two or more participants that exhibits a high degree of cooperation or accord.[1] I feel that Joint Productions give evidence of a high degree of concerted attention because speakers cannot disattend to or otherwise ignore talk to which they intend to interlock their own words. In order to contribute in a timely and relevant manner to the often ongoing utterance of another, the second speaker must be focused on the speech of that other.

In the following extract, the client, Sharon, is telling her therapist Marian, about her boss Tom's relationship with her, prior to her being transferred. In this example Sharon begins a sentence and Marian completes it with only a 0.2 second juncture between.

SHARON: **He's beginning to have a little bit to deal-to do:**
            with me now (.) uh=
MARIAN: **=now that he thinks he might**
            lose you.
SHARON: ºWell he told Mary that uh he thought I was so smart and that
            they had done me a disservice (.) they'd not been fair, but
            that they hadn't lost me yet . . .

Certainly the atmosphere of mutual trust and deep understanding fostered in psychotherapy may engender empathy, and Joint Productions may be one linguistic expression of empathy.[2] However, it is possible that Joint Productions are not only a signal of empathy but a means of creating empathy or the appearance of it. The *familiarity* that grows out of repeated psychotherapy sessions and the *concerted purpose* that accompanies a joint activity such as this one over time may actually be the relevant characteristics that facilitate this type of speech behavior. If familiarity and concerted purpose were sufficient conditions for Joint Productions to occur, then we could expect their occurrence, likewise, in a variety of situations where people were engaged in longstanding relationships, close working conditions, or otherwise had established rapport.[3] They also occur between caretaker and child. Ochs,

---

*Joint Productions are underscored and highlighted in boldface throughout.

Schieffelin, and Platt (1979: 251) note that children may learn how to articulate propositions by participating in a sequence in which they contribute a component of the proposition. One possible explanation for the frequent occurrence of Joint Productions in psychotherapy is that it may be an attempt through language to recreate the atmosphere of these early days when a proposition could be conveyed through a sequence of two or more utterances.

Another question that arises is: What social action does a Joint Production constitute? For example, whether or not it arises from empathy, familiarity, concerted purpose, or similarity to the closeness of the caretaker-child relationship, does its occurrence suggest to hearers any of these facets, and if so, could participants in therapy utilize these overtones in their discourse choices? I am concerned here with these and other questions as I investigate the social motivations for and syntactic characteristics of Joint Productions. I examine a subset of 30 instances of Joint Productions from four different therapy dyads, and, on the basis of syntactic constituency, prosodic cueing, interactional response, and length of juncture timed to the nearest hundredth of a second, determine the motivations for Joint Productions and their characteristics.

In addition to the importance of Joint Productions from an ethnographic standpoint of showing some of the underlying assumptions and practices of therapeutic discourse, consideration of Joint Productions bears upon several important issues in discourse analysis. Thus investigation of the phenomenon can contribute to the ethnography of communication, discourse analysis, cognitive science, and studies of social interaction.

Joint Productions pose three problems of theoretical interest to discourse analysts. First, they represent a little-studied but possibly universal discourse strategy. As one study of childrens' and caretakers' collaboratively built utterances pointed out, there are at least two important strategies for linguistically encoding an idea or proposition, but the encoding of propositions across utterances by different speakers is recognized by only a handful of scholars.[4] Research reported here contributes to a small but significant developing tradition of research on multiple party constructions and the audience as co-author.[5]

Second, an investigation of propositions conveyed through a sequence of two or more utterances from different speakers, such as Joint Productions, has implications for an understanding of the culturally defined notion of conversation and the rights and responsibilities of those who engage in it. Joint Productions are apparent deviations from the rules of turn taking described by conversation analysts for orderly transition to next speaker in Western conversation. Yet work by other analysts demonstrates that not all Western speakers share the same norms for discourse participation, and evidence is mounting that individuals as well as subgroups in a culture create their own styles of discourse.[6] As Tannen (1984, 1989) shows, the "conversational style" of many Americans is characterized by the creation of "involvement" through Joint Productions of sentences. The tradition of work contained in Duranti and Brenneis (1986) on the audience as co-author points to the cooperative achievement of all discourse and shows the inadequacy of "a straightforward communicative model presupposing a single speaker and unitary or relatively invariant hearer(s), with a single message being passed from one to the other" (Brenneis 1986:340). Similar concepts are the notion of a "conversational duet"[7] in which a sympathetic coparticipant to a multiparty conversation continues the turn lexically and prosodically just as a partner undoubtedly would have to the same audience, and the notions of cospeaker[8] and multiple-floored conversations.[9]

Joint Productions are also of interest to conversation analysts because the occurrence of Joint Productions reveals that speakers are aware of sequencing norms; they are attempts to bend but not break the conversational rule of one-speaker-at-a-time. When a speaker selects herself as next speaker before a prior speaker has completed a proposition, and that speaker makes the contribution synchronize with the semantic content, and crucially, the syntactic form of the previously initiated construction, she tacitly acknowledges a belief in the existence of some sort of system of turn taking. Just as there can be multiutterance turns (e.g., in narrative, instructions, lullabies), it appears that there exist multiturn utterances in the form of Joint Productions. Sequencing anomalies of any sort call into question assumptions about conversational rules.

Third, and most important for the creation of a theory of discourse, the existence of Joint Productions requires analysts to examine whether the collaboratively constructed clauses that are coproduced in Joint Productions constitute a discourse unit, whether speakers in fact co-construct a sentence, building it clause by clause or phrase by phrase, as psycholinguists[10] have argued. For some the notion *sentence* is merely a theory-internal grammatical construct.[11] However, Joint Productions suggest that, for some speakers of English, the sentence is a viable unit, a unit to which they

orient both syntactically and semantically and to which speakers
feel they can contribute. In the corpus, even lay people name the
sentence and make metalinguistic comment upon it, as in the following example, which demonstrates a metalinguistic awareness
of the notion *sentence* by the same dyad who construct several of
the Joint Productions in the corpus. I draw attention to the underlined portion, "Oh I wish I could just take that sentence out and
you know just cross-stitch it and put it up on your wall because I
think that's the story of your life. Say it again."

MS(4):163-165

MARIAN: I think you're terribly afrai:d of letting your anger come to
            the surface. You don't know what to DO with it. [You feel
            a:bsolutely stale]mated by it and so what do you do:? [You
            give them a reason]=

SHARON: [[No I don't know what to do with it] because I
            think [because I think]

MARIAN: =to be mad at you and you say, "Ah, now it's all clear. I'm
            not mad at the:m; they're mad at me."

SHARON: (1) I think they can do MORE to me than I can ever do to
            them. What difference does it make if I'M mad at them?

MARIAN: Oh I wish I could just take that sentence out and you know
            just cross-stitch it and put it up on your wall because I think
            that's the story of your life. Say it again. ((laugh))

SHARON: ((laugh)) I don't
            remember what I said NOW. ((laugh)) I think- What did I
            say? (2)

MARIAN: You don't kno:w? ((laugh))

SHARON: ((swallow)) What DID I say?

MARIAN: You you said that you thought that you were (.) that they- that-
            I'm not sure either ((laugh))

SHARON: ((laugh)) You don't know it either.

MARIAN: You want (.) to go back and listen to it? ((laugh))

SHARON: I forgot about that machine. ((recorder moved from record to
            play mode)

MARIAN: There. I'll cross-stitch it.

If interlocutors can take an active role in shaping the course of
a narrative, negotiating meaning, and the direction of talk,[12] can
they not shape other units of speech? Of course, the issue of what
constitutes a unit of analysis in discourse is far from settled. The
sentence, it can be argued (in English, at least), has syntactically
cohesive features such as subject-verb agreement, and displays some

suprasegmental features of pause, stress, and pitch, for example, weakening or devoicing sentence finally. In order to demonstrate the notion that speakers can jointly construct a single sentence I will provide several examples. In the course of discussion, four types of Joint Productions will be proposed and exemplified as types of social interaction. One common type is seen in the following extract from the first session between Gerald and Wilma. In this extract the topics under discussion are Wilma's general low esteem of herself and her boyfriend.

GW(1)31

WILMA: . . . And uh (2) I told him that night I said, "You need to find somebody that doesn't know anything about you," cause I know an awful lot about his past. It's not good. A male whore he was or is (.) and

GERALD: **Boy you sure talk about him in=**

WILMA: **=a negative way**

GERALD: Yeah.

WILMA: Most definitely. Think I hate him? I think a part of me does. The love-hate syndrome.

While the notion of cospeakers is gaining acceptance, due largely to work on overlap, repetition, and audience interpretation, there also exists a small body of work specifically on sentence completions. Joint Productions were described by Sacks, who first termed them *collaboratives*, later referring to them as *Joint Productions*.[13] Of the others who have worked on Joint Productions,[14] it is interesting to note that three draw examples from group psychotherapy sessions,[15] prompting the questions: "Are certain speakers, such as males, people with higher status, aggressive individuals, or those with certain cultural styles more likely to continue an utterance by another? Is the privilege symmetrical between interlocutors regardless of gender or role? This study touches on these and other questions.

Schegloff (1984:42) observes that the phenomenon indicates that "one person knows what the other person has in mind by saying it for him . . . completing his sentence." However, in the present corpus, rejection by recipients of some Joint Productions suggests that occasionally the completor of an utterance only *thinks* he knows what the initial speaker had in mind.

Another observation made in the literature is Wardhaugh's (1985) suggestion that speakers may attempt to use such words to complete another's remark and effectively interrupt by continuing to speak after the "completion." This imputes a floor-grabbing motive for Joint Productions. Wardhaugh (1985:154) proposes, "One way of interrupting and taking over a turn which is less offensive than attempting to drown out the speaker is by trying to complete something he is saying." For example, he suggests you can finish the sentence another is saying and "try to use that opportunity to lead straight into a sentence of your own, thus achieving a certain continuity of topic but a discontinuity of speakers."

The claim that Joint Productions are prefatory to interruptions is empirically testable. I raise the questions here: Do speakers always use sentence completions of another's utterance to wrest the floor away? Are Joint Productions always attempts to seize the turn? Using examples from the psychotherapy sessions I show that this generalization does not hold true for this special context and that there are other important motivations for Joint Productions in therapeutic discourse.

Data-based Considerations of Joint Productions

In this section, I suggest answers to three questions and illustrate with examples from four different dyads.

1. Is the privilege symmetrical between interlocutors regardless of gender or role?
2. Is the strategy a prelude to interruption, a bid to seize the turn?
3. Are Joint Productions ever rejected, and if they are risky, what motivates them?

In the therapeutic corpus there is no decided asymmetry among various classes of participants in who effects Joint Productions. Neither sex nor role appears to be a crucial factor, because both males and females, therapists and clients, complete each other's propositions. This lack of asymmetry may be surprising, but it does suggest that it is not the participants, rather, their setting or their relationship to one another that fosters the occurrence of Joint Productions. Of the 30 cases I closely scrutinized, slightly more were completed by therapists than by clients (18 completions by therapists, and 12 by clients). Seven of the nine participants in Texas (all but one therapist, Gerald, and one client, Norma) attempted to interlock utterances. For example, in the sample extract shown earlier, and repeated here, the client, Wilma, completes an utterance begun by her male therapist, Gerald. (She was discussing the breaking off of her engagement to a man she discovers is already married.)

GW(1)31

WILMA: ... And uh (2) I told him that night I said, "You need to find somebody that doesn't know anything about you," cause I know an awful lot about his past. It's not good. A male whore he was or is (.) and

GERALD: **Boy you sure talk about him in=**

WILMA: **=a negative way**

GERALD: Yeah.

WILMA: Most definitely. Think I hate him? I think a part of me does. The love-hate syndrome.

On the other hand, in the next example, it is the therapist, Marian, who completes the utterance begun by the client, Sharon. (In this sample, the client discusses her enthusiasm for beginning a more responsible job with the same firm that has been underemploying her talents. Her upcoming job will entail working under the supervision of a woman who is younger, less well educated than she is.)

MS5(12)

SHARON: ... but I think it's gonna be okay when I get back to Bellemeade and I'm working with new people. The woman I worked with this afternoon will be my boss there. She's-

MARIAN: You like her?

SHARON: Yeah. I think we'll do okay. I don't like her calling me honey, though and **I'm gonna have to find some way=**

MARIAN: **=to tell her.**

SHARON: to tell her. And this is not a person that (2) Somebody that's (.) 40 years older than me maybe can call me honey, but this is a woman that's not even my age. She's mid twenties and she's calling me honey.

The latched time for this example, denoted by the equal sign (=), as measured by computer is 0.2 second (See Fig. 4).[16] Here, following Marian's three-word completion "to tell her" of the propo-

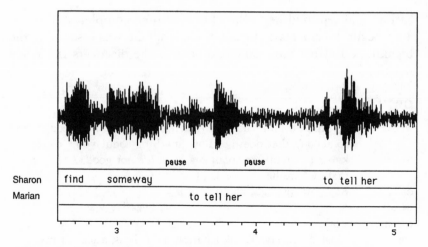

Figure 4 An example of Joint Production in Sound Cap notation.

sition initiated by Sharon, Sharon resumes talk. This example illustrates the fallacy of considering Joint Productions merely as interruptions or opportunities to lead straight into a sentence of your own.[17]

Close inspection of the utterance subsequent to a Joint Production and its source can reveal the answer to the question of whether or not they are attempts to seize the turn. In 29 out of 30 cases, the next utterance emanates from the initial originator of the proposition, not from the utterance completor or extender. This indicates that Joint Productions are not interruptions. In general, in almost all of the therapeutic discourse cases (97%; 29/30), the speaker who contributes a completing portion of an utterance makes no attempt to continue speaking. After a short completion (averaging three to four words in length), subsequent contributors do not proffer further comments; it is the proposition initiator who resumes talk. This orderly transition back to the proposition initiator shows that adult contributors to Joint Productions make their additions brief and immediately allow the proposition originator to make the next utterance. Thus, in the psychotherapy corpus, Joint Productions are neither attempts to seize the turn nor to change the topic.

We can conclude also that Joint Productions in this therapy data are not interruptions in the sense of Zimmerman and West's (1975) definition of "talk intruding into the talk of another." Joint Productions are convergent, whereas interruptions are divergent. In actual interruptions,[18] a second speaker starts up before a first speaker has terminated, but does so quite independently, without regard to the syntactic or semantic output of the first speaker. The result is a discontinued, less-than-complete proposition by the first speaker. Alternately, a Joint Production is a second speaker's attempt to contribute to the syntactic and semantic intent of the first speaker; it is an intrusion that is not disruptive.

If Joint Productions are not undertaken to seize the floor or as an opportunity to change topics in psychotherapy, there must be other strong motivations to supply words for another's thoughts, because, I argue, the practice involves risk. One potential complication arises from potential rejection by the initial speaker, and accompanying possible "loss of face." Such rejection is illustrated in the next example, in which the therapist does not accept the client's proposed completion, "is up to me," as indicated by the therapist's statement, "No," followed by the "challenge" to the client's competence as an adult conversational partner: "If you're following what I'm saying." (In this extract, Ralph, the therapist, is advising Lana, the client, to be cautious about revealing further intimate information to a male from her Alcoholics Anonymous meeting who has befriended her. She had described to him an unwanted encounter with an exhibitionist.)

RL(2)20

RALPH: Yeah. I think that you can still have more honest uh
          encounters with men through AA and outside of AA. You
          can work on some of that, intimacy issues with them, but
          without having that person be your confidante (.) [either way
          you're]
LANA: [I know] cause there are things I don't want to talk about.
RALPH: And see, you started out by making a rather large disclosure.
          He was there for you and that's great (.) but where
          you go after that is=
LANA: **=is up to me.**
RALPH: <u>No, if you're following what I'm saying. you know,</u>
          <u>you've already made it- it's almost too quick. a disclosure.</u>

In this extract, from the second hourly meeting, it is possible there is a double edge to the comment "No, if you're following what I'm saying," and that the double meaning of "following," (both "attending to" and "coming after," is played upon. The therapist appears to criticize the fact that the listener has anticipated the upcoming words, in effect preceding them rather than following sequentially. Note again, as elsewhere, that the proposition initiator (the therapist, here) resumes.

The next extract contains another example of a rejected Joint Production, from a different client and therapist dyad. Here it is the client who does not accept the contribution. At issue is the completion of the Wh-cleft, "What follows is . . ." The objector prefaces her disagreement with "well." (The client is describing the way she uses discussion of dreams to obscure the real problems she faces.)

MS2(15)

SHARON: **. . . If I throw enough tidbits then finally someday [maybe]**
MARIAN: **[I'll] get off the path (.) the trail?**
SHARON: Well, no the path won't get cold, but I won't have to deal with it either.

In the psychotherapy corpus, rejections of attempted splicings were made by therapists and clients alike, both male and female. Rejections of Joint Productions occurred 13% of the time, in 4 out of 30 instances. Thus, supplying words for another, completing an utterance, is a social practice not without danger. This factor of risk makes the motivation for such speech phenomena all the more puzzling. Why do speakers undertake Joint Productions if they might be rejected? If they are not attempts to steal the floor then there must be other, more complex reasons for speakers' attempting them. Based on prosodic cueing, syntactic constituency, and interactional response, I propose four subtypes of Joint Productions:

Types of Joint Production

1. Utterance Extensions
2. Predictable Utterance Completions
3. Helpful Utterance Completions
4. Invited Utterance Completions

The first class of instances is Utterance Extensions.[19] The feasibility that a sentence or sentence analog[20] can be extended by a second speaker beyond the point at which the first speaker consid-

ered it complete necessitates discourse analysis of all utterances
conjointly with the subsequent utterance(s) to determine if they are
in fact complete at the first possible completion point, or are continued by another. Here, the continuation of a syntactically complete utterance is shown in the following extract. (Ralph, the therapist, and Kurt, his client, are discussing Kurt's drinking habits in
their fourth session.)

RK4(15)

RALPH: So how have you been doing emotionally since I saw
you last week?
KURT: Well, still uh drinking fairly steady. Oh: I drank two
days in a row. Quit one day (.) two days. Had a drink
another day. Quit another day. I had a last, my last
drink yesterday. (2) Oh, I had noticed <u>one</u> thing
though. I never drink on Sundays. **The reason for
it is of course, I can't buy anything=**
RALPH: **=until noon.**
Yeah.
KURT: Uh-huh. A:nd on Sundays I haven't got the slightest
desire to drink. You know, it's just like if I can't get
ahold of it, you know, I don't have any desire for it.

Ralph latches a temporal adverbial phrase, "until noon" onto
Kurt's statement that the reason he doesn't drink on Sundays is that
he cannot buy whiskey. This qualifying remark by the therapist
refers to a "Sunday Blue Law" in Texas forbidding sale of alcoholic
beverages before noon on Sunday (when religious services are over).
A concern for the truth value of statements appears to be a motive
for utterance extensions, which serve as accuracy assurance. The
next example also follows the pattern of qualifying a potentially
misleading statement. (Sharon, the client, is discussing her present
supervisor at work.)

MS 5(43)

SHARON: I don't know. She talks about all the friends she's got.
She certainly <u>talks</u> about a lot of people. I mean, she,
you know [I know she plays tennis.]
MARIAN: [Well, you're happy. Let us] start here.
SHARON: **No, I'm not happy=**
MARIAN: **=to be around her.**

SHARON:	No.
MARIAN:	Do you think there're other people who would feel uneasy about being in (.) this woman's sphere of influence?
SHARON:	Oh I think so.
MARIAN:	Mmhm

The therapist, Marian, appends an adjective complement ("to be around her") as a clarification of Sharon's statement that she is "not happy." Rather than saying Sharon is not happy in general, Marian insists that it is one particular situation that makes her unhappy.

As these and other examples suggest, Utterance Extensions appear to be motivated by respect for the truthfulness of utterances. One of Grice's (1975) four maxims, along with the original Cooperative Principle, is that speakers make their contribution truthful. Where a statement is only partially so, interlocutors may append a truth-insuring extension. The commitment in psychotherapy to dealing with truth, avoiding distortions of it, may contribute to the occurrence of this type of Joint Production.

Consider a further example of extension by another beyond the point of syntactic completeness. In the following extract Marian adds a manner adverbial to qualify Sharon's partially true statement. (In a small context they are discussing a recent phone call from Sharon's mother, whom she resents and from whom she feels remote. In a larger context, the therapist is trying to encourage Sharon to access her feelings of anger, to confront them face on.)

MS5(32)

MARIAN:	Well, you <u>are</u> a good daughter. You're a very good daughter still.
SHARON:	No, not really.
MARIAN:	No? ((sniff)) (7) Now a really ba:d daughter might say when a mother says, "Ha ha still think of you" might say, "Bull<u>shit.</u>"
SHARON:	I guess if I'd been a really bad girl I would have asked her how many times she called (2) and what ti-
MARIAN:	Are you, oh! Now that's still verbal; it's intellectual.
SHARON:	We:ll?
MARIAN:	Say "I don't believe you. You're lying to me."
SHARON:	**Well, that would've- that's kinda part of what I was just asking [((laugh))]**
MARIAN:	**[((laugh))] [in a very polite way]**

SHARON: [You know I] ((laugh))
         You don't like to <u>bludgeon</u> people either. I don't do
         that very often.
MARIAN: I'm saying to you, "What are your feelings?" I'm not
         saying, "<u>Say</u> these things (.) or <u>do</u> these things."
SHARON: Sure.
MARIAN: I'm saying <u>play</u> with some access to those feelings.

Again, the pattern that emerges is that second speaker's extensions of a proposition by another (as shown in the boldface portion)
serve as a veracity check.

These Joint Productions are explicable as efforts to clarify, to
ensure completeness or correctness in terms of information and
truth value, and these semantic wishes are performed with syntactically compatible contributions by a second speaker to the first
speaker's utterance. The result is one sentence contributed by two
interlocutors. At other times the semantic incompleteness is less
salient than the syntactic incompleteness, as the next type of example will show.

A second type of Joint Production can be termed Predictable
Utterance Completion. Speakers project their intended utterances
well before their point of completion. Where a second speaker can
successfully anticipate the remainder of a proposition by another,
she or he may sometimes contribute the guessed portion. While not
always the case, the practice of predicting another's speech can
result in overlapped speech, with two persons speaking in tandem,
the second approximating the words of the other, in many cases
with uncanny accuracy. (In the following example, Sharon, the client, is recounting a well-known short story, "The Ransom of Red
Chief." The therapist makes a successful approximation of the
client's own intended words.)

MS(3)47

SHARON: Finally at the end of the story (1) when it was time
         for the ransom to really be given (2) the men that
         kidnapped this little boy wound up paying the parents
         to take this kid back. And the parents made them
         bring the boy back at night **because they wouldn't**
         be responsible for what the neighbors
         did to these guys if they saw them (.)
         [bringing the boy back.]
MARIAN: **[bringing the boy home.]**

SHARON: The last line in the story was something about one guy
            triple-legging it to Canada. I've thought a lot about
            that story lately. I don't know why (.) it's been on my
            mind, but ...

Again, the Joint Production does not preface an interruption,
but the utterance originator proceeds, without change of topic.

That listeners (or cospeakers) can successfully anticipate what
speakers will say next was shown empirically for words in sequence
by Goldman-Eisler (1958), who found 86% of the next words were
predictable with some probability. Butterworth (1980:16) argues that
although sentence types are potentially infinite, in practice, speakers use only a tiny subset and use them very frequently. As an
example of this projectability, the second female speaker in the
following extract is able to complete the sentence of the first female
speaker in a syntactically and semantically compatible way, supplying a conjoined verb phrase. (They are discussing Sharon's boss
Tom, a man who is sometimes a benefactor, sometimes neglectful.)

MS3(22)

MARIAN: **. . . He seems to like this idea that he takes poor**
            waifs o:n and and and [takes care of them.]
SHARON: **[takes care of them.]**
MARIAN: But you haven't played your role too well there either
            because you haven't created a <u>big</u> enough crisis.

Supporting the projectability of a sentence, a number of
researchers have argued for the clause as a basic planning unit in
real time speech production. They argue that as a given clause is
being uttered, the next one is taking shape and focus.[21] For example, Butterworth (1980:157) cites work by Goldman-Eisler as report-
ing that "listeners can make use of clause boundary pauses to carry
out cognitive work, but not pauses at other locations, probably
because these locations are predictable on the basis of current syntactic and intonational cues, whereas, for the listener, the location
of other pauses is unpredictable." Other empirical evidence suggests
that people plan and execute clauses within sentences basically one
at a time.[22] This research and that of Jaffe and Feldstein (1970),
pioneers of the study of pauses, suggest that discourse is more
complex than the simple concatenation of monologues into conversation and that discourse participants can frequently project what
another will say before it is said. I point out that this ability is less
mysterious than it may seem, because, prosodically, Predictable

Utterance Completions are often preceded by word stretches (elongated syllables), conjunctions, often repeated ("and and and"), brief pauses measuring less than a second, or by laughter.[23] The longest completion recorded in the therapy data is nine words in length, but the average is three to four words. Examination of the utterances just prior to the utterances containing the initiation and completion of a Joint Production shows that the utterance previous to the Joint Production also contains some hesitation phenomena, either pauses, elongated syllables, groping for a word (uh), fillers such as "you know," "I mean," or other fluctuation in tempo. This suggests that listeners can frequently project what speakers will say and indicates the mutual influence of the rhythmic patterns of speakers.[24]

A third type, Helpful Utterance Completion,[25] is a type of lexical help that many people automatically think of when considering the concept of Joint Productions. I see these as minimal additions offered by a listener who detects some difficulty on the part of a speaker in accessing an item in the mental lexicon. These momentary difficulties are typically signaled by "uh," or by a pause or by both in combination. Upon this signal, listeners often supply a missing vocabulary item but make no further addition. Their contributions are typically only one or two words in length and always phrasal rather than clausal, unlike the other types of Joint Productions. Quite often, recipients signal acceptance by repetition of the phrase. Again, there is no asymmetry in which participant contributes. The next two examples from different sessions between the therapist, Marian, and the client, Sharon, illustrate that both client and therapist can provide Joint Productions for one another. Likewise, both males and females can contribute.

MS2(18)

MARIAN: <u>Oh, you're throwing me little (.) [little scraps]</u>
<u>to</u>

SHARON: <u>[tidbits] Yeah</u>

MS5(21)

SHARON: <u>So:: you know, that takes part of the logiti-</u>
<u>legitimacy of my anger away, I think, because it</u>
<u>looks like uh=</u>

MARIAN: <u>=a response</u>

SHARON: <u>a response, uh a childish response, if you will, to</u>
<u>somebody being mad at me.</u>

Much more interesting than the simple contribution of a noun or adjective phrase is the next type of Joint Production. It plays a special role in therapy. I have termed this type Invited Utterance Completion. Unlike the other types, this class of Joint Production is overtly induced by the initial speaker's eliciting the sentence completion from the second speaker by means of a word stretch (syllable elongation) followed by a brief pause. This is a very useful discourse strategy in psychotherapy. These invited utterance completions are actually questions masquerading as statements, with the addressee intended to supply the missing Wh-information, (who, what, when, where, why).

This pattern is illustrated twice in the following extract. Ralph, the therapist, and Lana, the client, are talking about Lana's participation in Alcoholics Anonymous and the female supervision (or "sponsorship") she received. Pertinent here is the fact that the client Lana goes to therapy on a biweekly basis, and her therapist has not seen her since their last session two weeks ago.

RL(2)19

RALPH:	**Your sponsor befo::re =**
LANA:	**=was a woman.**
RALPH:	Yeah.
LANA:	But I only called her every three months.
RALPH:	**And your so your sobriety now, in AA:: [(is)]**
LANA:	**[is] at a**
	year
RALPH:	A year. Well, I'm not perhaps the expert in this case at all. However, I must admit that you're still young in (.) sobriety and I think that maybe still working with a woman for a while might be
LANA:	Yeah
RALPH:	in your best interest.

In both instances the therapist elicits information covertly from the client. Undoubtedly, these Invited Utterance Completions elicit information but have the further advantage interactionally of leaving ambiguous whether the initiator of an invited completion had knowledge of the answer. They are not overt, bald-on-record questions; they bear level rather than rising intonation, and thus can be interpreted by a listener as a mere hesitation. This is a useful ambiguity for the initiator of an invited completion to exploit. Users of the discourse strategy can elicit information without having to reveal whether they remember facts or had previous knowledge of the answer.

In the foregoing instance, for example, it is useful for Ralph, the therapist, in his second meeting with a new client who comes on the less common biweekly schedule, to leave unrevealed whether or not he actually remembers the precise biographical details from the first session two week ago. Therapists do not have encyclopedic minds, although clients often act as though they expect them to remember every detail from their biography. In fact, data from the consecutive sessions between this dyad indicate that Ralph *was* told these biographical facts in the prior session, but over the course of two weeks sees many other clients as well. The discourse strategy is thus a face-saving device. The technique causes the information to be reiterated without the interlocutor's having to ask directly for it. This type of Joint Production masks the fact that information is being requested. Such a gambit can be used to conceal the extent of knowledge or recollection while gathering information. In the psychotherapy setting it is especially appropriate as a tool for getting the client to talk. This in turn shows the importance of context in interpreting the meaning of an utterance.

Another important feature of invited completions is that they also provide support in the case for the sentence as a discourse unit since their force in eliciting a response may derive in part from the fact of their sentential incompleteness. In order to remain cooperative, interlocutors are forced into syntactically completing a sentence. In the following extract, for example, Gerald, the therapist, coaxes Wilma into completing the appositive (that be:ing) he has begun. She goes on to elaborate.

GW(3)8

GERALD: Okay. (1) ((cough)) How do you feel about the direction
            we're taking?
WILMA: I I felt good about it last last week. I really felt like after I
            left here that we hit on a good point.
GERALD: **Th-that be:ing=**
WILMA: **=the strong/weak side of me.**
GERALD: Ah.
WILMA: And feeling like I'm one way or the other, never an in-
            between.

The types of Joint Productions considered here indicate that synchronized sentence constructions arise from several motivations:

the desire to insure veracity, to help in word searches, and to elicit information covertly.

When we examine the wave form display created by the Sound Cap application to the Macintosh it shows the time juncture between utterances with accuracy and precision. The time juncture between Sharon's proposition, "I'm gonna have to find some way" and Marian's contribution, "to tell her," as measured, is a bare 0.2 second (Fig. 4). From an examination of a number of such first speaker–second speaker naturally occurring spliced sequences, it appears that 0.2 second is very close to the minimal margin between utterances, across speakers. In the psychotherapy corpus the shortest gap recorded and measured by Sound Cap is 18 centiseconds pause between speakers. To denote such interlocking, conventional transcription systems employ latching marks (=) or ziz zag lines. I suggest that precise measurements of fractions of seconds may prove valuable for assessing social meaning of this and other discourse phenomena, such as extent of overlap or interruption.

Although Joint Productions in individual therapy sessions between therapist and client are the focus here, it is not surprising to find synchrony of speech in other close or longstanding relationships, such as between couples, siblings, coworkers, prison inmates, or individuals in youth gangs or graduate seminars. If it is the case that Joint Productions appear in other discourse settings, then consideration of Joint Productions is important for analysis of discourse because the closely synchronized sequeling may transcend the topic of conversation and have more to do with the relationship between interactants.

A study of Joint Productions has important ramifications not only for understanding language use in psychotherapy but also for discourse analysis, because it challenges our notion of how discourse is produced and interpreted, how discourse units are constructed, and, indeed, what constitutes an appropriate unit of discourse. Joint Productions also invite methodological consideration of how time parameters of discourse are properly to be described, and contribute to research on the rhythm of talk.

The field of discourse analysis has evolved as a reaction to sentence-level grammar. A central tenet of discourse analysis has been the rejection of the sentence as the *primary* unit of analysis. Discourse analysts of all types insist on examining context, and agree that in order to understand a given string both prior and succeeding utterances must be taken into account. However, it is not necessary to reject the sentence as a valid construct altogether. While it is not a focal unit, and may not have recognized and labeled ("emic") status in any given language, it appears to be recognized and oriented to by speakers of English.

While earlier approaches to discourse examined only the *speaker's* role in the construction of discourse, the focus of this work is on the *interlocutor* as an active participant who can shape the course of a discourse unit. Such shaping of the discourse unit by interlocutors has been shown convincingly for narrative and, I claim, may hold true for smaller units as well. For example, evidence from a study of Joint Productions points to the fact that interlocutors can regard the sentence as *a discourse unit under construction*. Sentences are comprised of clauses (and can be further subdivided into phrases), and some people see the sentence as an opportunity to contribute to discourse and to shape its course semantically and syntactically (one clause at a time). The splicing of clauses by two or more speakers, resulting in a Joint Production, indicates that interlocutors are jointly constructing a unit. This study benefits from work by others who have raised the issue of whether listener and speaker are analytically separable in light of actual speech habits. Often these different participant roles collapse into a single body, and this in turn warrants theoretical consideration. The psychotherapy corpus reflects repeated orientation to and frequent naming of the sentence by the participants. Because Joint Productions are clearly a discourse strategy, recognition needs to be made that the definition of discourse analysis as analysis of units "larger than the sentence" does not exclude a study of the sentence itself, which may be a discourse unit for some speakers of English. Speakers can co-construct a sentence if each contributes a portion of a well-formed sentence by semantically and syntactically splicing together words.

Methodologically, Joint Productions can contribute to further refining the analytical techniques of discourse analysis. Because they involve crucial time junctures, Joint Productions offer the opportunity to refine some transcription techniques currently used in discourse analysis. The denotation of rapid succession of speaker change by latching (i.e., the use of equal signs (=) devised by Jefferson[26] can legitimately be criticized as impressionistic. It affords little differentiation between a pause of 0.2 or 0.8 second, although these differences certainly have social meaning. Discourse analysts can gain greater precision of measurement with the adjunct use of computerized timing devices, such as the Sound Cap application to a Macintosh, which provides an easy-to-use analog to digital measurement of timing and graphic display of the wave form.[27]

In conclusion, Joint Productions appear to be a deviation with social implications, that is, a discourse strategy. They nonetheless differ from interruptions in that they are a cooperative conversational style that involves cospeakers. Joint Productions are characteristic of therapeutic discourse. Joint Productions are not always successful. In the psychotherapy corpus, one out of seven is rejected. Consideration of the possibility of speaker rejection prompts the conclusion that there must be other strong motivations for them. The motivations within the psychotherapy setting range from the desire to insure verity, to offer lexical assistance, and to elicit information covertly. Joint Productions may also serve as an indicator or facilitator of empathy.

Finally, the exploitation of contiguity for discourse purposes suggests that the sentence itself may be regarded by some individuals as *a discourse unit under construction*, and that interlocutors have an opportunity to contribute to discourse, and to shape its course syntactically and semantically, even at the sentence level or below. Such contributions may either reflect empathy or build rapport in a therapeutic setting. Finally, consideration of Joint Productions suggests that the sentence may be a viable discourse unit for cospeakers. In this cooperative conversational style, which involves cospeakers, psychotherapy participants jointly construct discourse.

8

Afterword

In the course of writing this book I have frequently been asked, "Do you believe that discourse can be therapeutic?" "I certainly do," I reply. This book is an attempt to show not only that discourse can be therapeutic but also *how* discourse can be therapeutic. It is undoubtedly beneficial to have an empathic listener, and deep listening is one activity in psychotherapy. It is likewise probable that having the counsel of a therapist, someone experienced in human behavior, whom you can ask for advice is valuable. But this book focuses instead on the far more therapeutic aspect of the talk between client and therapist. An outstanding feature of therapeutic discourse and one from which the greatest benefit is to be derived is that such discourse is jointly constructed. Both client and therapist contribute to the construction of talk in the therapy hour. Each takes up a portion of the other's speech to interweave with his or her own, creating a dynamic and vibrant reality through words. When therapist and client jointly create an extended metaphor, splice together clauses to form a single sentence, or engage in playing out associations in dream tellings, they exhibit a concerted purpose with therapeutic effect.

Colleagues and friends have come forward many times to tell me of their own therapeutic experiences. From their reports, as well as from the data herein, I distilled an abiding belief in the individual's ability to gain insight into self and, above all, to change.

Can talking heal? It is not only therapists who believe so. The many thousands of people in the United States alone who seek out therapeutic discourse and are willing to pay are eloquent testimony to the efficacy of the talking treatment.

I can also report that, several years after allowing transcripts of her psychotherapy sessions to be made, one of the clients in this study, Sharon, has overcome her low self-esteem and destructive life patterns. She is now happily employed in another state as a professor in her field of specialization. Rising from a series of low-level jobs from which she was fired, she went on to achieve her full potential. Although she is no longer in therapy, she stays in touch with her therapist occasionally.

I am gratified to report Sharon's example. But many others who might get help are fearful of the unknown. Despite its familiarity to Western readers and its spread from Austria to Switzerland, Germany, England, the United States, Australia, New Zealand, and Canada, psychotherapy is not yet universally available. Nowhere is this more apparent than in Japan, where, as I write, I am teaching for one year. The eminent Japanese psychiatrist Takeo Doi has pointed out the scarcity of mental health facilities in Japan, where the Western talking cure is not a recognized community resource. It is my wish that this book will shed some light on the actual practices of talking about problems and make the process less opaque. By examining the actual words of experienced therapists and their clients as they mutually create a climate of change, I hope to remove some of the mystique and provide a better understanding. Perhaps more individuals will feel freer to explore the benefits of therapeutic ways with words.

To be fully human is to know the joint construction of reality. Largely, for most people, this is constructed through discourse, because talk is central to everyday life. I have tried to show that interweaving bits and pieces of your own and other's talk is the primary mode of creating a sense of your own place in the world. The basic need of every human being for others with whom to share discourse is seen in the plaint, "I just want someone that I can talk to."

Linguists as early as Sapir (1927) thought that linguistics could contribute to psychiatry. It is certain that words are central to both fields. And yet, what is said in the modern practice of psychotherapy is cloaked in secrecy. The average person is not allowed to glimpse the type of discourse contained in this speech-centered event. Likewise, even specialists and people in therapy have difficulty appreciating the language of psychotherapy because, unless it is tape-recorded, such language fades over time. This evanescent characteristic of language makes full appreciation of the skill and art involved in therapeutic ways with words difficult. It has been my feeling that opening up psychotherapy to the eyes of outsiders through a study of real language in use could not only reveal important discourse practices but enlarge understanding of a complicated social institution as well. I have included samples of situated language use in this book, taking real people's real words as the starting point of analysis. In this way I have hoped to reveal how words can be used therapeutically.

Discourse and the professions is a growing subfield of linguistics that recognizes that much of the work of any society, the very fabric of daily life, is carried on through language, often in skilled and creative ways by ordinary people as well as by medical, legal, and mental health professionals, and many others. Because psychotherapy as a modern institution is a complicated endeavor, no one book could fully explicate its many complexities. Through selected instances of talk in psychotherapy I have sought to show practitioners of psychotherapy and those with acknowledged curiosity about the event, as well as to remind discourse analysts, that discourse and language are really mutually constructed. People create meaning for each other, for example, in dream interpretation, by jointly creating metaphors, and they make their talk out of repeated bits of their own and others' talk. Each of the chapters in this book is related to the central idea that discourse is not a simple concatenation of monologues.

I've also taken the opportunity to comment on issues of interest in discourse analysis and to offer some methodological innovations. Some of the topics I treat are whether you can tell the same story twice, how phrasal and clausal repetition can be discourse strategies with social implications, how the sentence can be constructed interactively, how the narration of dreams is similar to yet different from that for personal experience narratives, and how word associations of one's own and one's interlocutor are mutually played out by partners in the therapy setting.

I locate my work alongside other works that concentrate on situated language use by real people. Most important, I go beneath the surface of what therapists and clients say about therapy to look at what they say *in* therapy.

Appendix A

Background of Clients Who Participated in the Study

The following is a brief orientation to the backgrounds of the clients who participated in this study. In order to protect the clients' anonymity, all names are pseudonyms.

Sharon is a woman in her midthirties who was abandoned by her father. She was raised in her grandparents' home in Arkansas by a mother whom she perceived as aloof and inattentive. As a child she was sexually abused by her twin brother and others. She nonetheless was the first member of her family to attend college and received a doctoral degree in one of the social sciences. She has been underemployed for the past four years in a succession of jobs. She was in therapy with Marian for two years. She has never been married. [Seven sessions collected.]

Kurt, a middle-aged, slightly hearing-impaired man from a rural part of suburban Austin, is employed as a mechanical engineer. He graduated from a school for the deaf but has never felt integrated into the deaf community. He has considerable artistic talent. He is single and has not been able to relate well to women his age. His sexual fantasies are of young girls and he is concerned that he might act on them when he is intoxicated. He is trying to give up addiction to alcohol and smoking. Several years ago he participated in a research program with a psychiatric intern. He has seen Ralph, his therapist, once before, in group therapy, but has just started individual therapy. [Seven sessions collected.]

Wilma is a pleasantly plump woman in her midthirties who has recently moved to Austin from a village in Missouri following the death of her mother and father, to seek wider employment possibilities. She previously owned a beauty shop in her small community of 400 and currently works as a secretary. She was divorced twice and has left her two children, aged 12 and 13, with their grandparents in rural Missouri. She lives with her boyfriend but has had trouble trusting him after finding out he is married. She wants to lose weight and explore ways to increase her self-confidence so she can begin a career. [Six sessions collected.]

Norma is an older returning college student from a large lower-class family in Missouri. She is grieving over the death of her father. She has begun work toward an undergraduate college degree several times and then quit because she doubts whether she is intelligent enough. She frequently becomes angry at her professors for not acting like parents. She admits to feeling strongly attached to her family, especially her older sisters, and is afraid of losing their approval if she stays in school. She is seeing the therapist Charlene. Norma withdrew from the study but gave permission for two of her sessions to be used. [Two sessions collected.]

Lana is a recovering alcoholic in her late thirties who is the mother of two teen-aged children who live with her. She is from Texas. She has been victimized by rapists several times. She is separated from her husband, an alcoholic, but they are on friendly terms. She is active in Alcoholics Anonymous and feels she is making progress toward sobriety. She enjoys her job as an administrative assistant. She has just begun therapy with Ralph. [Six sessions collected.]

Katie is a twice-married woman in her early forties, the mother of four children. She has entered therapy to gain confidence and to learn how to control her impulses. She feels that people frequently take advantage of her and that she is unorganized. She is having marital problems with her husband, a truckdriver. She was born and raised in a small town 20 miles outside Austin. She has just begun therapy with Gerald. [Three sessions collected.]

Shannon is a single woman in her midthirties who has recently experienced the death of her father, her only living relative. The trauma has reactivated the remorse she feels over having an abortion a few years ago and the loneliness she felt as a latchkey child of alcoholic parents. She has seen Marian 37 times. [Two sessions collected.]

Shelly is the 19-year-old daughter of a wealthy Austin family who has recently graduated from college and is experiencing her first long-term relationship with a man, after having been promiscuous for four years. She feels that her sexual curiosity is more intense than that of others and that it has caused her trouble with her parents since she was five. A gifted writer, she feels that the only time she gets positive attention from her parents, both professionals, is when she sells a short story to a magazine. She has been seeing Marian for a year. [Two sessions collected.]

Jake, in his midthirties, is an engineer with a college degree employed by a computer firm in Oklahoma. He grew up on the family farm and still works there on weekends. He has recently separated from his abusive wife. He complains that she is constantly hitting him unexpectedly and frequently beats her daughter, the child of a previous marriage. He has just begun psychotherapy with Bonnie, a clinical psychologist in training in her late twenties. [Six sessions collected.]

Howard is a hospital orderly in his thirties who was recently fired from a hospital in Oklahoma where he worked after some drugs were noticed missing. He later was reinstated with apologies from members of the administration, who acknowledged that he had been falsely accused. He holds a college degree and feels that his drug usage is preventing him from being ambitious. He is in therapy with Judy, a clinical psychologist in training in her late twenties. [Six sessions collected.]

Appendix B

Transcription Conventions Employed

The following is an adaptation of transcription conventions originally developed by Jefferson (Sacks, Schegloff, Jefferson 1974).

Symbol	Example	Explanation
[ ]	C: Well [maybe I need] to T: [you should]	Brackets indicate simultaneous utterances by differing speakers. The left-hand bracket marks the onset of simultaneity; the right-hand bracket marks the end of simultaneous speech.
:	We:ll no::	Colons indicate that the syllable preceding has been elongated. Two colons is twice as long a syllable as one.
___	I hate that woman.	Underlining is used to indicate heavier emphasis (in speaker's pitch or loudness.)
°	T: °Secrets. secrets°	A raised degree sign indicates a soft or low voice.
=	C: I don't like= T: = any hassles.	Equal signs indicate that "no perceptible time" has elapsed between the words "latched" by the marks. They are used when a speaker

Symbol	Example	Explanation
		starts to speak with little or no break between his and the previous speaker's utterance.
(1) or (.5)	C: I uh (1) wish I could. T: Why (.5) can't you?	Numbers in parentheses indicate the seconds and tenths of seconds of pauses between words or speaker turns.
(.)	C: I never (.) hurt so much.	A non-sentence-final period surrounded by parentheses on either side indicates a pause of less than half a second.
( )	C: She was wearing a ( )	Empty single parentheses indicate that something was uttered but that the transcriber was unable to determine the actual words spoken.
(monster)	T: He was a (monster).	Use of parentheses around a phrase or word indicates an estimation of what the actual words were when the transcriber is uncertain.
(( ))	T: ((laugh)) That's more like it.	Double parentheses enclose descriptions of additional relevant sounds that are not words [e.g., ((cough)), ((throat clear))].
↗	T: Do you think it's the tape?	An upward arrow indicates rising intonation.
↘	T: You felt betrayed. C: I felt betrayed	A downward arrow indicates falling intonation.
-	C: I tho-	A hyphen on an incomplete word indicates speaker break off, with glottal stop.

Notes

Chapter 3. Facets: Retellings in Therapeutic Discourse

1. I adopt the conventions for analysis of the internal structure proposed by Labov and associates. See Labov and Waletsky (1967); Labov (1972a,b,c, 1982); Labov and Fanshel (1977).

2. See Bauman (1986); Hymes (1985); Chafe (1977); Romaine (1984); and others.

3. Romaine's (1984) examination of three children's accounts of a fight involves a separate category, multiple versions of an event, not, as here, retellings by a single narrator. Likewise excluded are reciprocal narratives in which two or more people contribute stories in turn. [See Ryave (1978) and Kalčic (1975) for interesting treatments of reciprocal storytelling.]

4. Rickford (1988) observes that sociolinguistic studies usually draw single samples from large numbers of informants and seldom resample the same individuals. For this reason, retellings may not have appeared salient before. But compare the work of Hymes (1985) and Bauman (1986), who resampled the same person.

5. Polanyi (1981) poses this intriguing question for conversation.

6. Labov (1972a:371) notes that a story must be "reportable," "worth repeating . . . not ordinary, plain, humdrum, everyday or run of the mill." Labov and Fanshel (1977:105) argue that a narrative that is judged to be ordinary may be rejected after it is told by a withering "So what?" Elaborations on this view of reportability are to be found in Labov (1972a:370–371); Labov and Fanshel (1977:105), and Labov (1982:227). Compare also Chafe's (1977:44) concept of "event salience."

7. Hymes (1981) regards the notion of "reportability" as a reflection of sociocultural assumptions. He observes that after a walk, native American Indians report what they did *not* see, while he reports what he *did* see.

8. See Wodak (1981a) for other differences between interviews and therapy.

9. Hymes (1981) further observes that twice-told tales to Jacobs by Mrs. Howard are more fully realized in the second telling, containing onomatopoeia, inner speech, and formal close.

10. The evolution of a narrative over time is implicitly the focus of Hymes (1985) and Bauman (1986), who offer sensitive explanations for the mutations they observe.

11. A term used by Prince (1982).

12. For definitions of narrative functional elements see Labov and Waletsky (1967); Labov (1972a, 1982); Labov and Fanshel (1977).

13. Ryave (1978) has studied reciprocal narration where two narratives sharing a similar point are told by two different interlocutors to each other. Such reciprocal narration is common in conversation. Kalčik's (1975) study of sequenced narratives in women's consciousness-raising sessions also involves second and even third or fourth parties supporting the point of a prior narrative with an additional narrative of personal experience. I find that therapists only rarely tell stories. In the original 36 hours I recorded, for example, only three instances of therapists narrating occurred.

14. Schiffrin (1982b; 1987a) has indicated, in work on English discourse markers, that *like* has both a comparative and a restrictive role. While the comparative (*just*) *like* signals an analogy between two things, *like* in the restrictive sense indicates membership in a set.

Chapter 4.   Visions Through a Prism: Dream Telling and Interpretation

1. E.g., B. Tedlock (1981) on Quiché Mayan; Eggan (1949) on Hopi; Herr (1981) on Fiji; Kilborne (1981b) on Moroccan; Hallowell (1966) on Ojibwa; Bourgignon (1954) on Haiti; Wallace (1958) on Iroquois.

2. E.g., Kilborne (1981a); Bourgignon (1972); Eggan (1949); D'Andrade (1961); and Lincoln (1935).

3. Bourgignon (1972).

4. Bastide (1968:423).

5. Herr (1981).

6. Tedlock (1981).

7. Bernstein and Katz (1987:261); Grinstein (1968).

8. Kilborne (1981b).

9. Kuper (1979: 646).

10. See Jung (1974); Cahen (1966).

11. See Sloane (1979); Fleiss (1973).

12. Labov (1972b, 1982); Labov and Waletsky (1967).

13. E.g., Polanyi (1979, 1981, 1982, 1985); Schiffrin (1981, 1982a, 1984); Tannen (1982, 1983, 1989); Johnstone (1987a,b, 1990); Prince (1982); and others.

14. Compare *le/la plus* + adj; *une fois, un/une* in French narratives.

15. See Schiffrin (1982a) for commentary on the role of paraphrase as a bracketing device for narrative.

16. See Clark and Gerrig (1990) for discussion of the origins of quoted speech and Tannen (1989).

17. See Grinstein (1968:194).

Chapter 5. *Reflections: The Role of Repetition*

1. For example, Schiffrin (1982a:107) looks at the use of adjacent self-repetition as having an intensifying effect, Polanyi (1981) describes self-repetition in narrative as an evaluative device giving emphasis, and Johnstone (1987b) describes single speaker repetition in lexical coupling and in persuasion techniques in Arabic.

2. See Johnstone (to appear) for an overview and analysis of repetition in a variety of contexts.

3. Frédéric (1985) provides an overview of differing levels of repetition in French, and Norrick (1987) provides some crucial distinctions in an investigation of the plurifunctionality of repetition in English.

4. My use of "rejoinder" corresponds to Goffman's (1976) "reply."

5. For example, Cherry (1974) discloses one function of repetition in teacher-student discourse. Her example that follows illustrates a (1) query, (2) response, (3) rejoinder format:

TEACHER: What did you notice about the shape of the buildings, most
                    of them?
STUDENT: They were perfect.
TEACHER: Okay. They were perfect. (haha). I'm thinking more in
                    terms of geometry now . . .

In such Socratic style of questioning [see Labov and Fanshel (1977) and Walters (1984)], the teacher already knows the answer to the question, and repetition serves to confirm the correctness of the response and possibly, Cherry (1974) claims, to "rebroadcast" the answer so a wider audience can hear.

6. Discounted here are the type of one-word or formulaic echoes characteristic of greetings (e.g., A: Hi. B: Hi) or leave-takings (e.g., A: Bye. B: Bye). Instead, the focus is on novel, content-full utterances of three or more words.

7. *Echolalia* is the (usually) uncontrollable or senseless repetition of the words of another. It occurs when a patient repeats a question posed to him instead of providing an answer, as when an examiner says to a patient, "What is the capital of Texas?" and the patient says, "What is the capital of Texas?" See Chritchley (1970:11); Eisenson (1984:18).

8. *Palilalia* is a sort of "auto-echolalia," whereby an affected person frequently "repeats the last word or two of a verbal statement, the words trailing off in a diminuendo fashion, and with increasing rapidity," according to Chritchley (1970:11). Alajouanine (1972:28) describes the condition of palilalia as stemming from Parkinson's disease or other motor disorder or palsy. Citing Lebrun (n.d.), Frédéric (1985:105) gives the example:

EXAMINER: «*Etes-vous depuis longtemps malade?*»
              ("Have you been sick for a long time?")
PATIENT: «*Depuis longtemps, depuis longtemps, depuis longtemps,*
              depuis longtemps, depuis longtemps.»
              ("For a long time, for a long time, for a long time, for a
              long time, for a long time")

Chapter 6.   Glimmers: Therapeutic Uses of Metaphor

1. Psycholinguists (e.g., Ortony 1978, 1979, 1980), anthropologists (e.g., Basso (1979); Fernandez (1972, 1974, 1977); Howe (1977); Leach (1964), and Sherzer (1982b,1983), philosophers and linguists (e.g. Lakoff and Johnson 1980), and communication specialists (e.g., Martinich 1984) have provided valuable insights on the nature of metaphor. Crocker (1977) is a valuable starting point for the present focus.

2. Halliday and Hasan (1976).

3. See Chafe (1977, 1980); Tannen (1982, 1987a); Jakobson (1960).

4. See Lenrow (1966); Pollio and Barlow (1975); Pollio, Barlow, Fine, and Pollio (1977); Aftell and Lakoff (1985); Amira (1982) for work on the therapeutic nature of metaphor. Studies by psychologists on metaphor are usually in two different veins. The first is aimed at providing instruction for therapists in the practical aspects of utilizing metaphor, and the second involves quantitative measurement of type and extent of metaphorical language in actual case studies. Gordon's (1978) *Therapeutic Metaphors*, written for therapists, specifies how to create and deliver long, tailor-made stories with metaphorical content, which are pertinent for individual clients. Erickson's students, Lankton and Lankton (1983), explain the technique of using Ericksonian multiple embedded metaphors, a type of fabricated story that has metaphorical elements derived from a client's problem. The work of Barker (1985) is also a programmatic approach to constructing nonliteral anecdotes to fit an occasion. These three books instruct therapists how to construct allegories for clients and thus do not deal with metaphors of the type investigated here.

5. For example, *Language in Psychotherapy* (Russell 1987) devotes only one paragraph to metaphor.

6. Pollio and Barlow (1975).

7. Lenrow (1966:147).

8. Pollio, Barlow, Fine, and Pollio (1977).

9. This tripartite formulation is indicative of what Lakoff and Johnson (1980) see as structural metaphors.

10. As Lentine (1988) shows, attempts at clarification can take over the interaction and consume otherwise valuable time. Grinshaw (1980) shows how prevalent non-successes in talk can be.

11. E.g., Ortony (1980).

12. See Burbules, Schraw, and Trathen (1989) for one exposition of their differences.

13. Sherzer (1982b:175). See also Shevzer (1993).

Chapter 7. *Double Vision: Aligned Speech in Joint Productions*

1. *Attuned talk* is a term suggested by Nikolas Coupland. It encompasses any type of approximative language behavior. See Giles, Coupland, and Coupland (1991) and Ferrara (1991) for discussion of other types of attuned talk within the framework of accommodation theory.

2. See Kuno and Kaburaki (1977) for claims about other linguistic constructions that express empathy, also Havens (1979).

3. Joint Productions occur between couples, spouses, coworkers, in teacher-student dyads, and between others in frequent proximity on a regular basis. I have also observed them between interviewer and interviewee in telephone opinion poll surveys where a type of instant rapport was noticeable to independent coders. The latter cases, called to my attention by Judith Bean, are notable in that they show Joint Productions are not confined to face-to-face interaction. Falk (1980) sees camaraderie as a triggering device for a related phenomenon she describes as "conversational duet." For further discussion see Ferrara (1992).

4. Ochs, Schiefflin, and Platt (1979:251–252).

5. E.g., Falk (1980); Erickson (1982, 1986); Haviland (1986); Tannen (1987a,b, 1989).

6. See Schiffrin (1984) on Jewish argument as sociability; Tannen (1984) on conversational style; and Johnstone (1991), on individual variation.

7. Falk (1980).

8. See Haviland's (1986:259) observations on cospeakers in Tzotzil conversation.

9. See Erickson's (1982:51) work on Italian-American interpenetration of one another's sentences and clause units.

10. E.g., Holmes (1988); Butterworth (1980); Ford (1982); Garrett (1988).

11. See van Riemsdijk and Williams (1986); Morgan (1982) for discussions of sententiality.

12. As shown by Tannen (1984); Schiffrin (1987a); Polanyi (1989) for narrative.

13. See Sacks, Lecture 1, Fall 1965, pp. 2–7; Lecture 4, Fall 1967, pp. 9–15; Lecture 5, Fall 1968, pp. 1–9 for discussion of collaboratives and Sacks, Ms, ch. 3, p. 3 for discussion of Joint Productions. I prefer to use the neutral term, *Joint Production*, to the term *collaborative* originally applied by Sacks, because the term *collaborative* implies that the prior speaker willingly and knowingly participates in the joint construction, as in true collaboration, and this is misleading. Such is not always the case. The data show that speakers sometimes reject the proffered completions and occasionally indicate annoyance. In a similar way, the term *sentence completion* applied by Duncan (1974) does not allow for the possibility that a syntactically complete sentence can be extended by successive continuations from second or third parties or even the original speaker.

14. Duncan (1974), who called them *sentence completions;* Yngve (1970); Schegloff (1984:42); Wardhaugh (1985), and Lerner (1987, 1991). While Sacks (Ms, ch. 3) suggests that there is a typology of Joint Productions, he defines only two distinct types: sentence extensions and "helpful completions." Advantages of the current study are that it extends Sacks's notion that there are varying kinds of Joint Productions by examining three other types that have not previously been defined, as well as clarifying the two major types identified by Sacks (Ms, ch. 3). This chapter further elaborates on the syntactic junctures and interactional motivations for Joint Productions, neither of which has received extensive attention.

15. Sacks (Ms); Duncan (1974); Lerner (1987, 1991).

16. The selected portions were digitized by a computer system (the Sound Cap application to the Macintosh), and the speech wave was then represented on the microcomputer terminal. Using an editing function, designated portions of the speech were played back to establish the exact location of the juncture comprising the Joint Production. This permitted the length of each pause to be determined, measured to the nearest hundredth of a second. Permanent computer "snapshots" of each speech section were then made. An example is shown in Figure 4. The discourse extract in which the Joint Production occurs is given in footnote 18.

17. As Wardhaugh (1985:154) presumes.

18. A comparison of Joint Productions with interruptions is available in the following segment, as it contains instances of both. Note that Sharon breaks off speech, "Shes-" when Marian interrupts with "You like her?" The result of this interruption is one complete sentence and one broken sentence, whereas with the Joint Production shown in boldface the result is one sentence jointly constructed.

MS5(12)

SHARON: . . . but I think it's gonna be okay when I get back
             to Bellemeade and I'm working with new people.
             The woman I worked with this afternoon will be my
             boss there. She's-

MARIAN: You like her?
SHARON: Yeah. I think we'll do okay. I don't like her calling
            me honey, though and **I'm gonna have to find
            some way=**
MARIAN: **=to tell her.**
SHARON: to tell her. And this is not a person that (2)
            Somebody that's (.) 40 years older than me maybe can call
            me honey, but this is a woman that's not even my age.
            She's mid twenties and she's calling me honey.

19. Sacks initiated discussion of this type.

20. See Levinson (1983:18) for definitions.

21. See Garrett (1988); Boomer (1965:157).

22. Holmes (1988); Ford (1982).

23. Lerner (1987) also finds this to be true.

24. E.g., Erickson (1986); Haviland (1986); Jaffee and Feldstein (1970), Scollon (1981).

25. Discussed by Sacks (Ms, ch. 3).

26. Sacks, Schegloff, and Jefferson (1974).

27. For example, the minimal pause between the segments of a Joint Production that was recorded in the present sample was 0.18 (or about 0.2) second between speakers. A useful avenue of research would be to use empirical measurements of timed junctures as a basis for cross-cultural comparison of other instances of juxtaposed speakers. In this way we might determine how the interpretation of talk by cospeakers differs from culture to culture as well as from setting to setting. Work using computerized measurement of time is only beginning to appear, but may prove fruitful in comparing proposed conventions of Western conversational practices with a broader base. [Feld (1987) on "lift-up-over-speaking" and the strategic contrapuntal juxtaposition in Shokleng (Urban 1990) are two such examples.] Future work might probe what is or is not unique about the practice whereby speakers talk as if they "know what an interlocutor has in mind."

References

Aftell, Mandy, and Lakoff, Robin Tolmach. (1985). *When talk is not cheap or how to find the right therapist when you don't know where to begin.* NY: Warner Books.

Alajouanine, Theophile. (1972). Verbal realization in aphasia. In Martha Taylor Sarno (Ed.) *Aphasia: Selected readings* (pp. 19–36). NY: Appleton-Century-Crofts.

Amira, Stephen Alan. (1982). *Figurative language and metaphor in successful and unsuccessful psychotherapy.* Ph.D. dissertation, Vanderbilt University, Memphis.

Austin, J. L. (1962). *How to do things with words.* Oxford: Clarendon.

Bales, Robert F. (1950). A set of categories for the analysis of small group interaction. *American Sociological Review, 15,* 257–263.

Barker, Philip. (1985). *Using metaphor in psychotherapy.* NY: Brunner/Mazel.

Basso, Keith H. (1979). Portraits of the "Whiteman": Linguistic play and cultural symbols among the Western Apache. Cambridge: Cambridge University Press.

Basso, K., and Selby, H. (1976). *"Wise words" of the Western Apache.* Albuquerque, New Mexico: University of New Mexico Press.

Bastide, Roger. (1968). La divination chez les afro-américains. In A. Caquot and M. Leibovici (Eds.) *La divination,* Vol. 2. (pp. 393–427). Paris: Presses Universitaires de France.

Bateson, Gregory. (1958). Language and psychotherapy—Frieda Fromm-Reichmann's last project. *Psychiatry, 21* (1), 96–100.

185

Bateson, Gregory. (1972). *Steps to an ecology of mind.* NY: Ballantine Books.

Baugh, John. (1983). *Black street speech.* Austin: University of Texas Press.

Bauman, Richard. (1986). *Story, performance and event.* Cambridge: Cambridge University Press.

Bauman, Richard, and Sherzer, Joel. (1974/1990). *Explorations in the ethnography of speaking.* London: Cambridge University Press.

Bauman, Richard, and Sherzer, Joel. (1975). The ethnography of speaking. *Annual Review of Anthropology, 4,* 95–119.

Bernstein, Anne E., M.D., and Katz, Susan C., M.D. (1987). When supervisor and therapist dream: The use of an unusual countertransference phenomenon. *Journal of the American Academy of Psychoanalysis, 15* (2), 261–271.

Beutler, L. E. , Crago, M., and Arizmendi, E. G. (1986). Therapist variables in psychotherapeutic process and outcome. In S. L. Garfield, and A. E. Bergin (Eds.) *Handbook of psychotherapy and behavior change,* 3rd ed. (pp. 257–310) NY: John Wiley & Sons.

Bieber, Michael, Patton, Michael J., and Fuhriman, Addie J. (1977). A metalanguage analysis of counselor and client verb usage in counseling. *Journal of Counseling Psychology, 24* (4), 264–277.

Boomer, D. (1965). Hesitation and grammatical encoding. *Language and Speech 8,* 215–220.

Bourgignon, Erika. (1954). Dreams and dream interpretation in Haiti. *American Anthropologist, 56,* 262–268.

Bourgignon, Erika. (1972). Dreams and altered states of consciousness in anthropological research. In F. Hsu (Ed.) *Psychological anthropology,* 2nd ed. (pp. 403–434). Cambridge, MA: Schenkman.

Burbules, Nicolas, Schraw, Gregory, and Trathen, Woodrow. (1989). Metaphor, idiom, and configuration. *Metaphor and Symbolic Activity 4,* 93–110.

Butterworth, Brian. (1980). Evidence from pauses in speech. In B. Butterworth (Ed.) *Language production. Vol. 1: Speech and talk* (pp. 155–176). London: Academic Press.

Brenneis, Donald. (1986). Shared territory: Audience, indirection and meaning. *Text, 6,* 339–347.

Cahen, Roland. (1966). The psychology of the dream: Its instructive and therapeutic uses. In G. E. von Grunebaum, and R. Caillois (Eds.) *The dream and human societies* (pp. 119–144). Berkeley: University of California Press.

Chafe, Wallace L. (1977). Creativity in verbalization and its implications for the nature of stored knowledge. In Roy O. Freedle (Ed.) *Discourse production and comprehension* (pp. 41–55). [Vol. 1 in the series *Advances in discourse processes,* Edited by Roy O. Freedle.] Norwood, NJ: Ablex.

Chafe, Wallace L. (Ed.) (1980). *The pear stories: Cognitive, cultural and linguistic aspects of narrative production.* [Vol. 3 in the series *Advances in discourse processes,* Edited by Roy O. Freedle.] Norwood, NJ: Ablex.

Cherry, Louise. (1974). Sex differences in pre-school teacher-child interaction. Ph.D. dissertation, Harvard University.

Chritchley, MacDonald. (1970). *Aphasiology and other aspects of language.* London: Edward Arnold.

Clark, Herbert H., and Gerrig, Richard J. (1990). Quotations as demonstrations. *Language 66,* 764–805.

Crocker, J. Christopher. (1977). The social functions of rhetorical forms. In J. D. Sapir, and J. C. Crocker (Eds.) *The social uses of metaphor* (pp. 33–66) Philadelphia: University of Pennsylvania Press.

D'Andrade, R. G. (1961). Anthropological studies of dreams. In F. Hsu (Ed.) *Psychological anthropology* (pp. 296–337). Homewood, IL: Dorsey.

Duncan, Starkey. (1974). On the structure of speaker-auditor interaction during speaking turns. *Language in Society 2,* 161–180.

Duranti, Alessandro. (1986). The audience as co-author: An introduction. *Text 6* (3), 239–247.

Duranti, A., and Brenneis, D. (Eds.) (1986). The audience as co-author, special issue of *Text 6* (3). New York: Mouton de Gruyter.

Eggan, Dorothy. (1949). The significance of dreams for anthropological research. *American Anthropologist, 51,* 177–198.

Eisenson, Jon. (1984). *Adult aphasia,* 2nd ed. Englewood Cliffs, NJ: Prentice-Hall.

Elliott, Robert, Stiles, William B., Mahrer, Alvin R., Hill, Clara E., Friedlander, Myrna L., Margison, Frank R. (1987). Primary therapist response modes: Comparison of six rating systems. *Journal of Consulting and Clinical Psychology, 55,* 218–223.

Erickson, Frederick. (1982). Money tree, lasagna bush, salt and pepper: Social construction of topical cohesion in a conversation among Italian-Americans. In Deborah Tannen (Ed.) *Analyzing discourse: Text and talk.* Georgetown University Round Table on Languages and Linguistics 1981. (pp. 43–70). Washington, DC: Georgetown University Press.

Erickson, Frederick. (1986). Listening and speaking. In D. Tannen, and J. E. Alatis (Eds.) *Languages and linguistics: The interdependence of theory, data, and application.* Georgetown University Round Table on Languages and Linguistics 1985. Washington, DC: Georgetown University Press.

Ervin-Tripp, Susan. (1976). "Is Sybil there?" The structure of some American English directives. *Language in Society 5,* 25–66.

Ervin-Tripp, Susan. (1984). Expanding the notion of indirect requests. Paper presented at the 9th Annual Boston University Conference on the Study of Child Language, Boston, October 14, 1984.

Eysenck, H. J. (1952). The effects of psychotherapy: An evaluation. *Journal of Consulting Psychology, 16,* 319–324.

Falk, Jane. (1980). The conversational duet. *Berkeley Linguistics Society 1980.* (pp. 507–514). Berkeley: University of California Press.

Feld, Steven. (1987). Lift-up-over-sounding in Kahluli discourse. Paper given at Sociolinguistic Approaches to Discourse Conference, University of Texas at Austin, March 1987.

Fernandez, James. (1972). Persuasions and performances: Of the beast in every body . . . and the metaphors of everyman. *Daedalus, 101,* 39–60.

Fernandez, James. (1974). The mission of metaphor in expressive culture. *Current Anthropology, 15,* 119–145.

Fernandez, James. (1977). The performance of ritual metaphor. In J. D. Sapir, and J. C. Crocker (Eds.) *The social uses of metaphor.* Philadelphia: University of Pennsylvania Press.

Ferrara, Kathleen. (1991). Accommodation in therapy. In Howard Giles, Nicholas Coupland, and Justine Coupland (Eds.) *Contexts of accommodation: Directions in applied sociolinguistics.* Cambridge: Cambridge University Press.

Ferrara, Kathleen. (1992). The interactive achievement of a sentence: Joint productions in therapeutic discourse. *Discourse Processes, 15,* 207–228.

Fiedler, Fred E. (1950). A comparison of therapeutic relationships in psychoanalytic, nondirective and Adlerian therapy. *Journal of Consulting Psychology, 14,* 436–445.

Fleiss, Robert. (1973). Symbol, dream, and psychosis [Vol. III, Psychoanalytic series]. NY: International Universities Press.

Ford, M. (1982). Sentence planning units: Implications for the speaker's representation of meaningful relations underlying sentences. In J. Bresnan (Ed.) *The mental representation of grammatical relations* (pp. 797–827). Cambridge, MA: MIT Press.

Frédéric, Madeleine. (1985). *La répétition: Étude linguistique et rhétorique.* Tübingen: Max Neimeyer Verlag.

Freud, Sigmund. (1900). *The interpretation of dreams* (pp. 106–121). Standard edition, Vol. 4. London: Hogarth Condon, 1953.

Freud, Sigmund. (1917). *A metaphysical supplement to the theory of dreams* (pp. 219–235). Standard Edition 14. London: Hogarth Press, 1957.

Gaik, Frank. (1992). Radio talk-show therapy and the pragmatics of possible worlds. In Alessandro Duranti and Charles Goodwin (Eds.) *Rethinking context* (pp. 271–290). Cambridge: Cambridge University Press.

Garfield, Sol. (1986). Research on client variables in psychotherapy. In Sol L. Garfield, and Allen E. Bergin (Eds.) *Handbook of psychotherapy and behavior change,* 3rd ed. (pp. 213–256). NY: John Wiley & Sons.

Garfield, Sol, and Bergin, Allen E. (Eds.) (1986). *Handbook of psychotherapy and behavior change,* 3rd ed. NY: John Wiley & Sons.

Garrett, M. F. (1988). Processes in language production. In F. J. Newmeyer (Ed.) *Language: Psychological and biological aspects* (pp. 69–96). Vol. III in the series *Linguistics: The Cambridge survey.* Cambridge: Cambridge University Press.

Giles, Howard, Coupland, Justine, and Coupland, Nikolas. (Eds.). (1991). *Contexts of accommodation: Directions in applied sociolinguistics.* Cambridge: Cambridge University Press.

Goffman, Erving. (1974). *Frame analysis.* NY: Harper & Row.

Goffman, Erving. (1976) Replies and responses. *Language in Society, 5,* 257–313 [Reprinted in Baugh and Sherzer (1984)].

Goldman-Eisler, F. (1958). Speech production and the predictability of words in context. *Quarterly Journal of Experimental Psychology, 10,* 96–106.

Good, Colin. (1979). Language as social activity: Negotiating conversation. *Journal of Pragmatics, 3,* 151–167.

Gordon, David. (1978). *Therapeutic metaphors.* Cupertino, CA: Meta Publications.

Gottschalk, L. A., and Gleser, G. C. (1969). *The measurement of psychological states through the content analysis of verbal behavior.* Berkeley: University of California Press.

Gottschalk, L. A., Lola, F., and Viney, L. L.. (1986). *Content analysis of verbal behavior: Significance in clinical medicine and psychiatry.* Berlin: Springer-Verlag.

Grice, H. P. (1967/1975). Logic and conversation. In P. Cole, and J. L. Morgan (Eds.) *Syntax and semantics, 3: Speech acts* (pp. 41–58). NY: Academic Press.

Grimshaw, Alan. (1980). Mishearings, misunderstandings and other non-successes in talk: A plea for redress of speaker-oriented bias. *Sociological Inquiry, 50,* 31–74.

Grinstein, Alexander, M.D. (1968). *On Sigmund Freud's dreams.* Detroit: Wayne State University Press.

Gumperz, John J. (1982a). Fact and inference in courtroom testimony. In J. J. Gumperz (Ed.) *Language and social identity* (pp. 430–445). Cambridge: Cambridge University Press.

Gumperz, John J. (1982b). *Discourse strategies.* Cambridge: Cambridge University Press.

Halliday, Michael A. K., and Hasan, Ruqaiya. (1976). *Cohesion in English.* NY: Longmans.

Hallowell, A. I. (1966). The role of dreams in Ojibwa culture. In G. E. von Grunebaum, and R. Caillois (Eds.) *The dream and human societies.* Berkeley: University of California Press.

Havens, Leston. (1978). Explorations in the uses of language in psychotherapy: Simple empathic statements. *Psychiatry, 41,* 336–345.

Havens, Leston. (1979). Explorations in the uses of language in psychotherapy: Complex empathic statements. *Psychiatry, 42,* 40–48.

Havens, Leston. (1980). Explorations in the uses of language in psychotherapy: Counterprojective statements. *Contemporary Psychoanalysis, 16,* 53–67.

Haviland, John B. (1986). "Con buenos chiles": Talk, targets and teasing in Zinacantán. *Text, 6* (3), 249–282.

Herr, Barbara. (1981). The expressive character of Fijian dream and nightmare experience. *Ethos, 9* (4), 332–352.

Holmes, Janet. (1988). Paying compliments: A sex-preferential politeness strategy. *Journal of Pragmatics, 12,* 445–465.

Howe, James. (1977). Carrying the village: Cuna political metaphors. In J. D. Sapir, and J. C. Crocker (Eds.) *The social uses of metaphor* (pp. 132–163). Philadelphia: University of Pennsylvania Press.

Hymes, Dell. (1962). The ethnography of speaking. In Thomas Gladwin and William C. Sturtevant (Eds.) *Anthropology in human behavior* (pp. 15–53). Washington, D.C. Anthropological Society of Washington.

Hymes, Dell. (1964). Introduction: Towards ethnographies of communication. In J. Gumperz, and D. Hymes (Eds.) The ethnography of communication. *American Anthropologist, 66* (6), 1–34.

Hymes, Dell. (1967). Models of the interaction of language and social setting. *Journal of Social Issues, 23,* 8–28.

Hymes, Dell. (1972). Models of the interaction of language and social life. In John Gumperz, and Dell Hymes (Eds.) *Directions in sociolinguistics: The ethnography of communication* (pp. 35–71). NY: Holt, Rinehart & Winston. [Reprinted from Models of the interaction of language and social setting. *Journal of Social Issues, 23* (2), 8–28, (1967).]

Hymes, Dell. (1981). *"In vain I tried to tell you": Essays in native American ethnopoetics.* Philadelphia: University of Pennsylvania Press.

Hymes, Dell. (1985). Language, memory and selective performance: Cultee's "Salmon Myth" as twice told to Boas. *Journal of American Folklore, 98,* 391–434.

Irvine, Judith T. (1987). Domains of description in the ethnography of speaking: A retrospective on the "speech community." In Richard Parmenter, and Greg Urban (Eds.) *Performance, speech community and genre* (pp. 13–24). Working papers and proceedings of the Center for Psychosocial Studies, 11.

Jaffe, J., and Feldstein, S. (1970). *Rhythms of dialogue.* NY: Academic Press.

Jakobson, Roman. (1960). Closing statements: Linguistics and poetics. In T. Sebeok (Ed.) *Style in language* (pp. 350–377). Cambridge, MA: MIT Press.

Johnstone, Barbara. (1987a). "He says . . . so I said": Verb tense alternation and narrative depictions of authority in American English. *Linguistics, 25,* 33–52.

Johnstone, Barbara. (1987b). An introduction to perspectives on repetition. In Barbara Johnstone (Ed.) [Special Issue] *Text, 7* (3), 205–213.

Johnston, Barbara. (1990). *Stories, community, and place: Narratives from middle America.* Bloomington: Indiana University Press.

Johnstone, Barbara. (1991). Individual style in an American public opinion survey: Personal performance and the ideology of referentiality. *Language in Society, 20,* 557–576.

Johnstone, Barbara. (forthcoming). *Repetition in discourse: Interdisciplinary perspectives.* Norwood, NJ: Ablex.

Jung, Carl G. (1974). *Dreams.* Translated by R. F. C. Hull. Bolingen Series. Princeton: Princeton University Press.

Kalčik, Susan. (1975). ". . . like Ann's gynecologist or the time I was almost raped?": Personal narrative in women's rap groups. [Special Issue] *Journal of American Folklore, 88,* 3–11.

Kilborne, Benjamin. (1981a). Pattern, structure and style in anthropological studies of dreams. *Ethos, 9,* 165–185.

Kilborne, Benjamin (1981b). Moroccan dream interpretation and culturally constituted defense mechanism. *Ethos, 9,* 294–312.

Kuno, Susumu, and Kaburaki, Etsuko. (1977). Empathy and syntax. *Linguistic Inquiry, 8* (4), 627–672.

Kuper, Adam. (1979). A structural approach to dreams. *Man, 14,* (4) 645–662.

Labov, William. (1972a). The transformation of experience in narrative syntax. In William Labov (Ed.) *Language in the inner city* (pp. 354–396). Philadelphia: University of Pennsylvania Press.

Labov, William. (1972b). *Sociolinguistic patterns.* Philadelphia: University of Pennsylvania Press.

Labov, William. (1972c). *The social stratification of English in New York City.* Washington, DC: Center for Applied Linguistics.

Labov, William. (1982). Speech actions and reactions in personal narrative. In Deborah Tannen (Ed.) *Analyzing discourse: Text and talk.* Georgetown University Round Table on Languages and Linguistics 1981. (pp. 219–247). Washington, DC: Georgetown University Press.

Labov, William, and Waletsky, Joshua. (1967). Narrative analysis: Oral versions of personal experience. In June Helm (Ed.) *Essays on the verbal and visual arts: Proceedings of the 1966 annual spring meeting of the American Ethnological Society)* (pp. 12–44). Seattle: University of Washington Press.

Labov, William, and Fanshel, David. (1977). *Therapeutic discourse: Psychotherapy as conversation.* NY: Academic Press.

Lakoff, George, and Johnson, Mark. (1980). *Metaphors we live by.* Chicago: University of Chicago Press.

Lankton, S., and Lankton, C. (1983). *The answer within.* NY: Brunner/ Mazel.

Leach, Edmund R. (1964). Anthropological aspects of language: Animal categories and verbal abuse. In E. Lenneberg (Ed.) *New directions in the study of language* (pp. 23–63). Cambridge, MA: MIT Press.

Lenrow, Peter B. (1966). The uses of metaphor in facilitating constructive behavior change. *Psychotherapy, 3* (4), 145–148.

Lentine, Gentine. (1988). Metaphor as cooperation in therapeutic discourse. In *Linguistic change and contact: Proceedings of 16th annual NWAV conference.* Edited by K. Ferrara, B. Brown, K. Walters, J. Baugh. Austin: University of Texas, Department of Linguistics.

Lerner, G. H. (1987). Collaborative turn sequences: Sentence construction and social action. Ph.D. dissertation, University of California, Irvine.

Lerner, G. H. (1991). On the syntax of sentences in progress. *Language in Society*, 20, 441–458.

Levinson, Stephen C. (1983). *Pragmatics.* Cambridge: Cambridge University Press.

Lewis, Jerry M., M.D. (1978). *To be a therapist: The teaching and learning.* NY: Brunner/Mazel.

Lincoln, J. S. (1935). *The dream in primitive cultures.* Baltimore: Williams & Wilkins.

Martinich, A. P. (1984). *Communication and reference.* NY: Walter de Gruyter.

McQuown, Norman A. (1957). Linguistic transcription and specification of psychiatric interview materials. *Psychiatry*, 20, 79–86.

Mishler, Elliot G. (1986). The analysis of interview-narratives. In Theodore R. Sarbin (Ed.) *Narrative psychology: The storied nature of human conduct* (pp. 233–255). NY: Praeger Publishers.

Morgan, J. L. (1982). Discourse theory and the independence of sentence grammar. In Deborah Tannen (Ed.) *Analyzing discourse: Text and talk.* Georgetown University Round Table on Languages and Linguistics 1981. (pp. 196–204). Washington, DC: Georgetown University Press.

Norrick, Neal. (1987). Functions of repetition in conversation. In Barbara Johnstone (Ed.) [Special Issue] *Text*, 7 (3), 215–244.

Ochs, E., Schieffelin, B., and Platt, M. (1979). Propositions across utterances and speakers. In E. Ochs and B. Schieffelin (Eds.) *Developmental pragmatics.* NY: Academic Press.

Ortony, Andrew et al. (1978). Interpreting metaphors and idioms: Some effects of context on comprehension. *Journal of Verbal Learning and Verbal Behavior*, 17, 465–477.

Ortony, Andrew. (1979). Beyond literal similarity. *Psychological Review*, 86 (3), 161–180.

Ortony, Andrew. (1980). Some psycholinguistic aspects of metaphor. In R. P. Honeck, and R. R. Hoffman (Eds.) *Cognition and figurative language* (pp. 69–86). Hillsdale, NJ: Lawrence Erlbaum.

Passons, William R. (1975). *Gestalt approaches in counseling.* NY: Holt, Rinehart, Winston.

Patton, Michael J., Fuhriman, Addie J., and Bieber, Michael (1977). A model and a metalanguage for research on psychological counseling. *Journal of Counseling Psychology*, 24, 25–34.

Perls, Frederick S. (1969). *Gestalt therapy verbatim.* Compiled and edited by John O. Stevens. Lafayette, CA: Real People Press.

Pittenger, Robert E., and Smith, Henry Lee, Jr. (1957). A basis for some contributions of linguistics to psychiatry. *Psychiatry*, 20 (1), 61–78.

Pittenger, Robert E., Hockett, Charles F., and Danehy, John J. (1960). *The first five minutes*. Ithaca: Carl Martineau.

Polanyi, Livia. (1979). So what's the point? *Semiotica, 25,* 207–241.

Polanyi, Livia. (1981). Telling the same story twice. *Text, 1* (4), 315–336.

Polanyi, Livia. (1982). Linguistic and social constraints on storytelling. *Journal of Pragmatics, 6,* 509–524.

Polanyi, Livia. (1985). *Telling the American story: A structural and cultural analysis of conversational storytelling*. Norwood, NJ: Ablex.

Polanyi, Livia. (1989). *Telling the American story: A structural and cultural analysis of conversational storytelling*. Boston: MIT Press.

Pollio, Howard R., and Barlow, Jack M. (1975). A behavioral analysis of figurative language in psychotherapy: One session in a single case study. *Language and Speech,* 236–254.

Pollio, Howard R., Barlow, Jack M., Fine, Harold J., and Pollio, Marilyn R. (Eds.) (1977). *Psychology and the poetics of growth: Figurative language in psychology, psychotherapy and education* (pp. 101–157). NY: Halsted Press of John Wiley.

Prince, Gerald. (1982). *Narratology: The form and functioning of narrative*. Janua Linguarum. NY: Mouton.

Quirk, Randolph, Greenbaum, Sidney, Leech, Geoffrey, and Svartvik, Jan. (1980). *A grammar of contemporary English*. Harlow: Longman.

Rickford, John. (1988). The evolution of creole languages: Real and apparent time evidence. In *Linguistic change and contact: Proceedings of the 16th annual NWAV conference*. Edited by K. Ferrara, B. Brown, K. Walters, J. Baugh. Austin: Department of Linguistics, University of Texas.

Rodriguez, Richard. (1981). *Hunger of memory*. Boston, MA: Godine.

Romaine, Suzanne. (1984). The language of children and adolescents. Oxford: Blackwell.

Russell, Robert L. (Ed.) (1987). *Language in psychotherapy: Strategies of discovery*. NY: Plenum.

Russell, R. L., and Stiles, W. B. (1979). Categories for classifying language in psychotherapy. *Psychological Bulletin, 86,* 404–419.

Ryave, Alan L. (1978). On the achievement of a series of stories. In Jim Schenkein (Ed.) *Studies in the organization of conversational interaction* (pp. 113–132). NY: Academic Press.

Sacks, Harvey. Ms, chs. 3 and 4.

Sacks, Harvey. Unpublished lecture notes, 1965–1971.

Sacks, Harvey, Schegloff, Emmanuel, and Jefferson, Gail. (1974). A simplest systematics for the organization of turn-taking in conversation. *Language, 50,* 696–735. Also in J. Schenkein (Ed.) (1978). *Studies in the organization of conversational interaction*. NY: Academic Press.

Sapir, Edward. (1927). Speech as a personality trait. *American Journal of Sociology, 32,* 892–905.

Sapir, J. David, and Crocker, J. Christopher. (1977). *The social uses of metaphor*. Philadelphia: University of Pennsylvania Press.

Scheflen, Albert E. (1973). *Communicational structure: Analysis of a psychotherapy transaction*. Bloomington: Indiana University Press.

Schegloff, Emmanuel. (1984). On some questions and ambiguities in conversation. In J. M. Atkinson, and J. Heritage (Eds.) *Structures of social action: Studies in conversational analysis*. Cambridge: Cambridge University Press.

Schiffrin, Deborah. (1981). Tense variation in narrative. *Language, 57*, 45–62.

Schiffrin, Deborah. (1982a). Cohesion in everyday discourse: The role of paraphrase. In *Working Papers in Sociolinguistics, 97*. Austin: Southwest Educational Development Laboratory.

Schiffrin, Deborah. (1982b). *Discourse markers: Semantic resources for the construction of conversation*. Ph.D. dissertation, University of Pennsylvania.

Schiffrin, Deborah. (1984a). How a story says what it means and does. *Text, 4*, 313–346.

Schiffrin, Deborah. (1984b). Jewish argument as sociability. *Language in Society, 13*, 311–335.

Schiffrin, Deborah. (1985). Conversational coherence: The role of "well." *Language, 61*, 640–667.

Schiffrin, Deborah. (1987a). *Discourse markers*. Cambridge: Cambridge University Press.

Schiffrin, Deborah. (1987b). Discovering the context of an utterance. *Linguistics, 25*, 11–32.

Schiffrin, Deborah. (1987c). Sociolinguistic approaches to discourse: Topic and reference in narrative. Paper presented at the 16th annual New Ways of Analyzing Variation conference, Austin, October 1987.

Scollon, Ron. (1981). The rhythmic integration of ordinary talk. In Deborah Tannen (Ed.) *Analyzing discourse: Text and talk*. Georgetown University Round Table on Languages and Linguistics. Washington, DC: Georgetown University Press.

Searle, J. R. (1969). *Speech acts*. Cambridge: Cambridge University Press.

Searle, J. R. (1975). Indirect speech acts. In P. Cole, and J. L. Morgan (Eds.) *Syntax and Semantics 3: Speech acts* (pp. 59–82) NY: Academic Press.

Searle, J. R. (1976). The classification of illocutionary acts. *Language in Society, 5*, 1–24.

Sherzer, Joel. (1982a). Levels of analysis in sociolinguistics and discourse analysis: Two illustrative examples. Paper presented at the American Sociological Association Meetings, Sept. 1982.

Sherzer, Joel. (1982b). Play languages: With a note on ritual languages. In L. Obler, and L. Menn (Eds.) *Exceptional language and linguistics* (pp. 175–199). NY: Academic Press.

Sherzer, Joel. (1982c). Tellings, retellings and tellings within tellings: The structuring and organization of narrative in Kuna Indian discourse. In Richard Bauman, and Joel Sherzer (Eds.) *Case studies in the ethnogra-*

phy of speaking: A compilation of research papers in sociolinguistics (pp. 249–273). Austin: Southwest Educational Development Laboratory.

Sherzer, Joel. (1983). *Kuna ways of speaking: An ethnographic perspective.* Austin: University of Texas Press.

Sherzer, Joel. (1987). A discourse-centered approach to language and culture. *American Anthropologist, 89* (2), 295–309.

Sherzer, Joel. (1993). On puns, comebacks, verbal dueling, and play languages: Speech play in Balinese verbal life. *Language in Society, 22,* 217–234.

Shuy, Roger W. (1984). Linguistics in other professions. *Annual Review of Anthropology, 13,* 419–445.

Shuy, Roger W. (1983). Unexpected by-products of fieldwork. *American Speech, 4,* 345–358.

Sloane, Paul, M.D. (1979). *Psychoanalytic understanding of the dream.* NY: Jason Aronson.

Sound Cap. Tom Hedges, and Mark Zimmer (developers) (1987). Fractal Software. Minneapolis: McNifty Central.

Stiles, W. B. (1978). Verbal response modes and dimensions of interpersonal roles: A method of discourse analysis. *Journal of Personality and Social Psychology, 36,* 693–703.

Stiles, W. B. (1979). Verbal response modes and psychotherapeutic technique. *Psychiatry, 42,* 49–62.

Stiles, William B. (1981). Classification of intersubjective illocutionary acts. *Language in Society, 10,* 227–249.

Tannen, Deborah. (1982). *Spoken and written language: Exploring orality and literacy.* [Vol. 9 in the series *Advances in discourse processes,* Edited by Roy O. Freedle.] Norwood, NJ: Ablex.

Tannen, Deborah. (1983). "I take out the rock-Dok!": How Greek women tell about being molested (and create involvement). *Anthropological Linguistics, 25* (3), 359–374.

Tannen, Deborah. (1984). *Conversational style.* Norwood, NJ: Ablex.

Tannen, Deborah. (1987a). Repetition in conversation: Toward a poetics of talk. *Language, 63* (3), 574–605.

Tannen, Deborah. (1987b). Repetition in conversation as spontaneous formulaicity. In Barbara Johnstone (Ed.) [Special Issue] *Text, 7* (3), 215–244.

Tannen, Deborah. (1989). *Talking voices: Repetition, dialogue, and imagery in conversational discourse.* Cambridge: Cambridge University Press.

Taube, C. A., Burns, B. J., and Kessler, L. (1984). Patients of psychiatrists and psychologists in office-based practice. *American Psychologist, 39,* 1435–1447.

Tedlock, Barbara. (1981). Quiché Mayan dream interpretation. *Ethos, 9,* 313–330.

Turner, R. (1972). Some formal properties of therapy talk. In D. Sudnow (Ed.) *Studies in social interaction* (pp. 367–396). NY: Free Press.

Urban, Greg. (1990). Linguistic and musical parallelism. Paper presented at the NEH Conference on Repetition in Discourse, Texas A&M University, May 25–27.

van Riemsdijk, H., and Williams, E. (1986). *Introduction to the theory of grammar.* Cambridge, MA: MIT Press.

Wallace, A. F. C. (1958). Dreams and the wishes of the soul: A type of psychoanalytic theory among the seventeenth century Iroquois. *American Anthropologist, 60,* 234–248.

Walters, Keith. (1984). It's like playing password: Questions and questioning at school. *Texas Linguistic Forum, 24,* 157–188.

Wardhaugh, Ronald. (1985). *How conversation works.* Oxford: Blackwell.

Weiner, Susan L., and Goodenough, Donald R. (1977). A move towards a psychology of conversation. In Roy O. Freedle (Ed.) *Discourse production and comprehension* (pp. 213-226). [Vol. 1 in the series *Advances in discourse processes.*]

West, Candace. (1983). "Ask me no questions . . .": An analysis of queries and replies in physician-patient dialogues. In Susan Fisher and Alexandra Dundas Todd (Eds.). *The social organization of doctor-patient communication* (pp. 75–105). Washington: DC: Center for Applied Linguistics.

Wodak, Ruth. (1981a). How do I put my problem?: Problem presentation in therapy and interview. *Text, 1,* 191–213.

Wolfson, Nessa. (1976). Speech events and natural speech: Some implications for sociolinguistic methodology. *Language in Society, 5,* 189–209.

Wyatt, Frederick. (1986). The narrative in psychoanalysis: Psychoanalytic notes on storytelling, listening and interpreting. In Theodore R. Sarbin (Ed.) *Narrative psychology: The storied nature of human conduct* (pp. 193–210). NY: Praeger Publishers.

Yngve, Victor H. (1970). On getting a word in edgewise. *Papers from the sixth regional meeting of the Chicago Linguistics Society* (pp. 567–577). Chicago: Chicago Linguistics Society.

Zaro, Joan, Barach, Roland, Nedelman, Deborah Jo, and Dreiblatt, Irwin S. (1977). *A guide for beginning psychologists.* Cambridge: Cambridge University Press.

Zimmerman, Don H., and West, Candace. (1975). Sex roles, interruptions and silences in conversation. In Barrie Thorne and Nancy Henley (Eds.) *Language and sex: Difference and dominance* (pp. 105–129). Rowley, MA: Newbury House.

Index